What c
My Professoi

MW00800386

In a day when all of the forces of darkness are making every attempt to convince postmodern man of the folly of the Scriptures, it is not only refreshing, but reassuring to know that someone with such strong academic credentials and a heart wholly turned toward God cares to answer the faithless critics with a sound approach to the archeological and historical evidence of the absolute truth and veracity of the Holy Scriptures. I heartily recommend Dr. Tribelhorn's timely apologetic to everyone!

Mark Smith
Senior Pastor
Murdock Baptist Church
Port Charlotte, Florida

Dr. Tribelhorn has served for many years as one of St. Petersburg Theological Seminary's best loved and most respected professors. Now he extends his service to a broader community with this wonderful volume. In a most compelling and comprehensive—yet readable—way he marshals the evidence to answer questions and deal with issues that are frequently used to undercut a sound and reasonable Biblical faith. I have taught Apologetics courses for many years; this book will serve as one of my key texts from this point forward.

Rabbi John Fischer, Ph.D., Th.D.
Academic Vice President
St. Petersburg Theological Seminary

My wife and I traveled with Dr. Tom for a week on a Holy Land tour. During that time I saw Dr. Tom 'the shepherd' leading devotionals and prayer, counseling, baptizing, and reading Scripture passages as we filled our souls with the wonder of the Holy Land. When we were standing on the Tell at Jericho I saw Dr. Tom 'the professor' as he defended and supported with evidence the Biblical account of Joshua's destruction of that city. I realized then the severity of the battle that is raging over the Bible and that I was listening to a great modern day defender of the faith and the historical accuracy of the Bible. I strongly encourage you to read this book.

Brett Nordick
Minnesota

The historicity of the Bible continues to be under attack. With clarity and conviction, Dr. Tom addresses these assaults on Scripture with the eye of a scholar and the compassionate heart of a father in full support of the accuracy and truth of the Biblical text. This book is essential for any student of the Bible who has been confronted with the question of whether the Bible can be trusted historically. Using his knowledge of archaeology from the lands of the Bible, the author brilliantly presents compelling evidence for the accuracy of Scripture.

Dr. John DeLancey
Pastor and Holy Land Tour Leader
Stoneridge Church
Allison Park, PA
www.biblicalisraeltours.com

HEB 11:1

My Professor Says

The Bible Is A Myth

Before You Give Up on God –
Get the Facts

Thomas B. Tribelhorn, D.Min., Ph.D.

Hevel Media
International

Hevel Media International
P.O. Box 461592
Garland, TX 75046-1592

www.MyProfessorSays.com

On the whole . . . with editorial license in the interest of readability . . . we
have followed *The Chicago Manual of Style Online*, 16th edition, ©2010
University of Chicago, with the following clarifications: Direct quotations
appear with the traditional double quotation marks; quotations within quotations, 'scare/shutter' quotes and 'use-mention' quotes appear with single
quotation marks. Because the author disagrees with rule 8.102 (i.e. Mishnah
– Mishnaic; Koran – Koranic; Talmud – Talmudic; Bible – but biblical),
Biblical and Biblically have been capitalized at the author's request.
—The Editor

ISBN: 978-0-982948-80-4
Library of Congress: 2010934794

To my Dads—

Robert Tribelhorn
and
Richard Goodhart

Upon whose shoulders I stand, deeply grateful for, and indebted to, their lifetimes of faithfulness, hard work, and sacrifice for the Lord and their families

Acknowledgements

This book is the product of a collaborative effort. In many ways, it is the culmination of a lifetime's worth of work and study and experience . . . and there is a debt of gratitude owed to all of those people who offered support along that journey. Their names would fill more pages than we have available here. I do want to thank those who had a part in this immediate project. One of the greatest fears an author has in writing his Acknowledgements is that he will inadvertently leave out someone whose contribution is worthy of public gratitude. I have tried not to be guilty of this . . . but, if I am, I ask your forgiveness in advance. My neglect is truly an unintended oversight. That being said, I wish to acknowledge the following.

To all of our prayer partners, we are grateful to you for seeing us through these years of travel, research, and writing. The real battle is in the spiritual realm, and we thank you for embracing that truth and for taking seriously the critical role you have played in seeing this project through. We ask you to continue to pray in earnest that this book will enrich those who read it.

I owe a debt of gratitude to Dr. Peter van der Veen, who patiently answered my incessant queries for clarification during the writing process, and who graciously forced time into his demanding schedule to finish his critical review of the manuscript while in the middle of filming a documentary on Sennacherib's siege of Jerusalem for German Television.

I also want to thank Egyptologist and bestselling author David Rohl for watchfully walking me through the maze of Egyptian and Biblical chronologies, for answering my numerous inquiries over the years, and for his pointers, sharing his photos, and for his encouragement along the way.

I am grateful to publisher Rob Shearer (Greenleaf Press of Lebanon, Tennessee) for his encouragement, critical review of the manuscript, and helpful suggestions. Thank you to Cami McCraw of Stretch Productions Inc. for introducing us.

Special thanks to Dee Weston, who graciously carried his photography equipment half way around the world at the Spirit's prompting. It was not by chance that you came along on that November trip. Thank you, Dee, for your support of, and encouragement for, this project.

I am grateful to my good friend and colleague Dr. John DeLancey for inviting me to co-lead groups with him in recent years to Egypt, Jordan, and Israel. Finally we have been able to do some tours together like we day-dreamed about during our student days together at Jerusalem University College.

A word of thanks to Cindi Taylor for her persistence in locating some of the rare books I needed to double-check some obscure references during the process of writing.

A special word of thanks goes to Bob Massey for sharing his expertise to make www.MyProfessorSays.com a reality. And where would I be without Rob Supples, who so proficiently saved this project from the disaster that could have come to pass had he not been able to get the upper hand on those malware attacks, and reconstruct my operating system. Thank you, Rob.

On behalf of myself and my family I extend heartfelt thanks to Todd Beach for being our answer to a very specific prayer. Thank you for making possible our getaways to Orlando for needed R and R during this project.

It is with a grateful heart that we acknowledge an extraordinary group of partnering friends whose prayers and sacrificial giving (2 Corinthians 8:2) have over and over sustained us in this project. I pray that, as they now witness the fruition of this project, it will bring joy to their hearts and give them a deep sense of satisfaction for having rallied for the cause. They include: Rick and Pam Aanonsen, Carl and Grace Abrahamsen, Victor Antipov, Sam and Mary Barnes, Richard and Sharon Bauman, Randall and Melissa Breiwick, Cindy Case, Ek Hong Chang, John and Linda Charles, Tony and Donna Cortese, John Delancey, Ruth Denouden, Jim and Cyndde DeWeese, Gerry and Lynn Dodson, Eagles Assembly (RCCG), Carolyn Ebron, Rowland and Harriett Edwards, Debbie Eger, Jim and Barbara Franzen, Ed Gamble and the Southern Baptist Association of Christian Schools (SBACS), Louis and Lori Giovannini, Todd and Darla Griswold, Tom and Adriene Grob, Verne and Joyce Hiett, Steve and Sandra Holt, Michael and Patricia Howerter, Bud and Rozelle Johnson, Michael and Veronica Jones, Daniel and Sylvia Jordan, Eric and Susan Jorgenson, Pat Knippers, David and Linda Lowe, Kurt and Jill Luzius, Bob and Vera McSparin, Manny and Jeannine Medina, Richard and Shelby Munoz, Charles and Cherryl Nickerson, Brett and Sheri Nordick, Rob Nordick, Renee Plank, George Powell, Neal and Carol Raetz, Steve and Judy Ransom, Paul Rixmann, Wayne and Mary Rixmann, Dilys Smith, Cheryl Thomas, Ron Tower, Robert and Joyce Vaclav, Arnold and Ileen van Donselaar, Bill and Barbara White, Diane White, Adrean and Fran Wolbrink, Heather Wood, Marty Woodall, Richard and Georgia Yeskoo.

To my wife and best friend, Lynn, whose unwavering love and encouragement has made our lives together better than I could have ever imagined: thank you.

To my daughter Sarah, God's gift to us, whose loving smile and laughter fills each day with joy: thank you for being you.

To all who have helped in any way to make this book possible – publisher Dr. Katie Welch and her staff, my vigilant and supportive editor Bob Massey who was truly God's choice for this project and hopefully for many more to come, and my friend Ralph Nordick for catching the vision . . . making this project possible, – the author is deeply appreciative.

Foreword

As a scholar who has worked in the field of archaeology and ancient history for many years, I wholeheartedly recommend this book to you. Every Christian student should read this book; every pastor should read this book; indeed, every Christian parent should read this book, especially those who have sent their sons and daughters off to college.

While reading this book myself, many memories of my own college days came back to me. Having grown up in an evangelical Christian family in Holland – where the historicity of the Bible and its stories was always taken for granted – I never questioned during my childhood and adolescence if the events within its pages had actually occurred, or if any of the people had actually lived. As long as I can remember, I was always fascinated by the history and background of the Biblical world. Searching for complimentary evidence to support the Bible's claims became a way of life. Although there were times during my adolescence during which I had not lived a moral Christian lifestyle, I had also not questioned the reliability of the Bible as God's Word.

It was not until my days as an undergraduate student at an evangelical Christian college near Paris, France, that I started to seriously question what

I had been taught by my parents. Please understand that it was not the teachers at that college that caused my questioning and doubts (they all loved the Lord and were a great testimony). I suppose it was being away from home, trying to discover my own way of thinking, reading things my parents would never have allowed me to read. I started reading books by Rudolph Bultmann, the German New Testament scholar who had questioned the historical resurrection of Jesus Christ (he believed that Jesus had only risen in the minds of his followers). Although I wasn't quite willing to give up my faith in the resurrection, I started to wonder if certain aspects of the Bible were not, in fact, myth, and needed to be demythologized (as Bultmann himself called it) by finding a symbolic meaning behind them. I wondered about Jonah and his three days in the fish, I wondered about the Trinity – how God could be three in one. I wondered if everything in the Bible really needed to be true. Later on, after my time in France, I went through an even harsher time of questioning, and asked myself if God was really there.

But it was through the warm friendship and devotion of some of my professors at the colleges in France and Belgium that I learned to trust the Bible more and finally again. At the college in Paris, I met Dr. Tom Tribelhorn for the first time (he was my doctrine teacher then). It was professors such as he that made a difference in my life. They allowed me to talk freely about my doubts and queries without telling me that, if I doubted like Thomas (or, should I say, denied Him like Peter), the Lord would be angry and would punish me. With Dr. Tom, I was allowed to think, use my brain, and make up my own mind. I was not rejected when I spoke freely about my doubts. I always felt loved and taken seriously. I felt that teachers such as Dr. Tom gave me space to breathe.

Oh yes, I had other professors – unlike him – who acted very differently. They told me that it was wrong to question the Bible, even that my doubts were demonic. I felt intimidated; worse, I felt frightened. But their exhorting attitude did not draw me closer to God; it drove me away and made me wonder more about the truth of the Bible. Looking back, quite honestly, I don't know where I would have gone if people such as Dr. Tom had not been there. But they were there for me, and I thank God for His guidance.

In this heart-warming and thought-provoking book, Dr. Tom encourages his readers not to give up on their faith in the reliability of the Bible. He skilfully synthesizes and makes understandable the snares of several of the interrelated technical issues found in archaeology, philology, philosophy, and theology facing students today. Indeed, this seminary professor stands before us not only prepared to accept the Bible's theological message (as perhaps still a good many theologians are prepared to do), but rightly so and very consciously, he goes one step further: he also accepts the historical claims made by the Bible. In this day and age, very few archaeologists would be prepared to take the Bible at face value when it speaks about the existence of Abraham, a major Israelite Exodus out of Egypt led by Moses, or a large scale military conquest under Joshua. As you read this book, you will discover the academic reasons why he believes it is imperative not to swallow too hastily what certain scholars are teaching about the Bible. You will discover his resonating passion to give our students the tools they need to challenge the Bible-critical position.

While doing so, Dr. Tom takes us right back on a journey to the land of Israel to a time when he himself was confronted with many doubts about the historicity of the Bible. As you journey through Israel and Egypt with this doubting Thomas, he straightforwardly shares and explains that which he discovered for himself. His parents named him well, for in all the years I have known him, Dr. Tom is truly an "I need to see it for myself" person.

As an epigraphist, I am especially interested in ancient inscriptions from the lands of the Bible. It is the contemporary writings from the period of the kings of Israel and Judah that shed astonishing light on the world of the Biblical writers and the origin of the Biblical texts. Several inscriptions have been found in which personages known from the Bible (kings and officials) have indeed been confirmed. This brings the Biblical world very near to us. My work has not only helped to use these documents to establish firmer dates for the archaeological layers of the later Judean Monarchy Period, but also to identify several more Bible persons. Sometimes it seemed as if I saw them face to face. This is why I am thrilled that a book like this is now available for a more general Christian audience. The excitement of new discoveries awaits you as you read the chapters that follow.

Dr. Tom's uplifting book has one very important aim: to meet you, the reader, right where you are – with the doubts and questions that may have bothered you for some time. This book will help you think more critically, empowering you to determine if your doubts are based on solid evidence and balanced reasoning – or on someone's faulty and prejudiced worldview. It is my hope that this book will not only establish your faith more firmly in the Bible, but that it will also teach you how to handle your doubts and critical questions better in the future.

Peter van der Veen, Ph.D.

Biblical Archaeologist
Germany

Table of Contents

Archaelogical Time Periods

This chart will help you identify the various archaeological time periods as dated by the conventional and revised chronologies. The more traditional "BC" and "AD" are used instead of the "BCE" and "CE" categories used in scholarship and secular settings.

Conventional Chronology	Time Period	Revised Chronology
4500-3500 BC	Chalcolithic	c. 3300-2900 BC
3500-2000 BC	Early Bronze	c. 2900-1800 BC
2000-1550 BC	Middle Bronze Age	c. 1850-1300 BC
1550-1200 BC	Late Bronze Age	c. 1300-950 BC
1200-1000 BC	Iron Age I (Early Iron Age)	c. 1000-850 BC
1000-586 BC	Iron Age II	c. 850-586 BC
586-539 BC	Babylonian	same
539-332 BC	Persian	same
332-167 BC	Early Hellenistic	same
167-37 BC	Hasmonean	same
37 BC -132 AD	Early Roman	same
132-324 AD	Late Roman	same
324-638 AD	Byzantine	same
638-1099 AD	Early Islamic	same
1099-1291 AD	Crusader	same

Abbreviations

ANET	Ancient Near Eastern Texts, 3rd edition, edited by J. B. Pritchard
AKL	Assyrian King List
AOAT	Alter Orient und Altes Testament (Old Orient and Old Testament)
BA	Biblical Archaeologist
BAR	Biblical Archaeology Review
BICANE	Bronze to Iron Age Chronology of the Ancient Near East Study Group
CC	Conventional Chronology (aka standard/orthodox chronology)
C&C	Catastrophism and Chronology (See SIS below.)
CoD	Centuries of Darkness Chronology
HSM	Harvard Semitic Monograph Series
GM	Göttinger Miszellen
ISBE	International Standard Bible Encyclopedia, edited by G. W. Bromiley
ISIS	Institute for the Study of Interdisciplinary Sciences
JACF	Journal of the Ancient Chronology Forum
JSOT	Journal for the Study of the Old Testament
KJV	King James Version
NAS	New American Standard Version
NIV	New International Version
NLT	New Living Translation
OC	Orthodox Chronology (aka standard/conventional chronology)
PE	Post-Eden Source (a pre-Bible source theory explained in Chapter Seventeen)
PF	Post-Flood Source (a pre-Bible source theory explained in Chapter Seventeen)
PLO	Palestine Liberation Organization
NC	New Chronology (chronology proposed by David Rohl)
RC	Revised Chronology (all models)
SIS	Society of Interdisciplinary Studies
WAQF	وقف, Waqf is an Arabic word – the Muslim religious authority that oversees the Temple Mount (not an abbreviation)
ZÄS	Zeitschrift für Ägyptische Sprache

Introduction

Western culture is currently experiencing an unprecedented disconnect from the Bible, resulting in droves of next-generation students dismissing it as irrelevant. Perhaps you are one of them. If so, I want you to know you're not alone.

You see . . . I once came uncomfortably close to doing the same.

And I can tell you stories. Even amongst those who remain in the ranks, there are more than we realize (or perhaps care to admit) who go through all the motions of being a Christian while simultaneously concealing serious doubts about the Bible and their faith. These doubts are, by and large, the result of unanswered questions they have been too apprehensive to ask. Perhaps it's to avoid being ostracized, or out of pride, or a fear of being judged that they remain silent. (Be honest: how many times have you longed for a confidant with whom you could share your most intimate faith-related questions, without fear of reprisal?)

As a seminary professor, I see this happen all the time. That's why one of my goals is to provide students with a confidential 'safe harbor' where they can speak freely and openly about such matters. Hardly a semester has gone by over the years (especially during the last decade) that I haven't met a 'secret doubter' . . . someone raised in the church now on the verge of dumping it all . . . a student silently struggling to find genuine purpose and meaning in his or her life, perhaps even silently searching for a greater sense of security in our increasingly insecure world.

Nor are these twenty-first century questions and doubts confined to the campus. I have encountered secret doubters in pulpits, in front of classrooms, in congregations, in home fellowships, in small groups. There are secret doubters amongst those both following and leading.

My guess would be that you, too, may have had some plaguing doubt or question at one time or another. Living in what has become a post-Christian society, many have become confused, even disillusioned, by postmodernism and new-generation archaeology. They are intimidated by political correctness . . . they hide their bewilderment and misgivings for fear of compromising their positions . . . they allow the God-given process of thinking to collapse under the weight of peer pressure.

It is primarily this audience I wish to address. This book is especially for those on the verge of walking away from their faith, as well as those who, in their hearts, may have already done so – while still 'going through the motions' externally.

As is typical of the task of writing, decisions of inclusion and exclusion are continually being made. By no means does this book make a pretense of being a complete work of Christian apologetics, or anything close to that. It is doubtful such a book could even be written. My focus is admittedly and intentionally selective.

Broadly speaking, my prayer is that the Spirit of the Living God will anoint this work in order to encourage my readers, and provide them with a platform from which they can delineate and answer some of the intellectual challenges they are facing as twenty-first century Christians. My hope is that they become more aware of the dangers of the subtle challenges to a Biblical worldview that are being posed by the postmodern thinking that surrounds them on a daily basis. To avoid any appearance of condescension, I will draw upon my own years of combating doubt in presenting this material, when appropriate.

I have two primary objectives. My first objective is to introduce the interpretive faults of new-generation archaeology . . . and the limitations and prejudices of the arguments its practitioners level at the historicity of the Bible. I want my readers to recognize that the so-called 'indisputable' facts being used to declare the Bible a fraud are not as rock-solid as they are being led to believe. I want them also to recognize that any and all studies of the ancients will always be inconclusive works in progress. As a result, the case against the historicity of the Bible will always be far from solid. My readers need to realize that the burden of proof can be as effectively shifted to those who challenge the historicity of the Bible as to those who defend it.

My second objective is to introduce the inherent flaws and prejudices behind the continuing postulations that the Israelite religion of the Old Testament was nothing more than an adaptation of surrounding pagan religions. This so-called 'fact' is becoming increasingly prominent in textbooks and lecture halls. By walking you – my readers – through several ancient temples along the Nile, and showing you related non-Biblical texts, you will appreciate the similarities and differences between the Israelite temple in Jerusalem and the ancient temples of Egypt and the Near East, as well as the similarities and differences in ritual worship practices and linguistics. My goal is to accomplish this using an understandable, straightforward, reader-friendly format.

As I have said, I write from the perspective of having had to work through several of these intellectual challenges and doubts for myself . . . first as a graduate student in Israel, then in my post-graduate studies and subsequent years of research in Israel and Egypt, and in my seminary and college teaching in Europe and the United States. I remember too well feeling ostracized by the very Christians I had turned to for help during my own years of questioning the historicity of the Biblical narratives. (My friends in the world were more Christian to me than those who professed to be Christians.) As a result of that unpleasant experience, I continually ask God never to allow me to ostracize or belittle my doubting students or colleagues or others who are brave enough to share with me their questions, doubts, and faith struggles.

I believe the students who have been in my classes over these years will attest that this has been my pledge to every class. My goal with each of them has been to leave no stone unturned. There are no *dumb* questions. There are no wrong questions. There are no questions that are out of bounds, provided they are asked sincerely and respectfully. The only bad question is the one that remains unasked, when a solid, researched answer could have quelled a nagging doubt.

So I wish to thank my students (now too numerous to name) – especially those at the master's and doctoral levels who have encouraged this project for several years. I am deeply honored that they have trusted me with many of their personal questions, doubts, and fears. Their frankness and honesty have always been appreciated, and will always be admired. Granted, we did not always find the answer they may have been seeking . . . but, working together, we found many, and put to rest dozens of their disquieting questions. I trust they have found the interaction as valuable and helpful as I have – even on those occasions when we had to acknowledge that, in our finite understanding, some questions may never be answered this side of eternity.

I also write from the perspective that we, as citizens of the Bible-believing community, are here for one another, to build up one another in the faith. A friend of ours tells the story of the time she went to her pastor in Brazil and confessed that she felt she was running out of faith. Rather than condemning her, preaching at her, throwing verses at her, or shunning her, he very gently said, "Then it's time for the Body to have faith for you." If you find yourself running out of faith, connect with a fellowship that understands Biblical grace and the supremacy of love, or find a Bible-believing brother or sister willing to walk beside you during your journey of doubt.

In many respects I suppose this is the book I wish someone had handed me as a graduate student in Israel while standing on the tell of Old Testament Jericho (Tell al-Sultan) . . . while those around me tried to persuade me that I had been quite mistaken and naïve for thinking that I could synchronize archaeology with the narratives of my no-longer-relevant Bible. May this be a book that will expose some of the erroneous academic assaults to Biblical faith for what they are, and the bias from which they have come.

4

In my darkest journeys, I have discovered there is a light at the end of the proverbial tunnel, and that light is the Truth that comes from knowing God. May you find some of that – and Him – within these pages.

Tom Tribelhorn, D.Min., Ph.D.
Academic Dean
Chair, Doctoral Studies Program
St. Petersburg Theological Seminary
St. Petersburg, Florida USA

Read This First

There's something you need to know about the organization of this book. It is not meant to be read as you would an encyclopedia . . . where you can pick a topic and jump to it. The information presented here is cumulative. That is, the latter chapters of this book are built upon critically important foundations laid in the earlier chapters.

Therefore, please RESIST THE TEMPTATION TO SKIP AHEAD.

I organized the material in this book deliberately, in much the same way I would an on-campus or online course, or a lecture series. Each chapter is designed to be an essential building block for those that follow.

I understand if the topic of the recently discovered similarities in temple and temple worship practices pique your interest, but don't race ahead. You will get there soon enough . . . and you'll do it equipped with the prior information necessary to gain a full understanding of the subject.

So read the chapters in the order in which they are presented. That way, you'll be able to appreciate how powerful the evidence is for Biblical faith.

1

Why Students are Turning Their Backs on God

Lindsey's e-mail arrived in my inbox toward the end of the spring semester. Hers, like so many others, reflects the rising tide of Bible-believing college students who – as a result of having been enlightened by the so-called archaeological 'facts' – suddenly find themselves questioning the historicity of the Bible they grew up believing. She writes:

From: Lindsey
Subject: Question

I have a question from one of my religion classes that has been bothering me, so I thought I would send this out to people I feel are knowledgeable in this, that may be able to shed some truth on it.

Yesterday in my Bib Lit class, our assignment was to read the book of Joshua and then we had to read this chapter of a book called *The Bible Unearthed*. I will do my best to give you a recap of what it said.

Basically it was an archaeological account of the conquest of Canaan. There is supposedly evidence to suggest that Canaan was under control of the Egyptian Empire at the time. If this were true, the Egyptians never would have allowed such an invasion – at any rate, there would have at least been mention of it in the Egyptian records.

Supposedly there was no trace of a settlement in Jericho in the thirteenth century, and the settlement in the fourteenth century was of little consequence and was unfortified. There was absolutely no sign of destruction either.

Because of the Egyptian military influence in that region and provided protection, the famous walls of Jericho could not have collapsed because they never existed, according to Finkelstein. As a result of these findings, the famous scene of the Israelites marching around the wall carrying the Ark of the Covenant, blowing the rams' horns, and the walls crumbling to the ground was, according to Finkelstein, nothing more than a "romantic mirage." The entire event, along with other famous scenes from the book of Joshua, are argued to be nothing more than a folklore used as a literary device to depict what could happen if the Israelites followed the Law to the letter meant to unite the Israelites of the time of Josiah and give them a common and glorious past.

SO that being said . . . Thoughts?

Do you think what these archaeologists are saying could be true? Could my professor be right? This has really been bothering me! Can you help?[1]

You Are Not Alone

Every spring thousands of Christian students graduate and leave high school behind to attend college. The trouble is – as a recent research study indicates – an alarming majority of those same students leave behind their Bibles and their faith in God as well. Student ministry pastors from numerous Christian denominations estimate that between 65 and 94 percent of Christian students turn their backs on God and walk away from the faith after high school.

To help document these estimates, Fuller Theological Seminary's Center for Youth and Family Ministry launched a three-year study[2] in January 2005, called the College Transition Project.[3] The study confirmed that students who found themselves unable to defend their beliefs (or find someone who could help them defend their beliefs) typically walked away from their faith during their first year of college.

The Fuller study also confirms that *all* churches have had students who walked the narrow path in high school, but somehow made a U-turn and stumbled (or sprinted off in the opposite direction) when they went off to college.

In *Already Gone*,[4] authors Ken Ham and Britt Beemer cite research conducted by America's Research Group, which surveyed 'twenty-somethings' who used to go to church as kids but are no longer part of it. The church attendance of this age group (20 to 29) is as follows:

- 95 percent attended church regularly during elementary school.
- 95 percent attended church regularly during middle school.
- 55 percent attended church regularly during high school.
- 11 percent attended church regularly during college.

As these students got older, their church attendance dropped significantly. But why? Could the following statistics have something to do with it? Out of the students surveyed:

- 39.8 percent first had doubts about the Bible in middle school.
- 43.7 percent first had doubts about the Bible in high school.

- 10.6 percent first had doubts about the Bible in college.

By the time these students get to college, they are already riddled with questions . . . and felt either uncomfortable or too intimidated to ask them. That, or the Church did not give them satisfactory answers to assuage their doubts. They are by then, as the title of the book suggests, already gone. Oddly, the study[5] discovered that those who attended Sunday school (61 percent) are actually *more* likely than non-attendees (39 percent) to:

- Not believe that all the accounts and stories in the Bible are true.
- Doubt the Bible because it was written by men.
- Doubt the Bible because it was not translated correctly.
- Accept that gay marriage and abortion should be legal.
- Believe in evolution.
- View the Church as hypocritical.
- Become anti-church through the years.
- Believe that good people don't need to go to church.

If you are a member of this 'already gone' group, I understand your doubts – but I also urge you to continue reading. If you are a Christian parent entrenched in culture parenting, reading this book and pondering the documentation it provides will be well worth your time. There are answers – perfectly good ones – that may be able to turn the tide for the generations to follow.

Damage Control

Speaking as a seminary professor, my grade book says we are *failing* at passing the baton of faith to the next generation – and we must do better.[6] It never fails to shock (and sadden) me to read the statistics about how many Americans can't name a single Gospel, or can't identify Jesus as the person who gave the Sermon on the Mount, or who believe the entire Bible – *Old Testament* as well as New – was written shortly after Jesus's death.

Frank Page of the Southern Baptist Convention (the largest evangelical denomination in the United States) expressed alarm over the number of church dropouts in the SBC: "It is a disturbing trend, and part of it is that our churches have become one- and two-generation churches, and we've failed to learn how to reach this younger generation."[7]

The historicity of the Bible is not as inaccurate and far-fetched as our students are being taught to believe; quite the contrary. It is possible to use your mind and still trust the Bible in the twenty-first century. Too many of the upcoming generations have already written the Bible off as irrelevant myth – unnecessarily. There's work to be done. The content of the baton we are handing off must be brought continually up to date with that which is relevant to the intellectual challenges our students are facing. If a relevant baton is not passed, the next generation will not know God. It will continue down the road as a post-Christian generation. After the generation of Joshua died off, "another generation grew up, who knew neither the LORD nor what he had done for Israel. Then the Israelites did evil in the eyes of the LORD and served the Baals (Judges 2:10-11)." The prospect is frightening. And it happens before you know it.

Recently I was asked to speak to a group on the indictments being leveled against the historicity of the Bible and the alarming number of Christian students who are walking away from their faith. When the meeting was over, the majority of the audience began a slow but steady gravitation toward the front rather than heading for the exit . . . patiently waiting to speak with me. They didn't come forth because I delivered some kind of emotional altar call. These people were aching to share their own Christian student 'casualty' story.

The experiences were all familiar, as were the sorrow and deep sense of hurt on each of their faces. One question nagged at them all: How could it be possible that my son or daughter (or my nephew or niece or grandchild) – who had been the perfect baby, the perfect child, the perfect adolescent, who had always been so cooperative and never talked back, who had been so active at church, who had even been homeschooled – has walked away from the faith?

There were those whose son or daughter walked away not only from the faith, but from their parents . . . disowning them, severing all ties and communication . . . because they felt their parents had deceived them into believing the Bible is true when (according to their professors), it really isn't . . . as though they might as well have believed in Santa Claus.

If you are a student reading this book, and you've felt betrayed by your parents or grandparents or pastor in this regard, let me make this clear: *It is not necessarily their fault.* The Church goes along, doing its best – but it is unprepared to deal with the assault from the academic community. Even seminary students are too often inadequately armed to defend their faith against such criticisms. The graduates of these religious institutions – those who go on to become pastors and missionaries and teachers and (yes!) professors –find themselves ill-equipped to respond to barrages of such heavy academic artillery. In turn, they often adopt the 'irrefutable facts' espoused by the critics themselves . . . thus propagating error, and leading soul-searching students to believe that the Bible has been discredited in light of contradictory scientific 'evidence.'

If you are one of the wounded students reading this, I probably do not need to tell you how the Church and Christian education have failed you; you already know that well. In a lecture at Notre Dame University some thirty years ago, Christian apologist Francis Schaeffer warned that the church and Christian educators were teaching in joints and pieces at the expense of teaching a comprehensive framework (worldview) upon which students could hang the bits and pieces being thrown at them. This book is designed to help you construct that vital framework – one that will survive the assaults of the academic critics.

Be aware that the battle for the historicity of the Bible is not new. It has raged for more than two hundred years in liberal circles. Gradually the debate entered even more conservative circles[8] . . . and now, fueled by recent and ongoing archaeological discoveries, the controversy rages in almost all circles. As a result, scores have come to see the entire Hebrew Bible as little more than pious myth. What is it about the Bible that is being disseminated and taught so persuasively in colleges and universities that is causing students to walk away from their faith, the Bible, and God in such unprecedented numbers?[9]

To answer this question, we will survey what is currently being alleged about the historicity of the Bible. As we examine this broad canvas, understand that it goes beyond the scope of this book (or any other book for that matter) to assess every invective that attempts to divorce the Bible from reality.

Historical Theology and Philology

The term *archaeology* comes from two Greek words: *archaios,* meaning *ancient,* and *logos,* meaning *knowledge.* Strictly speaking, *archaeology* has come to mean the study of the material remains of the past. However, the discovery of written material is often the result of archaeological investigation. Although the study of written material belongs more properly to philology and epigraphy and the like, it is nonetheless inextricably related to archaeology in much the same way numismatics is related to archaeology.

The challenges being faced by students today that I've thus far discussed have been archaeology proper. Yet our survey would not be complete without considering the matters of linguistic and worship similarities, as well as similarities in the floor plans and structures of ancient temples with Solomon's Temple. Therefore, for purposes of this study, our survey will also need to include historical theology and philology. Historical theology, for the most part, defines itself: it is the study of the history of theology. Philology is the study of written records and the establishment of their authenticity – or lack thereof – including the establishment

philology
The study of literature, or language as used in literature.

epigraphy
The study of epigraphs, ancient inscriptions.

numismatics
The study of coins and metals.

hieratic
Referring to hieratic script, a simplified and abbreviated form of the hieroglyphic script.

of their original form and meaning.

During the early 1900s, archaeologists in Egypt began discovering various ancient Egyptian writings such as the two versions of the 'wise sayings,' or teachings of Amen-em-Ope. One version, housed at the British Museum in London, consists of twenty-seven pages written in hieratic Egyptian longhand on papyrus. It is generally held that Amen-em-Ope taught in Egypt sometime between 1250 and 1000 BC. Several portions of the teachings of Amen-em-Ope can also be found in our Bible (Proverbs 22:17 through 24:22). There are striking similarities pertaining to the counsel given by Amen-em-Ope and the verses found in Proverbs, as well as similarities in presentation and structure. Both begin with a general introduction followed by thirty wise teachings.

Amen-em-Ope begins, "Listen to what I say, Learn my words by heart."[10] The section in Proverbs 22:17-21 begins with much the same introduction:

> "Pay attention and listen to the sayings of the wise; apply your heart to what I teach, for it is pleasing when you keep them in your heart and have all of them ready on your lips.
> "So that your trust may be in the LORD, I teach you today, even you.
> "Have I not written thirty sayings for you, sayings of counsel and knowledge, teaching you true and reliable words, so that you can give sound answers to him who sent you?"

The Proverbs and Amen-em-Ope similarity is one of the better known examples we can cite, yet it's just one of a multitude of linguistic similarities between the Bible and other ancient texts.

Additionally, there are similarities between Solomon's temple and other ancient temples, and similarities pertaining to worship practices and rituals. These similarities are being used to support the notion that the Israelites invented their own religion by plagiarizing from the religions that surrounded them. The following paragraph pretty much sums it all up. Consider the magnitude of that which is being claimed:

The Bible is not "the word of God," but stolen from pagan sources. Its Eden, Adam and Eve were taken from the Babylonian account; its Flood or Deluge is but an epitome of some four hundred flood accounts; its Ark and Ararat have their equivalents in a score of Deluge myths; even the names of Noah's sons are copies, so also Isaac's sacrifice, Solomon's judgment, and Samson's pillar act; its Moses is fashioned after the Syrian Mises; its laws after Hammurabi's code.[11]

Our survey is not exhaustive. It is admittedly broad and selective with the goal of painting an expansive canvas of current academic thinking. By looking at this canvas, we get an idea of the difficult challenges our high school and college students are facing in their classrooms every day. I cannot emphasize to my graduate students enough the importance of reading critically, listening critically, and thinking critically, in all matters, not just in new-generation archaeological matters. Archaeology textbooks are not the only textbooks bombarding students with a biased anti-Bible, anti-Christian agenda.[12] The Bible, once revered and respected in American academia as the Word of God, has been reduced to just another ancient myth. And it is not only students who are being bombarded with this, but *all* Christians . . . through multiple media formats, both consciously and subconsciously.

Could it be that, after all, we have been wrong all this time . . . that the ancient narratives of the Bible are not real? What if the archaeologists are right? What if there is proof that the Biblical narratives are nothing more than elaborate fiction as is being claimed by so many scholars?

It boils down to this critical question: *Is there irrefutable evidence that proves the Bible is just one more record of ancient myth, as is being claimed?* As one who studied in Israel for several years . . . as one who once grappled with these same issues . . . and as one who has led numerous groups back to Israel, Egypt, and Jordan for many years, my goal is to help you to see that the answer to this question is **absolutely not!** Are there twenty-first century answers to these twenty-first century questions? I believe there are indeed answers – rock-solid ones (pun intended) . . . that are just as valid as those who are claiming otherwise.

Maybe you have a measure of faith that is so complete, it allows you to ignore the scholars who are insisting that what you have believed is a lie. Or maybe you're carrying an intellectual time bomb full of doubt that just hasn't exploded yet. Let me assure you that physical evidence *does* have its place in a Biblical worldview, since that worldview insists there is such a thing as truth, and that verifiable historical truth is important.

Did you ever stop to think how much of the New Testament is a defense of the faith? In his Epistle, John proclaimed, "That which was from the beginning, which we have **heard**, which we have **seen with our eyes**, which we have **looked at** and **our hands have touched** – this we proclaim concerning the Word of life . . .. We proclaim to you what we have **seen and heard**, so that you also may have fellowship with us. And our fellowship is with the Father and with his Son, Jesus Christ (1 John 1:1, 3)." John's original intent was to address those influenced by the emerging Gnosticism of his time, yet this passage also speaks to us today. That which we have seen with our eyes and touched with our hands is an important component of Christian apologetics.

If you are struggling (or someone you care about is struggling) in the quest for truth, then the chapters that follow are for you. We'll be talking more about the work of faith in the last chapter . . . but in the meantime, I would remind you of the words of Paul in Romans: "For by the grace given me I say to every one of you: Do not think of yourself more highly than you ought, but rather think of yourself with sober judgment, in accordance with the measure of faith God has given you (Romans 12:3)." Beware of spiritual pride. Before you judge others who may be struggling with doubt, bear in mind that all of us may be more vulnerable to the post-Christian environment that surrounds us than we realize.

As *Already Gone* warns: "Unless the facts behind the Christian faith are clearly and convincingly communicated in a way that students can learn and remember, their faith will not stand the assault of doubt from the world. It's not enough to just tell students, 'Believe in Jesus!' Faith that is not founded on fact will ultimately falter in the storm of secularism that our students face everyday."[13]

An Important Reminder

This first chapter has just been an overview. Now we're about to begin building a wall of defense . . . brick by brick . . . starting from the foundation and making our way up. Therefore, it's important for me to remind you to RESIST THE TEMPTATION TO SKIP AHEAD.

If you do not heed this recommendation, you won't have the tools to completely understand the information in later chapters . . . because groundwork was laid in earlier chapters. This is where we start digging for the *real* facts that determine whether the Bible can be considered historically accurate or not.

Come with me . . . and let's get our hands dirty, that our perception might be clean.

2

What the Experts Say About the Bible

Our concise summary of some of the current positions on the relationship of the Bible to archaeology should solidify this fact: new-generation archaeologists view Biblical archaeology as an incongruity. The relationship between the Bible and archaeology is now viewed as impossible, since the narratives of the Old Testament are considered to have never happened.

Let's look at a sampling of what some of the world's leading new-generation archaeologists and historians, and an evangelical professor are teaching about the Old Testament.

Meet the Experts

The narratives of Genesis, Exodus, and Joshua have, one by one, been dismantled, and their historicity academically dismissed as implausible. These Biblical narratives have been placed on the stack with other ancient myths, and the narratives of Judges, Samuel, Kings, and Chronicles are, if not already dismissed, viewed with a great deal of skepticism. An ever-growing number of archaeologists and scholars in general, as well an alarming number of Christian theologians, now hold that the Hebrew Bible either contains a large portion of – or is nothing more than – ancient myth. Now let's meet the various academics, and look at what they believe.

Bill Dever

"Joshua destroyed a city that wasn't even there," says William G. Dever.[1] Dever's specialty is the history of Israel and the Near East in Biblical times. He was professor of Near Eastern archaeology and anthropology at the University of Arizona in Tucson from 1975 to 2002. His career in archaeology is impressive, including his years as director of the Harvard Semitic Museum-Hebrew Union College excavations at Gezer from 1966 to 1971, 1984 and 1990, among other excavations. Dever joined the faculty at Lycoming College (United Methodist) in the fall of 2008, where he now serves as Distinguished Professor of Near Eastern Archaeology.

Dever has long been a frequent author on questions relating to the historicity of the Bible. He often wrote scathing comments about those who denied the Scriptures' historicity, even though he has never been a supporter of Biblical literalism.[2] A perusal of his books, especially his more recent writings, reveals a gradual inclination *away* from the historicity of the Bible.

"My view all along – and especially in the recent books – is first that the biblical narratives are indeed 'stories,' often fictional and almost always propagandistic, but that here and there they contain *some* valid historical information."[3]

Dever (like Michael D. Coogan, whom you will meet shortly) always maintained that the fictional and propagandistic narratives of the Bible still contained some valid historical information. More recently, Dever has been vocal about his joining those abdicating the historicity of the Bible. In an interview he and three other Biblical archaeologists had with Hershel Shanks, Dever said, "Originally I wrote to frustrate the biblical minimalists; then I became one of them, more or less."[4] Why has he changed his position? Why is he saying this?

Dever will tell you that he is saying this because the archaeological investigations conducted at Jericho have produced no evidence whatsoever that an inhabited city even existed at that location toward the end of the

Late Bronze Period. If you are unfamiliar with current thinking in this field, you may be doing a double take at his statement. If, on the other hand, you are familiar with current thinking in this field, you know that Dever's position is not out of the norm – it *is* the norm.

Frankly, there are few scholars left (evangelical scholar Kenneth Kitchen is one) who still advocate a full military invasion by Joshua. The majority of archaeologists and scholars of history find it impossible to reconcile the Biblical conquest story with the archaeological evidence. They will unilaterally tell you that there was no inhabited city in Jericho for Joshua to destroy when *and if* he passed through. True, they will acknowledge there is archaeological evidence that the city of Hazor was burned to the ground, but the stratum where the burn evidence was discovered is half a century or more *before* the dating of the conquest advocated by Kitchen. Further, they will point out, the central hill country settlements that emerged in Israel during Iron Age I were culturally the same as those from the preceding period. Accordingly, there could not have been an influx of aliens (non-Canaanites, i.e. Israelites) from a different cultural background during that time.

It's not just the story of Joshua and the battle of Jericho. The list of outrageous claims goes on and on:

- The Israelites were never slaves in Egypt.
- German archaeologist Edgar Pusch and his team have made some fascinating discoveries in city of Pi-Ramesse but they have not found Asiatic living quarters indicative of a large Israelite work force.
- Moses is a nice story, but he never really existed.
- The Exodus is a history that never happened; the Conquest of the Promised Land by Joshua simply did not happen.
- There's no evidence apart from the Bible for a King Saul.
- There's no archaeological evidence for a grandiose Jerusalem of temples and palaces during the supposed reigns of David and Solomon.

Are you getting the picture?

Finkelstein and Silberman[5]

There are numerous textbooks and media productions that we could cite to answer our question regarding what about the Bible is being taught that is causing so many students to walk away from their faith – but there is one book in particular that almost instantaneously comes to mind. Since the publication of Professor Israel Finkelstein and Neil Asher Silberman's *The Bible Unearthed: Archaeology's New Vision of Ancient Israel and the Origin of Its Sacred Texts*,[6] the practice of assigning readings from this text has become quite common. It is the book mentioned the most in e-mails just like Lindsey's.[7] (I once made a Freudian slip by referring to this work as archaeology's new *version* of ancient Israel and the origin of its sacred texts, but it was an honest mistake . . . I think.)

This text is well organized. Each chapter begins with a summary of the Biblical narrative and then discusses how recent archaeological discoveries and understandings controvert previously held perceptions of that particular text. Critics have suggested the book is ideologically controlled . . . and, for sure, it is . . . but according to the authors' stated purpose, I would think that was a given.

With caution I have encouraged several of my students to read this book for two reasons: (1) for its accommodating organization, and (2) for its ability to give my students a quick reality shock – especially if they are not familiar with contemporary teachings in Near Eastern archaeology. It should be read with vigilance, and balanced by the reading of a book such as Kitchen's *On the Reliability of the Old Testament*.[8] The Finkelstein text is biased and *does* have an *agenda* to destroy the historicity of the Hebrew Bible – a bias which is clearly acknowledged and stated by its authors. (I appreciate their forthrightness in saying so . . . rather than keeping it hidden, like a landmine ready to be tripped by the unwary reader.)

Here is one area where unsuspecting students get ambushed: Christian professors who assign readings from books such as this should be prepared to fill the apologetic void they can create. If you tear it down, rebuild. Don't leave the lot empty. There's a world of difference between tearing down to rebuild a better structure, and tearing down for the sake of tearing down.

"So whether you eat or drink or whatever you do, do it all for the glory of God. Do not cause anyone to stumble, whether Jews, Greeks or the church of God (1 Corinthians 10:31-32)."

Finkelstein is currently the Jacob M. Alkow Professor of the Archaeology of Israel in the Bronze Age and Iron Ages at Tel Aviv University, and is also the co-director of excavations at Megiddo in northern Israel. Previously, he was the director of the Sonia and Marco Nadler Institute of Archaeology at Tel Aviv University from 1996 to 2002.

He was born in Petah Tikva, Israel, and is a graduate of Tel Aviv University. He wrote his doctoral thesis on the Izbet Sartah excavations, for which he was also the field director. Considered a leading authority on Middle Eastern archeology, Finkelstein's specialty is in the early history of Israel. He has built his career being critical of first-generation archaeologists who interpreted the results of their excavations as confirming the Biblical narratives of the conquest. Over the years, Finkelstein has earned a reputation for controversy . . . being one of the first to describe tenth century Jerusalem (the period associated with the Biblical Kings David and Solomon) as a mere 'village' or tribal center. He also argues that the final edition of the Hebrew Bible was written in the Persian or Greek period, sometime after the return from the Babylonian exile.

Finkelstein is criticized by (among others) Michael D. Coogan, editor of *The New Oxford Annotated Bible*, who contends that Finkelstein and his colleague "move from the hypothetical to the improbable to the absurd."[9]

Finkelstein is a member of the new generation of Israeli archaeologists whose goal is to present how the latest archaeological discoveries have basically overturned our long-held beliefs and assumptions about the historicity of the Old Testament. Consider the implications and ramifications in these two key excerpted paragraphs:

> "It is highly unlikely that the Egyptian garrisons throughout the country would have remained on the sidelines as a group of refugees (from Egypt) wreaked havoc throughout the province of Canaan. And it is inconceivable that the destruction of so many loyal vassal cities by the invaders would have left absolutely no trace in the extensive records of the Egyptian empire. The only

independent mention of the name Israel in this period – the victory stele of Merneptah – announces only that this otherwise obscure people, living in Canaan, had suffered a crushing defeat. Some-

> **stele**
> (stē'lē, stēl) – An inscribed stone or wooden slab used as a monument, grave marker, commemorative tablet in the face of a building, or as a territorial marker to delineate land ownership.

thing clearly doesn't add up when the biblical account, the archaeological evidence, and the Egyptian records are placed side by side."[10]

"The process that we describe here is, in fact, the opposite of what we have in the Bible: the emergence of early Israel was the outcome of the collapse of the Canaanite culture, not its cause. And most of the Israelites did not come from outside Canaan – they emerged from within it. There was no mass Exodus from Egypt. There was no violent conquest of Canaan. Most of the people who formed early Israel were local people whom we see in the highlands throughout the Bronze and Iron Ages. The early Israelites were – irony of ironies – themselves originally Canaanites!"[11]

The Biblical narrative on Jericho, with the blowing of the rams' horns that resulted in the walls of Jericho crumbling to the ground, is (according to Finkelstein) nothing more than a "romantic mirage."

Thomas L. Thompson

For Thompson, combining the term *Biblical* with *archaeology* is antithetical because (as he sees things) there are no links between the two. Of his dozen-plus publications, I typically recommend my students read his *Early History of the Israelite People: From the Written & Archaeological Sources.*[12]

Thompson was born in 1939 in Detroit, Michigan. He is a Biblical theologian who lives in Denmark. Thompson obtained his bachelor's degree from Duquesne University in 1962, and his doctorate at Temple University in 1976. He has held several positions: instructor at the University of Dayton, assistant professor at the University of Detroit, research associate at Tuebingen, visiting professor at École Biblique, visiting associate professor at Lawrence University, and associate professor at Marquette University. He was named a National Endowment for the Humanities Fellow in 1988. Perhaps a little too radical for the educational climate in America, Thompson took a professorship at the University of Copenhagen in 1993 and became a Danish citizen.

The core of Thompson's work has been to highlight what he perceives to be the empty frontier that exists between the Bible (specifically the Old Testament) and archaeology. He made history back in 1974 when he released *The Historicity of the Patriarchal Narratives*. In this early work, he assaulted the then-dominant view that Biblical archaeology had confirmed the historicity of Abraham and the Biblical events such as the Exodus and the conquest of Canaan. He rattled more than a few cages in 1993 when he first released *The Early History of the Israelite People* (the premise of which is that the Israelites were a mythical – rather than historical – people). In *The Mythic Past: Biblical Archaeology and the Myth of Israel*, he argued that the Bible was a product of the period between the fifth and second centuries BC, a notion that has taken root in academic circles. His *The Bible in History: How Writers Create a Past* (1999) expands on the above. All of these books continue to be widely used in universities around the world.

Thompson has always been a controversial figure in Biblical studies, but now his views do not seem as radical as they once did. He has been joined by many others who hold that the Bible's history is not supported by any archaeological evidence. Thompson summarizes the relationship between the Bible and archaeology this way: Any attempt "to write a history of the late second – or early first-millennium B.C. in Palestine – on the basis of a direct integration of biblical and extra-biblical sources . . . must appear not only dubious but wholly ludicrous."[13] In his view, there *cannot* be a field of study known as *Biblical archaeology* – because there are no links between the Bible and the archaeological evidence whatsoever.

McCarthy and Sturgis

In November 2001, ITV in the United Kingdom began airing a Sunday night television series called *It Ain't Necessarily So*, hosted by John McCarthy. Born in 1956 of Irish Catholic origin, McCarthy is a British journalist. His name may be familiar to you, since he was the British journalist who was kidnapped by Islamic Jihadist terrorists in Lebanon in April 1986, and held hostage for more than five years. McCarthy was Britain's longest-held hostage in Lebanon, having spent more than five years in captivity until his release in August 1991. He shared a cell with the Northern Irish hostage Brian Keenan for several years. (His fiancée, Jill Morrell, had campaigned for his release, and most people assumed they would marry. The couple wrote a book together about his ordeal in Lebanon, but separated amicably in 1994.)

Matthew Sturgis wrote a book, *It Ain't Necessarily So: Investigating the Truth of the Biblical Past*,[14] to accompany McCarthy's television series. Both the series and the book are more entertaining than scholarly in format, but their shock factor attracted a large audience. Neither McCarthy nor Sturgis are scholars; they are both journalists.

Sturgis broaches the question: "If the children of Israel did not sweep into Canaan and conquer it, did they ever escape out of Egypt and cross the wilderness? Indeed, were they ever in Egypt? . . . For them (the majority of scholars) – in the absence of archaeological evidence – the Exodus – like the story of Joshua's conquest – remains an exploded myth."[15]

Sturgis makes a critically important observation. The very foundations of the Biblical record have been challenged and shaken. "A God-given conquest of the Promised Land and a distinct racial identity as God's Chosen People: these are the two great planks of Jewish tradition. Take them away and it seems to realign radically the accepted story of the Old Testament. It undermines the entire dynamic of the biblical narrative."[16]

And what of the grandeur of Jerusalem and Solomon's kingdom that the Bible talks about? "For most scholars the compass and character of Solomon's kingdom has dwindled," Sturgis says. "For some it has vanished to nothingness . . .. Solomon's grandeur remains stubbornly and disconcertingly mythical."[17]

Thus, the mythical nature of the Bible extends far beyond the creation story of Genesis. John McCarthy states, "When the site at Jericho was reworked in the 1950s, it was discovered that the walls had fallen down long before Joshua and his people were supposed to have arrived – and that at the time Jericho was almost certainly unoccupied . . .. [T]he conquest of the Promised Land by the Children of Israel began to evaporate into the thin hazy air. The fact that the archaeological evidence at Jericho – and other sites mentioned in the Bible – refutes the conquest story, came as a shock . . ..

"Archaeologist after archaeologist told me that not only was there no conquest of Canaan by Joshua and the Children of Israel, but that the Israelites were, in fact, Canaanites."[18]

McCarthy summarizes it this way: "There is no archaeological evidence whatsoever that Jerusalem was a great city of palaces and temples at the times of Kings David and Solomon. Archaeologists have found much material from earlier periods, and much from later, but from the tenth century BC there is nothing."[19]

McCarthy's statement is correct. The truth is: there is no evidence that Jerusalem was a great city in the tenth century BC. *This was one of the many discoveries that also rattled my own faith during my years of graduate study in Israel* (more on that later in this book). Before you jump to conclusions . . . know that we will be discussing *why* this 'specific evidence' is nonexistent in later chapters. (It's not what you think.)

Michael D. Coogan

One of the more conservative texts used on university campuses today is *The Old Testament: A Historical and Literary Introduction to the Hebrew Scriptures* (2006). I refer to this text myself when teaching my Old Testament classes. Its author, Michael D. Coogan, is professor of religious studies at Stonehill College (Roman Catholic). He is also director of publications for the Harvard Semitic Museum. Prior to his post at Stonehill, he taught at Harvard University, Boston College, Wellesley College, Fordham University, and the University of Waterloo (Ontario). He has participated in and directed archaeological excavations in Israel, Jordan, Cyprus, and Egypt.

Coogan is one of the leading Biblical scholars in the United States. In addition to the above mentioned textbook, he also authored or edited *The Illustrated Guide to World Religions, The Oxford Companion to the Bible, The Oxford History of the Biblical World, The New Jerome Biblical Commentary*, and The *Old Testament: A Very Short Introduction.*

You may have seen Coogan in the two-hour special *The Bible's Buried Secrets* on PBS's Nova series. The documentary investigated the origins of the ancient Israelites, the evolution of their belief in one God, and the creation of the Bible. Coogan, along with other leading Biblical scholars and archaeologists, provided in-depth information throughout the film (which, by the way, took more than four years to produce). Centered on the Old Testament, it examined the critical issues in Biblical archaeology about the true meaning of the historical stories of Abraham, Moses, and other Bible figures.

In his Old Testament introduction textbook, Coogan discusses the relationship of myth and the Bible as follows:

> "Ancient cultures were as intrigued as we are by beginnings, and they constructed elaborate myths – narratives in which the principal characters are gods – to explain their own prehistory. The establishment of the natural and social orders is typically presented in these myths as the work of a deity, usually the principal god or goddess of the city or region in which they were written. Like their Near Eastern neighbors, biblical writers made use of myths to explain the origin of their world. For both groups, however, the narratives of origins were not just myth, but history too. The modern distinction between myth and history probably is drawn too sharply, since mythic conventions informed the interpretation of the past in ancient historical writing, and accounts

of origins were the beginning of the record of a historical process that was guided divinely.

The early chapters of Genesis deal with prehistory and are largely mythical. In these Israelite expressions of the origins of the world, of society, and of civilization, the principal agent is the god of Israel. Although intended as the prologue to the larger historical narrative that follows in Genesis and beyond, these chapters are not historical in any modern sense: that is, they do not accurately represent what astrophysics, geology, paleontology, and other disciplines show took place, whether in terms of chronology or the origin of species."[20]

On the conquest of the land by Joshua, he says, "For much of the history of its interpretation, the narrative of the conquest of the land of Canaan by Joshua and the Israelites was accepted as an accurate account of what had actually taken place. That view, however, was irrevocably altered by modern study of the book and its biblical context and by archaeological evidence."[21]

Because Coogan leaves room for a kernel of actual history in the Biblical narrative, he is grouped with those considered to be conservative.

"For biblical writers, the United Monarchy, the reigns of David and Solomon, was a golden age, like Augustan Rome or Elizabethan England. Its success is presented as the result of divine favor and the fulfillment of the promise to Abraham . . ..

"It now seems unlikely that Israel's power over the territories that surrounded it was as wide-reaching or as continuous as this. *Nevertheless, underlying the apparently exaggerated claims is **a kernel of history**.*"[22] [Emphasis mine.]

Peter Enns

On 27 March 2008, the board of trustees at Westminster Theological Seminary announced that professor Peter Enns would be suspended from teaching at the conclusion of the 2007-2008 school year.[23] The often heated controversy that led to the board's decision began after the release of Enns's 2005 book, *Inspiration and Incarnation: Evangelicals and the Problem of the Old Testament.*[24]

In the book, Enns unflinchingly tackles some scholarly territory hitherto unspoken in evangelical circles. At the very heart of this controversy is his view of Biblical inspiration and hermeneutics, a view not traditionally held by evangelicals and, by and large, more commonly associated with liberal Biblical scholars. Since it is not within the parameters of the present study to delve into the Biblical inspiration, inerrancy, and hermeneutics debate,[25] I wish, for our purposes, to simply point out two things.

First, I would draw your attention to Enns's position on the Bible's relationship to ancient myth. Like Coogan, Enns states that the first chapters of Genesis are firmly grounded in ancient myth. Some of Enns's critics have suggested there is even a more serious danger to his views due to the stringent way he defines myth: "an ancient, premodern, prescientific way of addressing questions of ultimate origins in the form of stories." Based on this definition of ancient myth, Enns's views leave little to no room for the traditional evangelical posture on matters of the historicity of the Hebrew Bible.

Second, and the most important point of this section relating to Enns, is that the seminary administration confirms for us their belief that – even though too controversial for Westminster – Enns's "teaching and writings fall within the purview of Evangelical thought."[26] In other words, the myth of creation is now acceptably within the purview of evangelical thought. That's not the end of the world, but I do not believe such a statement would have been possible by a strongly evangelical seminary (at least in a public pronouncement) fifty or so years ago. But attending an evangelical Christian college or university in the twenty-first century no longer means that you will not be exposed to varying degrees of the 'Bible as myth' viewpoint. Perhaps you have discovered this already.

Now that we know what the experts believe about the Bible . . . we need to turn to a far more important critic: *you.*

3

What Do You *Really* Believe About the Bible?

For those who have embraced the Bible as their authoritative measure of faith and practice, this entire matter becomes quite personal and critical. Being told by archaeological experts that it can now be conclusively proven beyond any doubt that the Bible is myth can pierce and penetrate your heart far deeper than other dispassionate matters of scholarship.

Tell al-Sultan (Old Testament Jericho)

Toward the end of the first year of my graduate studies in Israel, my encounters with numerous textbooks, professors, archaeologists, ancient texts, and archaeological sites such as Tell al-Sultan (Jericho) were all beginning to take their toll. One weekend I wrote several letters

33

(much like Lindsey's e-mail to me) to my former professors and pastors whom I thought might be able to share some insight on these matters. Guess what? *No one* answered, save one – my New Testament Greek professor. His response was of no help, since he was honest enough to tell me that my questions went well beyond anything he had ever studied.[1] He promised that he would be praying for me, and asked that I share the answers with him when I found them.

Looking back, those were some bumpy years – spiritually and intellectually – for me. But when I see the challenges faced by today's students, I believe theirs are a thousand times worse. Their issues are far more thorny than mine ever were. Why? Because the society they have grown up in is far more disconnected from God and the Bible than it was when I was a student. Students today are required to also deal with entrenched postmodern challenges to Biblical faith that are assaulting the Church from every direction. In addition, they are faced with even tougher questions from archaeology, history, science, philosophy, eastern religions, atheism, agnosticism, Islam, the cults, our turbulent and confused culture, the media, and our own proclivity for self-deception . . . to name just a few.

A Critical Faith Lesson from Computers

I was nearly finished writing this book when I booted up the computer in my study just as I did every other morning. But soon the machine started acting strangely . . . doing things I hadn't asked it to do. It was getting slower and slower, and I knew something had to be seriously wrong when I could type faster than the computer could display it on screen.

Suddenly, everything froze. My keyboard and mouse were useless. To make matters worse, I had worked exceptionally late the night before and, exhausted, failed to back up my hard drive (as is my standard practice). With a knot forming in my stomach, I reached down and held the power button until the computer shut down. Thank God for Rob, my professional computer-expert friend who immediately came to my aid.

When Rob rebooted my computer using anti-virus software, he discovered and eradicated 'malware' – short for "malicious software" – in the form of several viruses and worms (a specific type of virus designed to propagate across many computers, typically by creating copies of itself in each computer's memory). He also removed two "Trojan horse" viruses that had been hiding in my Windows program for who knows how long. Like its Greek mythological counterpart, these viruses frequently conceal themselves by appearing to be something else. (That's what happened with the "Swen" virus that spread through e-mails in the early 2000s, disguised as a Microsoft update application.) Trojans normally do one of two things: they either destroy or modify data the moment they launch. They can erase a hard drive, or attempt to ferret out and steal passwords, credit card numbers, and other such confidential information – which was the 'back door' type I had caught. Trojans can be a bigger problem than other types of malware since they are designed to be destructive or annoyingly disruptive.

Today's malware is more sophisticated, using "obfuscation" . . . having built-in tools to defend against detection and removal. They not only hide, they can also ward off attempts to remove them.

Your computer can get infected by malware in several ways. Malware comes in a variety of forms. Software is considered malware when the perceived intent of its creator is to maliciously infiltrate, damage, or crash your computer system or steal the private identity data stored on your hard drive. One of the major risks you face when accessing the Internet is malware.

Malware is a growing and serious problem. According to Symantec, the release rate of malware likely exceeds that of legitimate software.[2] F-Secure claims that as much malware was produced in 2007 as in the previous twenty years combined.[3] Anti-malware laws have been added to the legal codes of several states.

After days of work and running multiple scans from Microsoft and other manufacturers, Rob discovered that, in addition to the first two back-door Trojans, there were fifteen other types of malware, ranging from medium to severe. As he worked to resolve the computer problems, I was strongly impressed with the reality that one of the major threats faced by believers in Jesus Christ in today's world is 'spiritual malware.'

Spiritual Malware

Think of it this way: Lindsey, the college student whose e-mail started chapter one, has had her mind and heart infected with a very sophisticated and dangerous spiritual malware of the twenty-first century.

As serious as malware is in the computer world, spiritual malware – doubts about the integrity of the Bible, suspicions that archaeological evidence doesn't corroborate historic events, reservations that God may not even exist, etc. – is even more serious.

On a computer, malware can hijack your browser, steal your personal identity data, redirect your search attempts to nasty websites, serve up unwelcome pop-up ads, track what websites you visit, cause your computer to behave bizarrely, damage your operating system, crash your computer or permanently destroy your data. Spiritual malware can hijack your mind and heart, steal your personal identity, redirect your search attempts to the wrong places, serve up unwelcome pop-up ads to sin, cause you to behave bizarrely, damage your Christian worldview operating system, or crash and destroy your faith data.

Worse, it's so very easy to get infected with spiritual malware. And once it's planted, it's difficult to remove. It behaves in the same way as computer malware. Many of your hidden doubts will 'reinstall' themselves – even after you think you have removed them. Spiritual malware can make a ruin of your heart and mind. It must be dealt with promptly.

Realize that there's a battle raging for your soul in the spiritual realm. Not everything you read, not every documentary you see on television, not every website or online study is accurate. And hear this: **not everything your professors tell you is necessarily trustworthy.** The anti-malware program on your computer is continually on guard against threats – and so must you be. Once you have allowed spiritual malware to be installed in your heart, it seeks to prolong its presence by staying concealed until ready to launch its attack. In your computer, techniques known as 'rootkits' permit this concealment by modifying your computer's operating system. Your worldview can also be modified, and it can happen so gradually you may never be aware that it has happened. Like rootkits on your computer, this malicious process can run without being seen, or keep its files from being read.

The analogies seem almost endless:

- Keep your heart's software patched and current.
- Both your Christian worldview operating system and your anti-malware apologetics must be updated on a regular basis.
- Run intellectual scans on a regular basis – and at the first hint of trouble.
- Only download from reputable sources. There are multiple sources that have the appearance of being reputable but are based on faulty or biased interpretations of the truth.
- Always think before you install something, weigh the risks and benefits, and be aware of the fine print.
- Install and use a firewall to protect that which you know to be true from unwarranted attacks.

Prevention is always better than cure. So I suggest it will be helpful for us to think of the next few paragraphs as your initial 'anti-spiritual-malware scan,' of sorts. As with computer scans, it has its limitations . . . in that it will be scanning for specific spiritual malwares related to the historicity of the Bible. Perhaps you are already aware of malware in your heart. Maybe it's already causing you havoc, and you're ready to crash. Or maybe you have *already* crashed, and need to remove the malware and rebuild your entire operating system.

If everything seems to be running well for you, great. But remember that computers can appear to function normally when infected, so it is always advisable to run scans even if you seem to be fine. Just as malware accomplishes its goals in your computer without being detected, the same holds true for your heart.

The obvious question is: how do you scan your heart for spiritual malware?

I'll tell you.

A Critical Question

Try this exercise: In your mind's eye, imagine yourself walking to wherever it is in your home or office that you keep a Bible. Now reach for it, pick it up and hold it in your hand. Look at it in your hands and ask yourself, "What is this I am holding?" The answer to that question – not just your quickly verbalized response, but the honest life-commitment answer – is what you need to ask yourself as you go through this study.

For example, is the Old Testament reality . . . or just another mythological tale from antiquity? Is the Bible you're holding *fact* or *fiction* . . . or is it both? Is it truth or fairy tale? Were the people of the Bible real historical figures or simply the invention of the storytellers? Are the Biblical narratives purely a collection of allegorical folktales?

If a majority of today's highly esteemed scholars (including too many Biblical scholars) and archaeologists were asked these same questions, they would vigorously proclaim that the Bible in their hands was nothing more than a collection of mythological fairy tales. Even some of the more conservative ones – in particular Biblical scholars (as we shall see in the next chapter) – would answer that, even though the Bible contains a percentage of truth, in reality it also contains a fair amount of exaggerated fairy tale. Liberal or conservative, the overwhelming majority of them would point to what they consider to be conclusive archaeological evidence to support their position that the narratives of the Hebrew Bible are nothing more than an invented history concocted to explain the emergence of Israel.

Was Joshua's conquest of Jericho (Tell al-Sultan) an invented history, as we are now being told by the experts, or did it really take place in time and space history as the Bible claims? Why are scholars now telling us that the Biblical account of the Israelite conquest of Canaan can no longer be considered verifiable history? Are the new-generation archaeologists of our day correct in proclaiming Biblical archaeology's final demise? These are not trivial questions; the integrity of the Bible and our Christian faith hang in the balance.

We must recognize the significance of academia's revised interpretations of raw archaeological data which dismisses the historicity of the Bible. These are not only a strike against the Bible and personal faith, they also undermine the very foundation and fabric of western culture. With Biblical moral absolutes out of the way, westerners can now legally redefine marriage and make arbitrary, relativistic determinations on what is right and wrong for an infinite number of issues. If the Bible is nothing more than myth, then our faith, our entire belief system, and our worldview are based upon myth. If the Bible is nothing more than myth, then the Judaeo-Christian foundation of western civilization is based upon myth. This has far-reaching ramifications. Even though many of today's scholars would rather disregard this fact, you cannot study the history of western civilization without acknowledging the Bible's central role. If we do not have a historical Bible, what do we have?

Each individual – including you who are reading this book – approaches the Bible with his or her own unique set of baggage. Each will approach it from a unique level of faith. Not everyone's computer is infected with the exact same malware.

Honest Unbelief

In the Gospel of Mark is an interesting account of a distraught father whose son had been plagued by an evil spirit since childhood.[4] First he came to the disciples, but they were unable to heal the boy. Then Jesus stepped in.

The father said to Jesus, "If you can do anything, take pity on us and help us."

"'If you can'?" said Jesus. "Everything is possible for him who believes."

Immediately the boy's father exclaimed, "I do believe; help me overcome my unbelief!"

Jesus did not rebuke that father – He rebuked the boy's evil spirit, and cast it out. To that man's honest doubts – and his honesty in confessing them – Jesus responded with compassion.

In the same way, God cares about the ambushes of intellectual doubt that sometimes plague us. It may seem as if the answers don't seem to come fast enough. But by the grace of God, they do eventually come, even if not all of them.

There's often a phobic panicky feeling that comes with the thought that what you have believed all your life may not be true after all. God is not like Santa Claus . . . where, when you get old enough, you discover he doesn't exist. He is real . . . and He can help you overcome your unbelief. Perhaps you are angry because you feel you have been deceived into belief by your Christian parents, or the person who led you to the Lord, or by the church. Maybe you're disgusted with the entire religion thing, denying the possibility that a journey of faith even exists; you just picked this book up out of curiosity. No matter where you are on life's journey or who you are, the Spirit of God likely has something to share with you in the days ahead.

I realize some of you reading this may have not even started on the journey of faith. Some of you may have begun the journey and then quit. Some of you have started the journey, but struggle with doubt. Each of us is stationed somewhere along this journey . . . solidly grounded with an unmovable faith . . . or battling with some degree of doubt or unbelief . . . or some place feeling disconnected or lost along the way. No matter what your station on the journey, God can help. He is there and He is not silent. God can and does answer – even requests such as the father of the demonized boy.

If you were reared in a Bible-believing Christian home or came to faith in Jesus Christ later in life, and you now find yourself in some setting feeling totally unprepared for the onslaught of anti-Bible, anti-faith, and anti-Judaeo-Christian values that are coming your way, I empathize with you, and hope God will persuade you not to start looking for the closest exit ramp from the journey of Biblical faith.

If you are currently a college student . . . the professors, textbooks, and other students you may have encountered on campus (you know . . . the ones that seem so hostile to your faith and Christianity in general) may be trapped in postmodernism. They are hostile toward anything or anyone making a clear claim to authoritative truth or meaning. It is likely that they have adopted a cultural context that automatically rejects what has been called the meta-narrative[5]: any single overarching view of the world and meaning. By rejecting the notion of any overarching system or ideology that purports universal truth or authority (such as the Bible), there can be no certainty. I am referring here to postmodernism, which we will discuss more completely in chapter four.

If you are currently struggling with doubt, let me encourage you by saying this: if you are experiencing anything similar to what I experienced as a graduate student in Israel, my guess is that the apologetics you were taught in your church, if any, have already started to crumble . . . that is if they haven't already totally failed you. In my years as a professor, I have witnessed this scenario over and over again. For too many, the constant diet of irrelevant entertaining fluff you were spoon-fed at your church student ministry doesn't even begin to cut it in the real world. With the technology we now have, our culture and the civilizations of our world are changing at such a rapid pace, it is impossible to keep up with things.

The news and educational websites and related search engines that make the rapid sharing of information (true and false) possible in our digital world . . . combined with YouTube, MySpace, Facebook, instant messaging services, Twitter, blogging, podcasting, and photo/video-sharing phones, etc. . . . have revolutionized our world. Maybe seminaries should institute a required course for pastors – something similar to netlingo.com – just so they can stay relevant. Sadly, there are many pastors who have not kept up (or even attempt to do so) with this technology . . . and, as a result, are unaware of the issues and challenges you are facing. It would be unfair (and impossible) to expect every pastor to have all the answers. But frankly speaking, too many clergy and non-clergy alike are sorely lacking in training when it comes to relevant Christian apologetics. They frequently find themselves at an embarrassing loss, or answer flippantly, when asked the hard questions. Never give up your faith because those you have looked up to in the past are now unable to answer your questions.

I tell you this because it almost happened to me.

How did my faith survive? There's one lesson I learned that you must learn, too. Let me share it with you.

The War of the Worldviews

Oxford chemist Peter Adkins said, "Science and religion cannot be reconciled."[6] This has been a widely held view for many decades. This same mindset has also become prominent in the field of archaeology, especially as it relates to what was formerly known as Biblical archaeology. Most archaeologists whose expertise is in the ancient Near East now espouse Adkins' mindset: archaeology and the Bible cannot be reconciled.[7]

But not all scientists are atheists. There are, for example, Christian scientists at the highest levels, such as the director of the Human Genome Project, physicist Bill Phillips, who won the Nobel Prize. There are still respected scientists who believe in a personal God who answers prayer.[8]

The conflict that exists between scientists who hold to scientific humanism and scientists who hold to Judaeo-Christian theism is *not* a conflict between science and religion. The conflict that exists between archaeologists who hold to scientific humanism and archaeologists who hold to Judaeo-Christian theism is also *not* a conflict between archaeology and the Bible. **The conflict is first and foremost a worldview conflict**.[9] In both cases – 'science versus the Bible' and 'archaeology versus the Bible' – it is not the evidence that is creating the conflict. It has more to do with the *interpretation* of the evidence, rather than the evidence itself.

Let's briefly consider the 2009 Copenhagen conference on climate change, which totally exposes this reality. This conference gathered together the top leaders and climate experts of the world. It was long touted to be the conference that would give birth to the international cooperation needed to end global warming. However, the conference quickly turned into a spectacular failure. The leaked e-mails and other documents from the Climate Research Unit at the University of East Anglia (nicknamed by the media "climate-gate") unquestionably revealed that leading climate scientists had deliberately destroyed and manipulated evidence in an effort to promote their position on climate change. They silenced the scientists who had strong doubts about the accuracy of the CRU data by preventing them from publishing their findings in peer-reviewed journals.

As reported by CBS news, "The e-mails show some of the world's top experts decided to exclude or manipulate some research that didn't help prove global warming exists."[10]

The lesson to be learned has nothing to do with global warming – it's this: what appears to be science is not always science; what appears to be documented fact is not always fact. Just as with the climate change scientists, it is equally possible (if not likely) that expert archaeologists – whose worldview presupposes that the Bible is myth – *will interpret the archaeological evidence through the lenses of their bias.* It is just as possible that some of the world's top archaeological experts might – again, based upon their agenda – *deliberately exclude or manipulate evidence* that doesn't help prove their Bible-as-myth position.

There's a joke about a man who believed himself to be dead. Some friends convinced him to see a therapist. After a long discussion, the therapist was exasperated because he was not able to convince the man that he wasn't dead. Then the therapist got an idea.

"Let me ask you a question," the therapist said. "Do dead people feel pain?"

"Absolutely not," the man replied.

The therapist then pulled out a needle and, without warning, stuck his patient.

"Ouch!" the man yelped.

"Did you feel that?" the therapist asked.

"Absolutely," the man agreed.

Satisfied with his demonstration, the therapist asked a question he thought would have an obvious response: "Since you agree that dead people are incapable of feeling pain – and you admitted you felt pain when I stuck you – what can you conclude?"

The man answered: "That dead people *do* feel pain."

As ridiculous as the punch line sounds, there are many people – even scholars and experts – who take the same attitude when they interpret evidence. Let me explain.

No matter how objective we try to be or think we are, everyone reads, writes, behaves, and interprets from within his or her own worldview. To a certain extent, everyone thinks epistemologically and metaphysically within the framework of their own presuppositions and worldview. And the reality is (as demonstrated by the scandal that clouded the Copenhagen conference): *an expert's objectivity can be compromised* – not only by their worldview, but also by a deliberate agenda.

> **epistemology**
> The branch of philosophy that has to do with the origin, nature, methods, and limits of human knowledge. Think of it this way. How do I know what I know? How do I know I know the things I think I know?
>
> **metaphysics**
> The branch of philosophy that treats the science of being (ontology), the reality of our existence, for example, and the origin and structure of the universe (cosmology), such as how we all got here.

As you sit in the lecture hall, or read a textbook or scholarly article, persistently keep in mind that the bias of the archaeologist's worldview or possible agenda has definitely played a part, to some degree, in how he or she has interpreted their so-called evidence against the Bible. Authoritative-sounding statements that boldly proclaim the Bible is nothing more than myth may, in reality, not be as factual as they appear to be. As we will document in the chapters that follow, archaeology is not a rigid science; artifacts do not come with labels. The archaeologist looks at the artifact and then tries to decide what it means (or decides what he or she *wants* it to mean), and labels it accordingly. An archaeologist with an anti-Bible worldview will likely interpret and label artifacts according to that worldview. Because one's worldview plays a major role in the labeling process, it is just as likely that another archeologist, with a theistic worldview, might interpret the meaning of the very same artifacts quite differently.

In the next chapter, we will begin our study by firstly examining the *worldview/agenda conflict* before we examine the particulars of the Bible's supposed conflict with the archaeological evidence.

Weathering the Storm

So . . . what are the results of your initial anti-malware scan? Only you and God know. As you read the chapters that follow . . . and we work through the serious challenges posed by postmodernism, historical theology, new-generation archaeology, and philology . . . I trust you will be encouraged to hold on to – perhaps even renew – your faith. My prayer is that you will be able to cling to your hope in God until the storm of questions, contradictions, and chaos passes, and things change for the better. May you find enough hope to carry on, even if your faith seems nowhere to be found.

"We wait in hope for the LORD; he is our help and our shield . . .. May your unfailing love rest upon us, O LORD, even as we put our hope in you (Psalm 33:20, 22)." When all is said and done, may yours be yet another story of a God-given faith that has overcome the malwares of disbelief and uncertainty only to emerge with a stronger revitalized faith. By the grace of God may you successfully expose and delete the dangerous malwares that have attacked – or may currently be attacking – your faith. And may that which you discover on your journey be useful in helping others remove their spiritual malware as well.

If that sounds farfetched at this point in your faith journey, I encourage you to read on. We're only just getting started.

4

Postmodernism's Attack on Biblical Truth

The America in which previous generations grew up was a society that, for the most part, respected the Bible. It was an integral part of every aspect of their lives. Public school classes opened their day with a reading from the Bible before the Pledge of Allegiance and morning prayers. The Bible was respected and integrated into our laws. The Ten Commandments were openly displayed in our courts of justice. Even politicians and entertainers were heard quoting a verse or two now and then.

Not all that long ago, George Gallup Jr., president of the American Institute of Public Opinion, declared 1976 the "Year of the Evangelical." A Gallup poll of 1,553 Americans conducted five weeks prior to his announcement had clearly confirmed the strength of the evangelical movement in the United States. The more conservative venue of American Christianity – evangelicalism – was once again on the move.

About half of the country's Protestants (34 percent of all Americans) said that they had had a 'born-again' experience, a definitive turning point when they committed themselves to Jesus Christ. They also believed that *the Bible was to be taken literally, word for word.* That projects to nearly fifty million Americans over the age of eighteen.[1] And this poll does not include those from groups such as the Roman Catholic and Eastern Orthodox Christian faiths who would also affirm respect for the Bible.

Today, however, we are living in unprecedented times. The West's once-held theistic worldview has been disassembled piece by piece and dethroned. During the latter half of the twentieth century, the West descended into an ever-expanding anti-Christian movement we might call post-Christian America. We have watched the twentieth century give way to a very secular and religiously antagonistic twenty-first century. There are increasing levels of intolerance for things Christian everywhere you look. We see this intolerance rising to heights many of us would have not believed possible, even in the Bible Belt of America. Public policy and the media have become openly hostile toward Christianity in general (especially the evangelical variety), seeing it as one of the main opponents to society's pluralistic common good.

How did the Bible, once so respected in western culture – even by the so-called non-religious – become so disrespected? How did the Bible, once so reverenced and esteemed in Christian circles, become so suspect and doubted even by the so-called faithful? The post-Christian and postmodern worldviews of our day assume a posture of suspicion and skepticism toward any claim to meaning or authoritative truth. Our culture has been conditioned to be suspicious of authority, and reject what today's philosophers call *meta-narratives* (over-arching or transcendent views of the world). A Biblical worldview, of necessity, is accordingly labeled *meta-narrative* because it provides an over-arching explanation for the world and reality. Consequently, this is why the professor in the front of your classroom so adamantly believes that the Bible must be rejected and discarded – because it claims to be authoritative truth.[2] The Bible and Christian faith are viewed in a postmodern society as a threat, a dangerous *meta-narrative* because it claims to make sense of the world through God's absolute, authoritative, unchanging truth.[3]

What is postmodernism? I'm about to explain that, as well as how it became the dominant ideology in the West. But I warn you: stay with me, because some of this gets complicated – if for no other reason than that it's so . . . well . . . *absurd.* Pay attention . . . and you'll see what I mean.

The Postmodern Paradox

It's difficult to define a term when the very thinkers and ideas often referred to as 'postmodern' typically disagree amongst themselves – usually significantly – as well as with existing dictionary definitions. Another reason is that postmodernism, as we shall see, denies the possibility of meaning in the written text. We are thus attempting to assign meaning to something that views meaning as impossible.

Postmodernism is a complicated and conflicting set of ideas. These ideas appear in a wide variety of disciplines or areas of study, including art, history, archaeology, architecture, music, film, literature, sociology, communications, fashion, and technology. Our purpose here is not to write a discourse on postmodernism, but rather to better comprehend this term as a means to understanding the current maze of thinking. With this in mind, we will now try to make some sense of it, since it plays such an important role in current thinking.

To begin, you will find the term *post-modern* in some writings and *postmodern* in others. This is not always by chance. The presence or absence of the hyphen can be used to clarify the author's understanding of the term . . . its meaning (in a system that denies meaning!) to distinguish between the two senses or uses of the word. When you see *post-modern* (with a hyphen) this typically indicates the author believes that post-modernism is the *continuation* of modernism, but in new directions (thus, after modernism – but modernism is still around and a part of it). When you see *postmodern* (without the hyphen), it indicates the author views the concept as something entirely new, *different* from modernism (thus *post*modern, or *after* modernism and separate from it, *replacing* it).[4]

In a nutshell, the postmodern thinker is skeptical, questioning all possibility of truth and clear meaning. The postmodern worldview is suspicious of all authority and motive. Postmodernism rejects:

- The idea that truth is universal.
- That truth can be absolute.
- That truth can be unchanging.

- That truth can be knowable.
- Imposed unities of meta-narrative and hegemony.
- Traditional frames of genre.
- Traditional structure.
- The possibility of stylistic unity.
- Categories that are the result of logo centrism.[5]
- And all other forms of what are viewed as having come from an artificially imposed order.

meta-narrative
A large-scale theory that claims to make sense of the world – an abstract idea that is thought to be a comprehensive explanation of historical experience or knowledge.

hegemony
Control, domination, supremacy.

genre
A set of criteria for a category of composition that establishes some type of boundary; often used to categorize literature and speech.

Within postmodernism, "Historical events could not be verified even if we had a video recording."[6] We see then that the postmodern worldview not only challenges the Bible, it also challenges the conventional historian. In his article "*An Engagement with Postmodern Foes, Literary Theorists and Friends on the Borders with History*," British Professor Patrick K. O'Brien believes that "a majority of professional historians will, I predict, obdurately refuse to incur the costs of engagement at a philosophical level with the postmodern challenge to the very foundations of their craft as practised in Britain, Europe and Japan."[7]

Professor Marwick argues for the necessity of the conventional view of history and meaning on the grounds that "Without knowledge of the past, we would be without identity, we would be lost on an endless sea of time."[8]

Whether they admit it or not, conventional historians are actually arguing many of the tenets of a Biblical worldview. "In epistemology we know a thing is there because God made it to be there. It is not an extension of His essence, it is not a dream of God as much Eastern thinking says they are. It is really there."[9] Our universe and the planet we live on have an objective reality. There is a correlation between the observed and the observer because that's the way God made it. There is a correlation between the knower and the known, between the subject and object, between the noun and the verb. There is a correlation between the who, what, when, where, and why. And we can be truthful when reporting on a certain correlation – or we can lie about that correlation. *To do history at all, one must assert the rational existence of truth.*

Everything we have talked about thus far in this chapter is especially important for those of you born after the mid 1980s. You have been born into a post-Christian, postmodern society. You have grown up having to deal with this prominent philosophical landscape as an obstacle to developing a Biblical worldview and Biblical faith. Our western secular colleges and universities . . . and the textbooks students read . . . have, on the whole, bought into postmodernism. And since much of our media has sold out to post-Christian postmodernism as well, even those who were born well before the 1980s are also being influenced by postmodernism to some degree or another.[10]

The Sun of Theism Sets in the West

So how on earth did the West go from a theistic to a postmodern world-view?

The Bible has had its adversaries in every generation. That's a given. But there was a time (not that long ago, in the grand scheme of things) when text still had meaning . . . when absolute truth was still viewed as possible . . . and when general respect for the Bible in academic circles – and popular attitudes toward the historicity of the Bible in western culture, on the whole – were much the opposite of the prominent anti-Judaeo-Christian worldviews of our postmodern and post-Christian societies of today.

The first chartered institution of higher learning in the American colonies was Harvard College in Cambridge, Massachusetts. It was founded by the Puritans in 1636 so that their local churches would have literate pastors. The college received its name three years after its founding when John

Harvard, a young preacher in nearby Charlestown, died of tuberculosis. He willed half of his estate and his library of four hundred books to the college. The total sum of what this young pastor left the school was not all that much. Books, however, were very expensive at the time. Thus, the value of his books and the Christian spirit with which they were given led to naming the school after Pastor Harvard.

The New England Puritans also founded Yale and Dartmouth when they believed Harvard had been infected with some of the liberal ideologies of the Enlightenment. The Great Awakening in America resulted in the founding of even more Christian universities, such as Princeton in New Jersey . . . where the great missionary preacher Jonathan Edwards became its president in 1757.

All of these great schools of higher learning were founded with the goal of *training pastors for the ministry of sharing the gospel of Jesus Christ* – but *none of them* has kept to the original purposes of their founders. Today, these very same schools are primarily secular in emphasis, deeply entrenched in postmodernism, and tout that most of the Bible is rooted in ancient myth.

Plato (427-347 BC) taught that if there are no universals (absolutes), then the individual things (particulars) have no meaning. This concept is essential not only in abstract thought, but also in everyday life. What did he mean? Individual things are just that. Individual blades of grass make up my front lawn, a universal. My front lawn is an individual thing belonging to my yard, a universal. My yard is an individual thing belonging to my neighborhood, a universal, and so forth. We are all individuals who ultimately belong to the human race, a universal. The individual things find their meaning in the universals to which they belong. In the absence of a universal (absolute), the individual (particular) has no meaning.

French existential philosopher Jean-Paul Sartre (1905-1980) built upon Plato, as did most western philosophers. Sartre utilized Plato's universal/individual viewpoint to explain his growing concern over the direction western civilization was taking in the twentieth century. What was the universal (absolute) that would unify and give meaning to the individual things (the particulars) of living? Sartre, in some ways recapitulating Plato, warned that a *finite* point is absurd if it has no *infinite* reference point.

Sartre's model can be most easily understood in the area of morals. If there is no universal (absolute) moral standard, then an individual cannot say what is right or wrong with any degree of certainty.[11] With no moral universal (absolute) beyond the ideas of men, there is no final appeal to judge between men (or groups of men) whose moral values and judgments conflict. Sartre's concern was that the finite (human beings) would be left without an infinite . . . thereby leading to a society of absurdity, a society of entirely conflicting opinions on moral issues. My, that has a familiar ring to it, doesn't it?

We also need a universal (absolute) in order to define ourselves and find the meaning of the existence of humankind, and as a starting point for knowing. Without a universal (absolute) how do we know we have a solid epistemology? We don't. And that is where the secular world is at. Bottom line: without a universal (absolute) . . . without an infinite reference point . . . the finite points such as morals, values, the meaning of existence, and a basis for knowing are all lost. As you surf the Internet, read the newspaper, and observe the behaviors and attitudes of society, you can surely recognize the meaninglessness and confusion that is occurring in the absence of the universal (absolute). Court rulings seem more absurd every day. Our world has lost its way because, ultimately, we refuse to acknowledge that we can only find meaning in our Creator.

Non-Christian philosophers from the time of the Greeks until modern times were rationalists. That is, they believed they could start and end with humans alone, that humans were capable of creating their own universals (absolutes). Rationalists reject any possibility for knowledge outside the finite, outside of humankind itself. By reasoning, humans should be able (thinking in terms of antithesis) to determine truth from falsehood, right from wrong. We note that Christian philosophers of this time frame likewise believed in reason, and rightfully so . . . but it was reason unified with true knowledge from God as found in the Bible.

Postmodernism replaced modernism, so we need to back up and first be sure we understand the notion of modernism.

No Good Reason

It is generally accepted that modernism can be thought of as being synonymous with, or much the same as, the humanist philosophy of the Enlightenment, which began in the seventeenth century. This would include the philosophical notions that came approximately at the time of the Enlightenment (thus during the seventeenth and eighteenth centuries). The Enlightenment is also called the Age of Reason.

Preceded by the Renaissance, the Enlightenment elevated humanism and human reason as the final arbiters of truth. The expectation was that truth could be discovered by means of human reason and the natural sciences . . . and that these would replace superstition, irrationalism, fears, and beliefs that had been held unquestioningly by previous generations. It was hoped that this would lead to an ordered world in which men thought for *themselves* – instead of following the superstitions of the past. It was at this time that the first encyclopedias were written. Philosophers scrutinized all conventional knowledge and authority by this new-found ability to reason for themselves, especially as regards religious and political thought.

"The utopian dream of the Enlightenment can be summed up by five words: reason, nature, happiness, progress, and liberty. It was thoroughly secular in its thinking. The humanistic elements which had risen during the Renaissance came to flood tide in the Enlightenment. Here was humankind starting from itself absolutely. To the Enlightenment thinkers, humankind and society were perfectible."[12]

The Enlightenment and resultant modernism were concerned with the metaphysical. While it taught that fundamental truth existed, it also taught that there is truth that lies beyond what we consider to be reality, and that it had to be searched for beneath the surface of human existence. Modernism is exemplified in the works of Karl Marx, Sigmund Freud, Albert Einstein's general theory of relativity, the questions posed by quantum theory, and others.

Now . . . postmodernism comes along and questions whether these ideals of the Enlightenment and modernism can actually exist at all! In many respects, we can think of postmodernism as *anti*-modernism. Humankind, having now come full circle, has given up on rationalism – its reasoned effort in modernism – in exchange for an irrationalism in postmodernism. It is skeptical of the very possibility of the truth and meaning that had been encouraged by the Enlightenment. This outcome was predicted by Francis Schaeffer back in 1976.[13]

Some adherents of postmodernism claim it was disillusionment and cynicism with modernism's failures, economic and social conditions, and abuses of what is described as 'late capitalism' that pushed society into this new historical period. We can see the result of this thinking in the current push toward socialism in the United States. Scholars who view postmodernism as a distinct period view society as having collectively eschewed the ideals and notions of modernism, and replaced them with ideals that are in reaction to the restrictions and limitations of modernism.

Alex Callinicos (who sees post-modernism as an extension of modernism), a leading member of the Socialist Workers Party (Britain) – a Marxist organization of the International Socialist Tendency[14] – makes an interesting assessment of postmodernism. He argues for a post-modernism that "reflects the disappointed revolutionary generation of '68 (particularly those of May '68),[15] and the incorporation of many of its members into the professional and managerial 'new middle class.' It is best read as a symptom of political frustration and social mobility rather than as a significant intellectual or cultural phenomenon in its own right."[16] The current move toward 'progressivism' in the West, which leans toward state capitalism, is a direct byproduct of postmodernism. However, this entire phenomenon goes far deeper than arguing the merits of capitalism versus socialism. The true root of this frustration is first and foremost the logical result of man (the particular) reaping what he has sown when trying to live without God (the universal).

Without endorsing his existentialism, we can observe that Sartre was more of a prophet than he realized . . . for we have arrived where he warned we would be. We live in a society where what is right or wrong is more and more being determined by the most popular opinion or the arbitrary ruling of some judge . . . void of universals (absolutes) and any infinite reference point. Even the *possibility* for a universal has now, for the most part, been ruled out as well. (I warned you it would get complicated – and absurd.)

Eclecticism comes from the Greek term εκλεκιτός, meaning *selective.* Eclecticism, consciously or subconsciously, tells us not to follow any one system of, for example, philosophy or theology or worldview. Rather we should select and follow whatever feels right, whatever we consider true . . . that is, whatever we determine to be the best from the multiple systems available to us. We are free to select whatever is on the menu.

Simultaneously, the postmodern worldview is challenging the very possibility of the existence of *any* meaningful truth from which our menu selections can be made. The resultant contradictions and chaos, and the notion that there can be no ultimate meaning – even in the written text – become viewed as the norm. As a result, we find people all around us whose outlook on life has become pessimistic and skeptical. You live in a day when many around you feel disillusioned and empty. If the Bible that once defined our civilization is only a myth . . . if we do not have a historical Bible . . . *what do we have?*

(Something to ponder: What new universal (absolute) will a lost and groping western world, having deposed the God of the Bible, turn to next?)

How Postmodernism Affects Archaeological 'Truth'

Shortly after Napoleon Bonaparte conquered Egypt in the spring of 1799, he led his troops northward to conduct the first European military campaign into the Holy Land since the Crusades. In that year, the vast region of Palestine (sometimes referred to by archaeologists as the Levant[17]) had no political frontiers or national boundaries. (Previous to this, the region was seldom visited by Europeans, except for the occasional traveler who ventured to the interior cities of Nazareth, Jerusalem, and Bethlehem.) In political terms, the region had been part of the Ottoman province of Syria. Napoleon's conquest of the Near East reopened the fascinating world of ancient Egypt and the Holy Land to Bible enthusiasts, western explorers, and scholars. French and British scholars began making exciting finds in this rediscovered ancient Biblical world.[18] It is important that you make note of the fact that this happened during a time when popular attitudes in Western Europe were still generally respectful of the Bible and the theistic worldview.

The Victorian era was the zenith of the British Empire. In many respects it was an amazing period. The British Industrial Revolution was at its apex, and the masses of wealth it generated permitted the intelligentsia to indulge in large libraries, academic pursuits, and the funding of expeditions to the Near East. The imperial nations of Europe were at the height of their power and influence. It was the heyday, if you will, for intercontinental adventures and discoveries. The returning booty generated further wealth to fund even more discoveries.

Keep in mind, this was a moralistic society. It was important to be viewed as upstanding and generous. Philanthropy was revered. Emphasis was placed on the family and family values, Sunday worship, and families were all grounded in the narratives and teachings of the Bible.

Accordingly, archaeologists who were funded to go to the Near East were sent to search for archaeological *proof* for the Biblical narratives . . . and they were expected, by those footing the bill, to return with some. Granted, not everyone went to the Near East for this purpose; there were fortune seekers and those purely interested in enterprise as well. Nonetheless, the early years of exploration and excavation were dominated by those who set out with a Bible in one hand and a trowel in the other. While we might commend them for their Victorian-era respect for the Bible, this approach (as we shall see later) may not have been the best . . . for it backfired on subsequent generations – including our own.

A well-liked hymn from this era reflects the reverential and esteemed position of the Bible in that day. "How Firm a Foundation" is a classic that was sung at the funerals of American presidents Theodore Roosevelt, Woodrow Wilson, and Andrew Jackson. It goes:

> How firm a foundation, ye saints of the Lord,
> Is laid for your faith in His excellent Word!
> What more can He say than to you He hath said,
> To you who for refuge to Jesus have fled?

The Protestant Reformers played a large role in re-establishing the Bible as the firm foundation of faith and culture in the western hemisphere. In Victorian England, the Bible was respected enough that it was not openly challenged. Even in the area of political reforms, the results of the Reformation are impressive. However, the humanistic elements which had surfaced during the Renaissance became a torrent during the Enlightenment and the rise of modern science. By the turn of the century, the idea of an authoritative Bible had become more and more confined to conservative Christian circles. The outcomes of the Enlightenment were in antithesis to those of the Reformation.[19]

As the West's theistic worldview crumbled, the attacks on the integrity, inspiration, and inerrancy of the Bible increased. As respect for the Bible waned, so did the archaeological proofs for the Bible. For more and more people, the 'firm foundation' that had once seemed so unshakable began to shake, crack, and crumble beneath them. More recently, in the postmodern and post-Christian era, this progression of decay continues even in the faith journey of individuals who have called Jesus the Lord and Savior of their lives. For some – including prominent Christian leaders – their view of the Bible and trust in its words has changed so dramatically, they have given up their faith altogether. Others have had one or more faith meltdowns but have recovered. Teachers and leaders who have experienced a faith crash and fail to recover typically not only walk away, they begin preaching their rejection of Christianity with the same fervor with which they once preached the gospel message. The spirit of Drs. Hymenaeus and Philetus of 2 Timothy 2:17-19 is still alive and well.

A Faith Based on Fact

As a young graduate student, I was required to read Colin Brown's *Philosophy & the Christian Faith*. I can't tell you now most of what was in that book – but there was one page that left an indelible mark on my life and I pass it along to you:

A faith which goes on believing regardless of the evidence is not a faith worth having. The biblical idea of faith is trust in God because of what God has done and said. If it could be shown that there were no good reasons for believing that God had said or done these things, the faith would be empty and vain. In saying this, we are not tying faith to the latest book of the scholar who happens to be most fashionable at the time. But we are saying that scholarship has a real place . . .. (W)e are only carrying on what the biblical writers themselves were doing. The Bible is not a promise-box full of blessed thoughts. So much of it is devoted to arguments, demonstrations and appeals to history. To get to the point, we need think no further than the Epistles of the New Testament or of the opening words of Luke's Gospel which stress the historicity of the story of Jesus as the basis of faith. It is upon the truth of such arguments that Christian devotion depends. The ordinary believer is not required to work out all the arguments. But someone has got to do it somewhere for the sake of the faith.[20]

Surely you must think evidence is important to faith . . . or you likely wouldn't be reading this book. Thank God for a new generation of Christians who are stepping up to the plate and choosing to do hard things for God. Your generation can turn the tide. Your generation can make the difference. Because you have grown up in our postmodern culture, you have learned to constantly be aware of the dangers of the postmodern thinking that surrounds you . . . this worldview that encourages and fosters doubt and skepticism. It can give birth to a crisis of faith when you least expect it. Don't exchange the truth of God for the lie of meaninglessness (Romans 1:25).

How tragic that so many of you have grown up in churches that continue to think they are winning or losing the battle based on attendance. Their focus is on entertaining students and playing the numbers game. The battle is so much more sophisticated than that. The church has lost sight of what it means to disciple . . . to teach and thoroughly equip its members . . . becoming a devoted and educated community to support one another, and to carry a relevant Gospel into our postmodern society. We have failed to pass on to our students the firm foundation for a faith that has roots deep enough and strong enough to survive the secular onslaught. Doesn't anyone else find it ironic that, after the billions of dollars the Christian West has spent on student pastors and student ministries and Christian media and music events, we have produced a generation of young Christians the majority of whom – when challenged – know next to nothing about their own faith and the Bible? Yes, they can tell you how they feel about it, but they do not know why they should obey the so-called old-fashioned morals taught in the Bible, or even what comprises the essentials of Biblical faith. Too many of them are vulnerable, ignorant of the Bible (especially the Old Testament), and are unprepared for the academic and social pressures they face in college. Quite bluntly, rather than preparing our sons and daughters to face their first year of university, we are instead often setting them up for failure. We are either oblivious to the challenges they face, or else we're ignoring their hard questions as if they didn't exist.

Thank God there are those rising up from within this "generation that knows not God" who are encouraging their own to step outside the box of the narcissistic society into which they were born, and follow Jesus and His ways. Dismayed by the lack of content and challenge in the baton that was handed them, these kids want to use their intellect for God and others rather than for themselves. They do not want to live their adult lives chasing after infantile materialistic cravings that never satisfy. They actually say that they don't want others to do their thinking and living for them. They *want* to do hard things, using the mind God has given them to make wise decisions prayerfully. They take the time to read and actually study their Bibles and develop an interior spiritual life. They affirm the fact that houses, cars, money, prestige, fame, and power do not define true success.[21]

If you are struggling with doubts, I'll do my best to help you begin working them through. When you do, I can assure you God will use what you have learned to rescue your friends from the emptiness of our postmodern world. There is a correlation between the observed and the observer because that's the way God made it. That's why **a faith not supported by evidence is a faith not worth having**; that's the way God made it. There is a correlation between the knower and the known, between the subject and object, between the noun and the verb. There is a correlation between the who, what, when, where, and why of the past. And we can be truthful when reporting on a certain correlation – or we can *lie* about that correlation. To learn from history at all, one *must* assert the rational existence of truth. In the next chapter, we will begin looking at the evidence.

5

Where Has All the Archaeological Evidence Gone?

First-generation Biblical archaeologists – from Sir William Flinders-Petrie to William Albright and John Bright – all claimed they had found confirmation of the Bible's narratives in their excavations. The Christian world was ecstatic. Leonard Woolley's excavations at Ur (in Southern Iraq) indicated West Semitic Amorites (or Martu) had come to rule close to the time of Abraham's residence in the city. Hammurabi of Babylon was identified with Amraphel of Shinar, one of the four kings confronting Abraham in Genesis. Excavations in Egypt were said to have confirmed the existence of the 'store cities' of Raamses[1] and suggested that Apiru (Hebrews) had been engaged in building projects for Ramesses II. The discovery of the Israel stele that mentions a battle between Egypt and Israel in Canaan was viewed as proof of the settlement of the land after the Exodus by the Children of Israel. John Garstang's excavations at Jericho found large walls split by cracks that confirmed Joshua's attack as reported in the Bible.

Albright claimed he had confirmed the identification of the city of Ai, conquered by Joshua during the settlement of Canaan by the Israelites shortly after the Battle at Jericho.[2] Somewhat later, in the twentieth century, Yigael Yadin and others found what were claimed to be Solomon's city gates

<table>
<tr><td>

ashlar walls

Walls made from cut, rectangular stone as opposed to rubble walls made from irregular, uncut stone. Important for archaeological dating.

</td></tr>
</table>

and associated fortification ashlar walls at the fortress cities at Megiddo, Hazor and Gezer.[3]

But new-generation archaeologists insist the first-generation archaeologists were sorely mistaken in all of their findings. So what happened to the archaeological proofs this previous generation discovered? I believe I can best answer this question by telling you more about my graduate studies in Israel.

First of all . . . Indiana Jones I am not. Archaeology was not my major at Jerusalem University College, but it was *very* much a part of my master's program in Judaeo-Christian studies. Our class had the privilege and thrill of studying the Bible *in* the land of the Bible, examining the Biblical sites firsthand, while sitting under the teaching of several esteemed professors

from Hebrew University (including Anson Rainey, Isaiah Gafni, and Gabriel Barkay as well as the excellent faculty at JUC). Hands down, it was an awe-inspiring, life-changing, almost surreal experience . . . and one that I have always treasured. (And it's why I enjoy sharing Israel with others so much; perhaps you can join me some day.)

Tell Dan

Of all the sites of antiquity we studied, Tell Dan (near the sources of the Jordan River) remains my favorite. Originally known as Laish, it was subjugated by the Phoenicians of Sidon (Judges 18:7, 27ff). Leshem is a variant spelling of Laish (Joshua 19:47). When the tribe of Dan felt the pressure of the Amorites, they packed up and left their original territory and moved northward. In a surprise attack, they captured Laish from the Phoenicians and renamed it Dan (Judges 18). I'm not sure if it is the exciting history . . . the tell . . . the beautiful trees and foliage . . . the taste of the potable pure spring water . . . the fact that it was here archaeologists found the "House of David" inscription . . . or a combination of the above that has always attracted me to

tell
A mound composed of the remains of a succession of previous settlements.

this place (but if you visit the north of Israel, you must make the time to experience Dan).

While I can look back and treasure those years now, it was also a time of questioning, doubting, inner conflict and turmoil . . . even more so in the time following my years of graduate study in Israel.

The First Conflict

I was born and raised into a Baptist home. At the age of five, while watching Oral Roberts Sr. on television, I responded personally to the gospel message and acknowledged my need of the Savior. I remember going across the living room and touching the screen as a symbol of my decision (and then running to the kitchen to tell my mom what I had done). I was young, but it was real and genuine.

For the most part, I grew up in a Baptist environment . . . basically a theologically conservative environment. By my teen years we had changed to another Baptist church in an adjacent township, where I was baptized and had my first church membership. It was there that I began teaching Sunday school – a class of first graders – when I was in junior high school. In fact, I cannot remember a time when I *wasn't* an officer of some sort in our small youth group of about twenty.

At one of our Sunday night youth meetings, during my senior year in high school, I was asked to speak to the group on Joshua 6. I believe we were working our way through the book of Joshua, and chapter six had fallen to me. Using my trustworthy *Halley's Bible Handbook* (which I liked because it always included *amazing archaeological discoveries)*, I began preparing my talk.

My twenty-third edition of *Halley's Bible Handbook: An Abbreviated Bible Commentary* was published by Zondervan Publishing House in 1962. In the foreword, Henry H. Halley (1874-1965) wrote, "In the main, it is a book of FACTS, Biblical and Historical. I have sought to avoid featuring my own opinions on controversial subjects."[4]

Although Halley never traveled to the Holy Land, he was fascinated with Biblical archaeology. His two prized books were McGarvey's *Lands of the Bible* and J. T. Barclay's *City of the Great King*. His fascination and love of archaeology is pre-eminent in all of his writing. Throughout his handbook, Halley infused the facts of his amazing archaeological discoveries, which he used to provide archaeological proofs for the Biblical narratives under consideration.

The foreword continues, "In my efforts to familiarize myself with archaeological findings, it has been my good fortune to meet, or be in correspondence with, a number of archaeologists. I have been greatly impressed by their courtesy, and also by their open-mindedness. *They are men who deal with facts*, and seem to be more free from dogmatic tendencies than many men of academic calling."[5] [*Emphasis mine.*]

In discussing Joshua's conquest of Jericho in Joshua 6, Halley went to great lengths to draw attention to the links between the Biblical record and archaeological discoveries on the Old Testament tell. To do this, he cites the findings of Garstang, who excavated from 1930 to 1936. Halley writes:

Dr. John Garstang, director of the British School of Archaeology in Jerusalem and of the Department of Antiquities of the Palestine Government, excavated the ruins of Jericho, 1929-

> **scarab evidence**
> A symbol, seal, amulet, or gem fashioned to resemble the scarab beetle, sacred to the ancient Egyptians. Important for archaeological dating.

36. He found pottery and scarab evidence that the city had been destroyed about 1400 BC, coinciding with Joshua's

date; and, in a number of details, dug up evidence confirming the Biblical account in a most remarkable way.

'**The wall fell down flat.**' (v. 20) Dr. Garstang found that the wall did actually 'fall down flat.' . . . Dr. Garstang found that the outer wall fell outwards, and down the hillside, dragging the inner wall and houses with it, the streak of bricks gradually getting thinner down the slope.[6]

"**They burnt the city with fire.**' (v. 24) Signs of the conflagration and destruction were very marked. Garstang found great layers of charcoal and ashes and wall ruins reddened by fire. The outer wall suffered most. Houses alongside the wall were burned to the ground. The stratum generally was covered with a deep layer of black burnt debris, under which there were pockets of white ash, overlaid with a layer of fallen reddish brick.

'**Keep yourselves from the devoted thing.**' (v. 18) Garstang found, under the ashes and fallen walls, in the ruins of the store rooms, an abundance of food stuffs, wheat, barley, dates, lentils, and such, turned to charcoal by intense heat, untouched and uneaten: evidence that the conquerors refrained from appropriating the foods.[7]

In the next section on Joshua 7 and 8 (titled "Fall of Ai and Bethel") – like the section on chapter six – Halley spent the bulk of his writing on the archaeological notes. This time, he cited A. F. Albright's discovery that Bethel had been destroyed at a time precisely coinciding with Joshua. This was all great stuff, especially for a senior in high school soon to be off to college. It was exciting to have the narratives of your Bible (and your faith) shored up with facts.

While studying for my talk, I explored everything I could find (which has always been my nature) on Joshua's conquest of Jericho. In doing so, I found some disturbingly negative articles that contradicted my *Halley's Bible Handbook*. According to an archaeologist by the name of Kathleen Kenyon, Garstang's dig was inaccurate – he had dated the tell improperly.[8] I remember at the time wrestling with Kenyon's conclusions . . . but, in the end, taking comfort in Merrill Unger's explanation, which seemed adequate. After all, his handbook was published by Moody Press, and that was the publisher everyone could trust, wasn't it?

Unger wrote, "Remains of the massive walls and the city that fell to Joshua (c.1400 BC) have largely eroded, since Jericho was constructed of mud brick. The excavations of Kathleen Kenyon since 1952 reveal that most of the extant mound is 16th cen. B.C. or earlier. Joshua's Jericho has thus *largely been washed away.*"[9] [*Emphasis mine.*]

The night of my presentation, I cited Halley as my main source, mentioned Kenyon's liberal findings, and then presented Unger's position just in case the Halley commentary was wrong. I dismissed the whole thing and the issue never resurfaced during Bible college or seminary. But it was in my high school years that I developed an ever-growing yearning to study in Israel and see these things for myself one day.

That one day arrived.

Go to Israel? It Would Take a Miracle

Beyond doubt I made it to Israel by the Lord's miraculous provision. I borrowed the $35 application fee from a seminary friend. After being notified I had been accepted into the graduate program, I was doing pulpit supply at a Baptist church in Basking Ridge, New Jersey, one Sunday evening . . . and *several people began slipping checks and cash into my pocket* as they left the church. What's uncanny is: *none of them knew anything about my plans.*

I had been holding a reservation for a one-way ticket from New York to Tel Aviv for some time. The deadline was quickly approaching when I would be forced to pay for the ticket or lose the reservation. Frankly, I had no idea how I was going to pay for it. But on that Sunday evening after the service, as people were shaking my hand and making their way to the door, I distinctly remember two people saying to me that they didn't know what this was all about, but they felt strongly that God had directed them to *give me a specific amount of money* . . . as they slipped small white envelopes into my sport jacket. One boy, wanting to give something because his parents had given me a check, apologized that he didn't have much to give, and handed me some loose change from his piggy bank. And specific it was, for when I got home that evening and emptied my pockets, *the checks, cash, and change added up to the money I needed* to meet the deadline of midnight the next day to pay for my one-way ticket to Tel Aviv. By the way, it was young Kurt's change (the change he had apologized about) that made everything add up to the amount needed. There is no way anyone could have known my need, the amount of my need, or the situation. I could not and cannot explain it to this day . . . other than, as they say, it was definitely a 'God thing.'

Some weeks later, I visited my aunt and uncle in their apartment at the Bible conference center where they worked. I didn't know it at the time, but they had arranged for me to be introduced an elderly summer conference guest that Sunday afternoon.

Sitting across from me in my aunt's living room, this new acquaintance wasted no time with small talk. She got right to the point and said, "Your aunt tells me you want to study for a master's degree in Israel."

"Yes," I replied, "It's a program in Judaeo-Christian studies. It's a study of the Jewish roots of Christianity. This is something I've wanted to do since my high school days."

"It must cost something, no?" she said.

Before I could answer, she continued, "How will you pay for it?"

"Well, at the moment, I'm not exactly sure," I admitted.

Her stern demeanor lightened as she smiled excitedly.

"I believe the Lord has been telling me in my heart for quite a long time that I was going to meet a young man this summer here at this Bible Conference that I was to help with study expenses," she said. "I now believe God's Spirit is confirming in my heart that it is you. So how much does this master's degree at the university in Israel cost?"

I was stunned, and told her with some hesitation the amount I needed. I thought her mouth would drop open, and that would end our conversation. Instead, with growing excitement in her voice, she said, "OK, that's tuition. How will you live? You can't eat on tuition money."

I then explained that, the way the program was set up, the original amount I had given her included room and board as well as tuition.

"Well then," she said without hesitation, "if you can drive me to my bank in Irvington tomorrow, I would like to get you a bank check and pay for your tuition, room and board. Can you take me?"

Thus, *in less than eight minutes, the total funding for my graduate program in Israel was taken care of.* This is what I meant by "Beyond doubt I made it to Israel by the Lord's miraculous provision." Some may call it coincidence, but I will always believe the Lord miraculously granted my dream to study the Bible in the land of the Bible, and complete a master's in Judaeo-Christian Studies at Jerusalem University College. But what I didn't know was that I was about to embark on a journey to the place where I almost lost my faith.

The Evidence Begins to Crumble

Keep in mind that the background and training that accompanied me to Israel that August was quite conservative. I can remember as if it were yesterday the shock wave that swept over me one day at Tell al-Sultan (Jericho) during my first semester of study. I distinctly recall our historical geography professor saying from under his large-brimmed straw hat:

"Here's the problem. On the one hand, the account given in *Halley's Bible Handbook* is wrong because the city walls that have been found that we are looking at today are actually circa 2200 BC – not circa 1400 BC. That's a problem because the city as reported by Garstang (which he called "City IV," with its own impressive fortification walls) is actually circa 1600 BC. On the other hand, the account in *Unger's Bible Handbook* is wrong because the walls are still here. Nothing was washed away here in this desert. The dilemma (he paused and continued) – and this is significant (he paused again) – that we, as evangelicals face, is that the walls are dated circa 1600 BC. This means that by the time Joshua and the Israelites arrived here, where we are standing today, this city may have already been destroyed by someone else and deserted. So we have to entertain the possibility that Joshua may have made up the conquest narrative in the Bible based on the fallen walls that were already here when he arrived. Unfortunately, as evangelicals, we have no answers for this one."

He turned and we descended the tell to our awaiting bus.

Toward the end of that school year, I found myself in yet another faith-disturbing situation at Lachish. Identified with Tell al-Duwayr, Lachish was a Canaanite and Israelite city located southwest of Bet Guvrin. Here, the

foundations of an Israelite city, later to become the second most important town of the Kingdom of Judah, were laid by David or Solomon. Rehoboam included Lachish in the list of his fortifications (2 Chronicles 11:9). Here, conspirators killed Amaziah (2 Kings 14:19). Here, a large water shaft project was

Lachish

abandoned, most likely by Hezekiah. From here, Sennacherib sent messengers to Jerusalem (2 Chronicles 32:9; Isaiah 36:2; cf 37:8) after besieging and capturing Lachish.

And it was here, on a very personal note, I experienced yet another deep sense of disappointment and shock. As if it were yesterday, I can remember standing beside Judy, a friend who was overseeing the summer dig at Lachish, when she turned to me and said, "If our Bibles are right, we should have come to a burn layer here." And after a long pause, she finished her thought, "And we didn't. It's just not here."

According to most archaeologists today, there is no evidence of a conquest (as we noted in chapter two). There are exceptions . . . and Lachish is actually one of them, together with Bethel, Hazor, and others, where some destruction has been found. But many archaeologists suggest these were caused by a conqueror *other* than Israel. After all, the empire of Egypt had a powerful hold on that region during the time at which the conquest has been dated. Surely a strong Egyptian empire would never have allowed a significant entity such as Israel to conquer the hill country they controlled.

For me, these issues – together with issues that had been raised in the classroom – began opening the door of doubt. Lachish was yet another hard pill for me to swallow. But for Judy, I'm sure this did not come as any great surprise; she was expecting it. I am also sure she would have been delighted if a burn layer that matched the Biblical date had been exposed. Perhaps because she had been studying in Israel for years before I had gotten there, she had already grown somewhat calloused to such discoveries. And besides, as I used to tease her, she was raised in the Episcopalian church, not in the literalistic Baptist church.

The faith quandary presented by the so-called lack of archaeological evidence to verify the Biblical narratives was only the first crack in my faith armor. It got worse. As my graduate studies went on, it seemed as if almost every class and every book I read challenged yet another underpinning of my Christian faith – and the cracks began to add up. Some of you have been there . . . some you are there now . . . in the midst of questioning, doubting, inner conflict and turmoil which breeds more questioning, doubting, inner conflict, and turmoil.

Nor was it the most comforting experience to discover that the Christian professors I had looked up to now seemed clueless when I wrote them. Had I been betrayed by the people I had trusted . . . by evangelical scholarship, my pastors and professors from Bible college and seminary? Had they been hiding the truth about these things? Had we all based our lives on myths? Were the narratives about God's mighty hand leading His chosen people an invented history?

Over that year I had written to several of my former professors and pastors. In the end, only one actually responded, my New Testament Greek professor, a humble sincere dairy farmer who – in order to make use of his language talents in Christian ministry – had left his cows, returned to school, and completed his PhD in Semitic languages at Brandeis University. He was a man who never rose to heights above his humility or sincerity, the one who had the courtesy to write back. He was the one I came away from this experience respecting the most, because he had the integrity to confess that the questions I was asking were beyond what he had studied. But he wrote to encourage and affirm me, stating that he was looking forward to the day I would share some answers with him when I found them.

I clung to the hope that surely God had not provided the means for me to study in the land of the Bible in such a unique way, only to have my faith destroyed – even though that is what seemed to be happening. In the years that followed . . . as the fog of doubt would come and go . . . I often recounted the miracle of His provision in my own life. It was one of my lifelines of hope through the worst faith storm of my life.

So what happened to evidence touted by the previous generation archaeologists?

The Maximalist-Minimalist Debate

It helps to synthesize what has occurred over the past century or so by using two common descriptors: *Biblical minimalism* and *Biblical maximalism*.[10] These are essential for understanding what happened to the previous generation's archaeological proofs for the Bible's historicity.

Biblical minimalism began as a school of exegesis stressing that the Bible is not an accurate historical account of antiquity, and should therefore be read and analyzed principally as a collection of narratives. Its roots can be traced to Copenhagen in the late 1960s, thus the original name for this position being the *Copenhagen school*. Minimalist theology evolved out of the need of scholars to explain the contradictions and absence of chronological links between the Biblical record and the emerging findings of archaeology in Israel and surrounding countries. The presumed discrepancies between the archaeological record and traditional interpretations of the Biblical record initiated the minimalists' elevation of archaeology to the place of primary source for reconstructing the history of Israel. In their system, the Bible, as a secondary source, should then be refitted within the context suggested by historical archaeology.

Minimalist theologians thus began viewing the Biblical record as historically inaccurate. Further, they advocated that it is improper to apply the literalist hermeneutics used by conservative Christians to the Bible (such as

Albright), because this results in an unhistorical understanding of the text. Rather than using all the more recent archaeological finds to confirm the Bible, they were being systematically interpreted and deliberately deployed to undermine the credibility of it.

> **hermeneutics**
> The methodical interpretation of ancient texts, especially regarding the Scriptures.

Gradually the theological use of the term *minimalist* began appearing in archaeology and related scholarly disciplines. You will also see archaeologists and scholars from related disciplines of study being labeled *minimalist* or *maximalist*. Also called *Biblical revisionists* (and even *Biblical nihilists*), archaeologists and other scholars who hold the minimalist position view the narratives in the Bible as being mythical in nature. For them, the Biblical narratives are not an attempt at disinterested historical reporting; rather, they are the ploy of later generations to develop and lay claim to a historical identity.

Biblical maximalism evolved as the term to describe the antithesis of Biblical minimalism. Maximalists (theologians and archaeologists) generally hold the view that the Old Testament (or Hebrew Bible) is based on the actual past. But a word of caution: *maximalism* is *not* synonymous with *Biblical inerrancy*. True, conservative Christians who hold to the inerrancy of the Bible might also fit the maximalist category, but the few maximalists who are even left seldom view the Bible as being without error.

To help you understand the current discussion, I would also remind you that there is often considerable tension between the two positions. Apparently, minimalists and maximalists exist in bi-polar opposition allowing for no middle ground. Each would say if you are not for me, you are against me. That is, you must be one or the other. Anson Rainey, for example, has often been called a maximalist by the minimalists. Having attended his lectures in Israel, I would see him as someplace in between the two poles. It has been my observation that if you are not a minimalist, then you are condemned to ranks of the maximalists.

So what had happened to the archaeological proofs discovered by previous generations? Over the past 150 or so years, when Biblical archaeology was first introduced by the zealous intruders of the late 1800s, most were maximalists. Accordingly, there were very few minimalists. (Neither term existed, but that is how we would identify them today.) Now . . . more than a century later   . . . the pendulum has completely shifted: most archaeologists are minimalists. Therefore, the previously held proofs have been *reinterpreted within the framework of a new worldview* that is in complete antithesis to the Biblical worldview under which the previous generations had worked. Granted, this is an intended oversimplification . . . but it's enough to serve as the groundwork so that we can move on.

6

A Dutch Student Sets Me on the Journey of My Life

Looking back to some of the hardest days in our lives, there are times when God gives us a glimpse of how He was carrying us along . . . even when He seemed far removed, and even when we didn't realize it. In retrospect, I can now see quite clearly how God began answering several of my most plaguing questions the year I was a visiting professor at a small Christian college just north of Paris. Although I was not aware of it at the time, God had actually physically placed in my hands – through an undergraduate student of mine – the preliminary research that would, years later, lead to some solid answers to several of my questions. Here's what I found, and how I found it.

During that year I was given the third-floor apartment (in Europe that would be known as the second-floor flat) that connected with the south tower of the château housing the European Bible Institute in Lamorlaye. Most every morning I was awakened long before my alarm – not by the sunlight, but by the sound of clomping horses' hooves on the pavement. The horses were headed for their early morning lunging and grid work exercises in the white-fenced fields across the main road in front of the château. At that time, I had just finished two years of intense class and field work in Israel, and I was working on research and writing my thesis (as well as trying to prepare for my upcoming comprehensive exams). A friend of many years had asked if I could come over from Israel to the college in France as a visiting professor because they were short one instructor in my field. I was honored to oblige. I have to say that I thoroughly enjoyed my classes in the English-speaking division, which was composed of students from more than a dozen European countries.

We had a somewhat unique student body that year. One of the things that made this particular student body so memorable was their enthusiasm. They truly had an awe-inspiring and intense love for archaeology . . . so much so that they had requested (and received permission from the college administration) to conduct their own dig on the acreage behind the château.

I remember very little about the direct history of the old château, but do recall the contours of several large semi-circles that could be seen through the grass on the back lawns, which had instigated the student-led excavations. The project was short-lived, however, as it had to be given up because of flooding. The excavation was too close to the river that ran through the cam-

Campus of Institut Biblique Européen,
Lamorlaye, France

pus. To their delight, though, the students *did* find pottery that gave evidence of an early medieval occupation, and I believe the semi-circles also had something to do with that. In the forest behind the château, remains were found of a Roman road dating back to the days of Julius Caesar! This was an exhilarating place to teach, I must say.

The château itself went back to the sixteenth century, but was heavily restored . . . as it had been destroyed in a fire at some point. It had been inhabited by a relative of Napoleon Bonaparte in the nineteenth century, and a statue of the 'Little Corporal' graced the entry hallway. Friends in the village said that the Nazis were in the building during the Second World War, and that it had been one of the many residences of Hermann Göring.[1] This is why the Greater Europe Mission (the founder of the school) was able to buy this beautiful estate so cheaply after the war. No French buyers could be found at the time because the Nazis had owned it. (It's also why I used to get the creeps thinking I was using the same bathtub that might have been used by Hitler's number two man.)

Even though this was a very conservative Christian college by European standards, I found the academic freedom I was given quite refreshing. It was wonderful being able to openly and frankly share my own faith trials with the students. I would not have been able to accept the invitation to teach there had that not been the case.

One morning in January, during an eight o'clock class (when it was still dark outside, since sunrise was much later that season of year), I shared some of my story and archaeological concerns with the class. That day after class I was politely and empathetically approached by one of the Dutch students, a member of the group that had dug up the back lawns. He asked me if I had ever heard of the new studies suggesting a revision of the standard ancient chronology.

"Excuse me, sir, but have you heard of Egyptologist David Rohl and his colleagues in Great Britain?" the student asked. "I think you would find their research most fascinating."

I was unfamiliar with Rohl and James and their revised chronology proposals, so he volunteered to bring me information the next day.

That student would later become a good friend – and a scholar in his own right: Peter van der Veen, PhD, head of the Biblical archaeology branch at the Christian Research Foundation Wort und Wissen in Germany. (In case you can't tell . . . I'm extremely proud of him.)

As promised, Peter handed me several dog-eared mimeographed A4 sheets and copies of articles with references made to a so-called Glasgow and Rohl-James Chronology (a history of these models appears in Appendix C). There were articles by John Bimson, lecturer of Old Testament and Bib-

Dr. Peter van der Veen
working in the Kidron Valley
(Photo by Richard Wiskin)

lical archaeology at Trinity College/Bristol . . . an Egyptologist by the name of David Rohl . . . a scholar of ancient history named Peter James . . . as well as a few others. At that moment Peter had actually handed me what would re-establish my 'firm foundation' . . . through which I would eventually find the answer to where the archaeological proofs had gone that I had learned and studied in my adolescent years. It would eventually become the catalyst from which I would conduct my own research and teaching, and would culminate in the writing of this book.

I read through the pack of material, found it captivating, and then promptly put it on a back burner. Since I was aware that other 'quacks' had submitted chronology revisions – virtually all of which had been ruled untenable – I set it aside until I could examine it more vigilantly, as has been my nature and practice. A week later Peter asked what I thought of the revised chronology idea. I politely thanked him for the information and excused myself, hurrying to my next class.

Eventually I *did* investigate the information further. I knew, quite obviously, that I would not be able to reconstruct what the architects of the revised chronology models – David Rohl, Peter James, John Bimson and others – had actually envisaged. (After all, archaeology was not my major . . . nor was Egyptology or ancient history, for that matter.) But being a 'doubting Thomas' – by name *and* nature – I knew I would never be satisfied until I examined the proposals more carefully, including returning to Israel and Egypt multiple times to see the proposed evidence for myself. I also wanted to wait and see how it was received by other historians, archaeologists, and Egyptologists. I assured Peter van der Veen I would revisit the chronology study in the years ahead . . . which, of course, I did – and in much more depth. As soon as I began to dig, I sensed he really was on to something; his excitement was justified. It was mainly through studying David Rohl's work (which was most lavishly presented in his books and television documentaries in Great Britain and America) that I got acquainted with what the revised chronologists were actually suggesting.

Meet the Maverick . . . David Rohl

When Egyptologist David Rohl was introduced at a conference at Reading University in the United Kingdom, he was described tongue-in-cheek as "the furry caterpillar in the Egyptological salad" – an analogy acknowledged with great applause. That's because Rohl has always tried to be contentious for the truth in his maverick approach to Egyptology and the world of the ancients. I believe that his initial research in Egypt, coupled with his subsequent books and media venues, have demonstrated to the public at large an important position: we cannot simply accept the foundations of the conventional chronology as being sufficient – and we have no reason to think the Biblical account is the myth of pious frauds.

Egyptologist David Rohl

It is probably not an exaggeration when I say that had it not been for Rohl's writing of *A Test of Time: The Bible – From Myth to History*,[2] his popular television documentaries and the research and writing of the several other "revised chronologists" who shaped the revised chronology landscape, we would not be having this conversation today. Without doubt, Rohl's books and DVDs have widely exposed the revised chronology platform to the general public; however, you also need to know that he is not the only voice contending for a revised chronology. Appendix C provides you with a short history on the "other voices" of the revised chronology project. For now, we need to move along.

Rohl first traveled to Egypt as a 9-year-old boy when he took King Farouk's paddle boat up the Nile from Cairo to the Temples of Abu Simbel and Nubia. That was the start of his passion for Egyptology and the beginning of a lifelong career.

I first met David through his unpublished writings long before we met in person. David is an agnostic. He never set out to prove the historicity of the Bible. As an ancient historian, he was primarily interested in what he perceived to be flaws in the accepted timeline of ancient Egypt. His desire to correct the ancient Egyptian chronology led to the rediscovery of the historical background of several Biblical stories – an unexpected byproduct of his research. Thus he cannot be accused of setting out with a preconceived agenda or Christian ax to grind.

David Rohl has received considerable popular attention through his books and media productions, especially in the United Kingdom. However, academics have been reluctant to engage him in any meaningful dialogue. From my perspective, I have come to view the cause of this enigma as at least twofold. First, his conclusions are foreign to postmodern thinking. Rohl's research in Egyptology shows that the Bible, once dismissed as myth, can be academically restored as an accurate credible historical record of real Near Eastern history, a text with real meaning tied to time and space history. Second, he is grouped with the maximalists, which can be a curse in and of itself . . . since minimalism is now politically (or at least, academically) correct. He has been accused, in my presence, of having an evangelical Christian agenda to restore the historicity of the Bible – which has been quite interesting when I point out that he is an agnostic.

Setting the Academic World on Its Ear

The more strongly Rohl's work was criticized and rejected, the more I studied it. I remember thinking that Rohl must be on the right track, otherwise the status quo of academia wouldn't be protesting so loudly.

Naturally, as I have worked through his proposal, I can understand that there may well be some valid reasons why scholars may have objected to some of his propositions, but certainly not all of his work. (I have heard it said that Rohl is a quack and not a scholar, but the "label and dismiss" tactic is often inappropriately employed for this purpose.) Since new theories are almost always rejected out of hand when standard views are being seriously challenged, I believed the revised chronology models deserved a careful testing. At least their proponents had no doubt demonstrated that the traditional standard chronology of the ancient world was not as stable as I (or other scholars) had previously estimated.

Although I, too, was a skeptic at first, I slowly came to respect the solid work done by revised chronologists such as Rohl . . . and grew to see many of them as organized and able scholars. Obviously, I could not come even close to beginning to reconstruct their many years of research, but (as I confessed earlier) I was constrained to travel to Egypt to examine the artifacts and temples – especially the ones Rohl had been talking about – for myself. It has also been my pleasure to share these sites with others, leading groups through this fascinating part of the world.

Having discovered the intermittent lack of objectivity in scholarly circles for myself, I also began to admire that Rohl and his colleagues had been unafraid to challenge the sacred cows of Egyptology and the conventional chronology of the ancient world. Again – and this is important – it is not because they (especially Bimson, Rohl and van der Veen) were bent on proving the historicity of the Bible, but simply because they wanted to know the truth. I found that approach alone to be refreshing and stimulating.

When Rohl's proposals were first published, the Sunday Times described his work as "a scholarly theory that has set the academic world on its ear." That it has. And the heat he has taken for his questioning the sacred cows of his discipline has, at times, been intense. Regardless of the heat, he is a consummate communicator who writes and lectures brilliantly. Several of his critics could take a lesson. (And I am not saying this just because, during this process, he has also become a treasured friend.)

Peter van der Veen has compiled (together with his colleague, Professor Uwe Zerbst) a detailed and scholarly work titled *Biblische Archäologie am Scheideweg?* (Hanssler-Verlag, 2002, published in German) . . . in which they test Rohl's theories as well as other less radical revised chronologies. After twenty-seven years of examining and testing Rohl's work, van der Veen states, "(M)any of the aggressive criticisms raised against David's work by certain academics are unwarranted and do not actually stand up to examination. . . . As an ancient historian and Biblical scholar, I recommend his work even if his theory remains a work in progress and will undoubtedly need to be carefully scrutinized and refined."

Most people in the United States who have heard of or know anything about Rohl and his "new chronology"[3] were introduced to the topic through Rohl's television documentary that aired in the United States in 1995, "Pharaohs and Kings: A Biblical Quest," which was based on his book of the same name. In January 2004, our seminary students and their guests had the privilege of hearing Rohl present his new chronology in person . . . thanks to Peter van der Veen, who was instrumental in making the connections for this brilliant lecture series, "The Bible – Myth or Reality?"[4]

For obvious reasons, trying to present Rohl's complex proposals in this small book would not be feasible, nor is it my purpose. To adequately cover the vast terrain of revised chronology studies (which goes well beyond the work of Rohl) . . . with all of its historical references and links . . . takes, at bare minimum, a semester of intense graduate-level study. (Incidentally, I would love to welcome you to one or more of my classes on campus.) You can read more on Rohl's proposals in *Pharaohs and Kings*[5] (425 intense pages), along with the seminary DVD presentation mentioned above.

Girding Yourself for Battle

I have found it valuable to share with my seminary classes a synopsis of the 'conventional' versus 'revised' chronologies debate, and the significance of this debate to Biblical archaeology and Christian apologetics. Again, I acknowledge my indebtedness to David Rohl and Peter van der Veen for so patiently sharing and interacting with me on this topic over many long years, including the hours spent together discussing the subject (usually while our wives were off shopping at the mall).

By the end of our classroom discussions on the revised chronology, my students understand that I guardedly concur with several proposals made by revised chronologists such as Rohl, van der Veen, and Bimson. We will talk more about that later. Nevertheless, I have found walking my classes through the basic tenets of the revisionist proposals opens an important door for them . . . a door that helps them understand for themselves that any and all studies of the ancients are always going to be inconclusive works in progress. This is my goal in walking you through several key aspects of the revised chronology here.

In Appendix C at the back of this book, you will find a summary on the history and current developments within the academic turf of the various revised chronology studies. You'll see that this discipline has a long history of its own . . . one that takes us right back even to the very early days of modern Egyptology and Levantine archaeology. But for now, let's move forward.

> **Levantine archaeology**
> An archaeological term meant to be non-political used to describe the land mass between Egypt and Mesopotamia. Today that area politically includes Syria, Lebanon, Jordan, and Israel as well as parts of north-western Iraq and southeastern Turkey.

The next few chapters reflect the introductory lecture material I have been presenting to my seminary classes. The introductory synopsis in the immediate chapter is aimed at providing you with some basic understandings, and to help you build your own platform. I trust this will leave you empowered to discuss this topic with assurance – especially the erroneous teachings of new-generation archaeology.

7

How the Past is Being Controlled

"Who controls the past controls the future: who controls the
present controls the past."

– George Orwell[1]

The Vatican recently had to order an ultra-traditionalist bishop to pub-
licly recant his views denying the Holocaust. A statement from the Vatican
said Bishop Richard Williamson must "unequivocally" distance himself
from his statements in order to continue serving in the Roman Catholic
Church. The Pope had not been aware of the bishop's views when he lifted
excommunications on him and three other bishops in December 2008. A
senior cardinal acknowledged the Vatican had mishandled the issue, making
clear the Pope's decision to end Bishop Williamson's excommunication was
based upon an unrelated matter. The decision justifiably caused a bitter row,
in that the British bishop denied six million Jews were murdered by the
Nazis in World War II. According to Williamson, it's a history that never
happened.

"I believe that the historical evidence is strongly against – is hugely against – six million Jews having been deliberately gassed in gas chambers as a deliberate policy of Adolf Hitler," Bishop Williamson said.[2]

As a result, Williamson was relieved of his position as director of the La Reja Seminary in Brazil. The head of the Society of Saint Pius X, Father Christian Bouchacourt, made it clear that Williamson's position did not in any way reflect the position of the Brazilian congregation.

Williamson's distorted view of this very real historical event is not unique – unfortunately. Holocaust denial movements are active in many parts of the world including countries in the Near East, Western Europe, North and South America. They relegate the Nazi regime's systematic mass murder of six million Jews during World War II to propagandist myth and reject any evidence that does not support their position. The Holocaust, they claim, is a Zionist conspiracy invented to plunder the nations of their resources and wealth using politicians to dominate the world's power, wealth, and media based upon the world's sympathy for a Holocaust that never happened.[3]

If enough people keep saying – and start believing – the Holocaust is a lie, then modern Zionism is delegitimized . . . as well as the modern state of Israel. Think this is not possible?[4] Today in Europe, men and woman in their old age who still bear the tattoos of concentration camps see a continent where Jewish lives and Jewish property are once again coming under attack. The European public debate has once again been poisoned by a level of anti-Semitism we thought had been once and for all dumped into history's garbage heap.[5]

> **Zionism**
>
> International religious and/or political secular movements that sought to secure the return of the Jewish people to Eretz-Israel. Modern political Zionism (in response to growing anti-Semitism) was initiated by Theodore Herzl, culminating in the foundation of the modern state of Israel. The modern Zionist movement was opposed by those Jews who believed divine intervention was being usurped by human intervention. Modern Zionism seeks to support Israel.

But postmodern thinking legitimizes the denial of historical events. If the historicity of the Holocaust (in *recent* history) can be so easily denied, then how much more so can the historicity of Biblical events (in *ancient* history). If enough people keep saying – and enough people start believing – that the narratives of the Bible are a history that never happened, the Bible is delegitimized . . . as is the God of the Bible, Judaism, Christianity, and the Biblical foundations and fabric of western culture. "Who controls the past controls the future: who controls the present controls the past." With this in mind, we need to revisit where all the archaeological proofs for the Bible have gone.

Defining History

U.S. President Harry S Truman once said, "No two historians ever agree on what happened, and the damn thing is they both think they're telling the truth."

Voltaire said, "History is the lie commonly agreed upon."

Napoleon Bonaparte said, "History is the version of past events that people have decided to agree upon."

While we might consider some of these statements somewhat extreme, they do hit upon a critically important reality: history is not necessarily the past, it is a recorded *interpretation* of the past. To accurately view the past, we would need to invent a time machine to transport ourselves back there. But then we would still need to acknowledge that what we witnessed would still be *our interpretation* of what we had seen. Written histories are not only literary, they are empirical. As objective as chroniclers may try to be, their works cannot escape their authorship. Take, for example, the Second Temple period historian Josephus. Historians have especially learned to approach Josephus with caution . . . for his interpretation of the events depends upon who was paying his salary at the time he wrote them. When we recognize this, the difference in the slant of his historical record becomes quite obvious.

What is history? We answer this question by first acknowledging what history is not. History is **not the past**. History is the recorded **interpreta-**

tion of the past, and the chronologies that have been created by historians are just that – *created* by historians, to help us *interpret* the when of the what, where, and whom.[6] As we shall discover, historical accounts are not necessarily bare statements of fact, especially as regards the dating of the ancient past.

Two Types of Dating

Relative dating fixes a geological structure or event to a chronological sequence that is "relative" to another or other geologic structures or events. The Bible, like Egyptian and other ancient sources, uses relative dating. The entire ancient world for that matter, is relatively dated.

The word of the LORD came to Jeremiah, for example, in the thirteenth year of the reign of Josiah son of Amon king of Judah, and lasted until the reign of Jehoiakim son of Josiah king of Judah, down to the fifth month of the eleventh year of Zedekiah son of Josiah king of Judah, when the people of Jerusalem went into exile (Jeremiah 1:2-3). *But there is no universal calendar* upon which we can determine precisely what year the fifth month of the eleventh year was.

Absolute dating fixes the specific date of a geological structure or event to an already existing specific calendar. Some prefer to use the terms *chronometric* or *calendar dating* for fear the word "absolute" implies a certainty and precision that is not possible in *any* method of dating, ancient or modern.

We live our lives based on absolute or calendar dating. You know, for example, that you had a dentist appointment at 2:45 p.m. on 12 September 2010. You also know that you did not get in to see the doctor until precisely 3:07 p.m. because she was running late, which in turn made you late for your 4 p.m. afternoon appointment with a Realtor. We have absolute birthdates and anniversary dates, mortgage payment due dates and so forth. We live and record the events of our lives by absolute dating, using a fixed calendar.

Here's an example of relative versus absolute dating plain and simple.

<u>Relative Dating</u>: During the last month of the last year of the reign of George W. Bush, a US Airways jet made a successful emergency landing in the Hudson River between Manhattan and New Jersey after a flock of Canadian geese struck its engines.

<u>Absolute Dating</u>: On Thursday, 15 January 2009, minutes after its 3:26 p.m. takeoff, a US Airways jet made a successful emergency landing in the Hudson River between Manhattan and New Jersey after a flock of Canadian geese struck its engines.

Why is it important that we understand the difference between relative and absolute dating? Because the ancients used *only* relative dating. Their historical records, typically kept on tablets and papyri stored in archives (as well as on stele), were dated *relative* to other events, *not using a universal calendar with absolute dates.*

It is also important to understand that, prior to the 1800s, no attempt was ever made by historians or Bible scholars to absolute-date the events of the ancient world. **The chronology used by current scholars is largely a modern attempt to absolute-date the events of an ancient world that knew nothing but relative dating.** For that matter, Egyptology and Biblical archaeology as fields of study are also fairly new disciplines.

Absolute Dates for a Relative-Dated World?

The only way possible to attempt the absolute dating of the people and events of the ancient world was to develop a chronology, a timeline that was constructed upon observed synchronisms with other chronologies (an arrangement in chronological order showing historical events that happened, or people who were alive around the same time) found amongst the Egyptian, Assyrian, Canaanite, and Israelite Biblical records and artifacts, as well as astronomical (typically lunar) dating discovered on certain papyri.

> **papyri**
> Plural of papyrus, a material on which to write, made from the pith or stems of the papyrus plant.

When comparing the records about a person or event found in most or all of the ancient sources, if a synchronism is discovered, an 'anchor date' or an 'anchor-point' has also been discovered. Working from the anchor dates, backward and forward, absolute dates for people and events were then determined. Because the ancients did not absolute-date their historical records (in terms of a large chronological framework using BC and AD, as we do today), western scholarship has superimposed its absolute dating over the relative dating of the ancient world like an overhead transparency.

> **regnal year**
> A year in the reign of a sovereign.
>
> **interregnums**
> The time in between pharaohs.

Understand that the absolute or calendar dating of the ancient world was not handed to us as a ready system to be applied to our own absolute chronological BC/AD framework. It was largely nonexistent before the 1800s. The ancient Egyptians used no single system of dating . . . no consistent system of regnal years. We have never discovered anything that would indicate they practiced naming years (like those used in Mesopotamia). Using relative dating, Ancient Egyptian chroniclers compiled lists of pharaohs . . . but the lists – even if they were comprehensive – still had significant gaps in their texts (such as the Turin King List). Some of the lists discovered were textually complete but still failed to provide a complete list of rulers. And then there was the problem of interregnums.

Add to this quandary that there can be conflicting information *within the same regnal period* from different versions of the same text (referred to as textual problems). We know, for example, that there once existed a history of Egypt by the Egyptian historian Manetho because of the extensive references made to it by subsequent writers, such as Eusebius. But even with this source, the dates for the same pharaoh time and again varied substantially, depending on which intermediate source was used. Thus, we do not have an accurate count for the length of the reigns for most of the kings of Egypt.

At the end of the eighteenth century (as discussed in chapter four), in the wake of Napoleon's conquests, there followed the greatest rush to the

Holy Land since the Crusades. Anxious explorers, Bible scholars, and entrepreneurs from France, Germany, Austria, Italy, and Victorian England were drawn to the region. Keep in mind that these men were firmly rooted in the Biblical traditions of their era. They held a Judaeo-Christian worldview, holding the Bible in high esteem. Their purpose was to search for archaeological evidence in support of the historicity of the Bible. They viewed the Bible as absolute truth, the historically reliable Word of God, so they quite naturally used the Bible as their point of reference. Assuming the Biblical record was truth, they then set out looking for synchronisms in the Egyptian and Assyrian records. This was their mindset.

Dropping Anchors

By the early nineteenth century, modern Biblical archaeology (as we know it) was launched by those who ventured to the newly opened Near East, Napoleon's expedition being the catalyst. Specifically in relation to Egypt, though, it was enshrined in the articles of the Egypt Exploration Fund (later Society), founded 1882 in the United Kingdom . . . which specifically states the objective that its archaeological missions would partly be for the purpose of "illuminating the Bible." Its very first dig was in the Eastern Delta at the site believed to be the Pithom of Exodus 1:11. As its website states: "The early emphasis on work in the Nile Delta was intended to attract sponsorship from those interested in finding evidence to support Biblical stories concerned with ancient Egypt, and many of the Fund's early donors were members of the clergy."[7]

As we can see, it was the zealous intruders (as Naomi Shepherd labeled them) who established the first anchor-points in what was to become the conventional chronology *still used by scholars today* to *absolute-date* the ancient world. What is known as the conventional or orthodox chronology began with Champollion's identification of Shoshenk I as Shishak in 1828, and then was gradually developed over the next century so that it was pretty well established by the 1930s. It has been revised downwards by about 20 years since then (based upon the recommendation of Kenneth Kitchen).

What I want you to see here is that **the conventional chronology that we use to try to absolute-date the ancient world has not been fixed in stone** for time and eternity. The chronology used to date the ancient world is itself a youngster. Its roots only go back to the nineteenth century . . . and, in reality, is nothing more than a modern synthesis of the ancient past.

Going back to the question "what is history?" . . . the chronology used by scholars to date the ancient past is based upon westerners' *interpretations of the past*, not necessarily the past itself. The people groups of the ancient world left us their relative-dated records and artifacts that are fragmentary, mere sketches of an overall picture. The historical puzzle of the ancient past still has many missing pieces as well as 'found' pieces which just don't fit.

As a result of this . . . if there remains any interest in academic objectivity . . . we have to acknowledge that it is possible the conventional chronology may have been founded on one or more *completely false* anchor dates. We would have to acknowledge that the conventional chronology itself may have been assembled incorrectly . . . and consequently could be a misaligned interpretation of what actually happened in the past. But this is a topic few want to consider . . . for the result would mean the dates in millions of textbooks might need to be corrected, and some 'sacred cow' politically correct assumptions overturned. Often purposefully ignored, the chronology is fundamental to our interpretation of the ancient past and our interpretation and understanding of ancient history. Rather than questioning the possibility that the conventional chronology might be wrong, the Bible's historicity is immediately dismissed instead – because dismissing the Bible's historicity (rather than challenging the *assumptions* of the conventional chronology) is politically correct.

In February 2008, Ben Stein's film *Expelled: No Intelligence Allowed* was released in a thousand theatres in the United States. The film exposed the case of three scientists fired and blacklisted[8] because they had the courage to challenge the prevailing, politically correct worldview that all life on earth evolved capriciously from a single-celled organism. Each of them, motivated by objective inquiry (not religious conviction), had questioned the inadequacies in evolutionary theory. They also dared to make reference, in one way or another, to the evidence they had discovered pointing in the direction of some type of intelligent design. (Isn't that what scientists are sup-posed to be doing – questioning and observing?)

Whether you agreed or disagreed with the position of this film . . . or watched or didn't watch it . . . I found Stein's metaphorical use of the Berlin Wall as a reflection of what's going on in the current academic world to be right on the money (and, as we'll see, money is definitely involved). Stein espouses an *ideological* Berlin Wall has been erected within scientific acade-mia to thwart serious discussion of anything challenging evolutionary dogma. The academic freedom touted in university marketing applies *only* for those *who are on the right side of the wall* – and are not challenging the consensus. I propose that this 'Berlin Wall' likewise exists in the science of archaeology (perhaps not to the extreme as evolution versus intelligent de-sign, but close). No matter how brilliant or how impressive their credentials, revised chronologists who dare to challenge the conventional chronology dogma in favor of a revised chronology (that just so happens to support the Bible's chronology) typically find themselves swimming against the very strong current of academic dogma.

Some of the scientists interviewed by Stein spoke on camera anony-mously. Why? This may or may not surprise you, but there's a potential loss of money – lots and lots of money – at stake. Of course, that's nothing new. The early Biblical archaeologists were funded to go to the Near East to search for archaeological *proof* to *substantiate* the Biblical narratives . . . and they were expected, by those footing the bill, to return with same. Today, the clear majority of archaeologists who get funded are sent to search for archaeological *proof* to *discredit* the Bible . . . and they are expected, by those footing the bill, to return with same.

I am sure you have heard the expression *money talks*. Those who ques-tion academic dogma (the *consensus*, as it's called) have found themselves denied jobs, unable to get published (an activity essential for scientists), and are starved of research grants. Yes, Stein is right on the money. When we see what goes on behind the scenes, we understand how very efficient deny-ing jobs and cutting off grants can be as a way to repress an opposing point of view.

Faculties are not the only ones being impinged upon by academia's 'Berlin Wall' (I will be borrowing this metaphor throughout this book); students as well are being held to the fire.

What I appreciated most about Stein's film was the way he laid bare the tolerance level of the liberal academic machine: use your intelligence, dare to question the *assumptions of the consensus,* and you are expelled from the cult! When questioning and objective investigations are suppressed . . . and well-credentialed scholars and students are afraid to speak for fear of retaliation . . . *all* true scholarship has been hopelessly lost. So I urge you, do not give up on the integrity of your Bible based on 'scholarly,' politically correct *assumptions*!

8

When Timelines Don't Add Up

British Egyptologist Hugh Evelyn-White, a respected scholar who had served well at Oxford University, was one of the first to enter the newly discovered tomb of Tu-tankhamen (located in the Valley of the Kings) in 1922. Two years later, at the age of forty, he committed suicide. Why? Our only clue: moments before he hanged himself, he wrote (supposedly in his own blood, but that may be spurious), "I have succumbed to a curse." Evelyn-White was implying he

Entrance to the tomb of Tutankhamun
Valley of the Kings, Egypt

was the target of an otherworldly spiritual phenomenon. As the story goes, because the members of the expedition had 'violated' Tut's tomb, they all died (some say mysteriously) – save for Howard Carter – not long after their entrance. Archibald Douglas Reed, who had X-rayed the Tut mummy before it was transported to the Museum in Cairo, got sick the next day and was dead three days later. Others, who died a little later, were said to have suffered and died from what was diagnosed as blood poisoning. Understandably, Evelyn-White's basic assumption was that he and the others had vexed the gods; they had all been cursed for daring to enter the tomb . . . and he had hanged himself to avoid falling victim to a more ghastly death due to what came to be known as the King Tut Curse. (Five years after Evelyn-White's 1924 suicide, the King Tut Curse gained even more notoriety when Richard Bethell, Carter's secretary and the first person behind Carter to enter the tomb, died in 1929 of respiratory failure at the young age of thirty-five.)

Today we are quite certain that the 'curse' was more likely their exposure to a deadly mold which had caused a severe allergic reaction. Being the first to open the tomb, these early explorers paid no mind to the pink, gray, and green patches of fungi on the walls. The fruits and vegetables that had been placed in the tomb for the pharaoh had, through the centuries, given rise to deadly molds.[1] Clinical studies have proven that mycotoxins produced by fungus can cause severe neurological abnormalities . . . including tremors, convulsions, lesions on the central nervous system, toxic encephalopathy,[2] and death. (Today we can visit the tombs in the valley quite safely.)

Let's think about this. Evelyn-White's basic assumption was that he and the others had somehow been cursed for entering the tomb. We now know that his basic assumption was incorrect, and that it led to his making an incorrect conclusion with a tragic outcome. The point of my telling you this story is quite simple: incorrect assumptions typically lead to incorrect conclusions, which can produce disastrous outcomes. If the basic assumption is incorrect, then the conclusion is likely incorrect. If the basic assumption is suspect, then the conclusion is suspect. (Granted, correct assumptions do not necessarily guarantee correct conclusions, nor do incorrect assumptions guarantee incorrect conclusions in every situation. But the odds favor the 'correct assumption equals correct conclusion' scenario.)

An assumption is a statement that is assumed to be true, and from which a conclusion can be drawn. It is something we take for granted . . .

typically something we previously learned from a textbook or lecture and never had any reason to question.

If you were to walk down the hallway and stand outside the Critical Thinking class in session as I write this, you would hear how important it is to clarify and challenge assumptions. *Not* challenging assumptions can lead to fallacious reasoning. Fallacious reasoning can keep us from knowing the truth; more importantly, the inability to think critically can make us vulnerable to manipulation. Because assumptions are not always obvious, or made explicit, an especially important part of critical thinking is to identify what are called the *hidden* or *implicit assumptions* of a conclusion or argument.

Think back to some of the stated conclusions of new-generation archaeologists in chapter two: Thompson's conclusion that there is no direct integration of Biblical and extra-Biblical sources possible; Finkelstein's conclusion that there was no mass exodus from Egypt and no violent conquest of Canaan; Dever's conclusion that Joshua destroyed a city that wasn't even there; Sturgis's conclusion that Solomon's grandeur is mythical; or Coogan's statement that our view of Joshua has been irrevocably altered by archaeological evidence (I would call your attention to his use of *irrevocably*).

Is there a hidden assumption inherent in each of their conclusions? Yes, there is. But, you might protest, their conclusion that the Bible is myth is based upon hard archaeological evidence. Seems logical, doesn't it? However, *the hard archaeological evidence is based upon an implicit or hidden assumption.* The hidden or implicit assumption necessary for each of these conclusions is that the *modus operandi* used to absolute-date the relative dates of the ancient world – namely, the conventional chronology together with all of the anchor-points used to create it – achieve an accurate historical interpretation of the past. Remember: *if the basic assumption is incorrect, then the conclusion is likely incorrect . . . and vice versa.*

Some of the material we are about to cover in this chapter is complicated . . . but my goal has been to make it understandable. When you grasp the implications of the assumptions being made to discredit the Bible, you'll be amazed – and likely more than a little upset that the academic world criticizing the Scriptures has sold you a bill of goods – but only the bill; the goods are strangely absent. Pay attention and follow along . . . because this is extremely important.

Four Critical Anchor-Points – and Why They're Suspect

Never setting out to prove the historicity of the Hebrew Bible, Egyptologist and historian David Rohl, while absorbed in his life-long research of pharaonic Egypt, exposed some compelling evidence that *challenges the implicit basic assumption that the conventional chronology is itself accurate.* What he has discovered revolutionizes how we interpret (date) the linking of Biblical characters and events with the archaeological data. Rohl says archaeologists have been looking in all the right places for archaeological evidence for the Israelites, but completely *in the wrong time* due to erroneous anchor-points that support the conventional chronology. Rohl believes his new chronology, when applied to the raw archaeological data, reveals a truer historical interpretation of the past. Interpreting the archaeological data with the new chronology rather than the conventional chronology amazingly realigns the Biblical timeline with the ancient past. As a result, there is an *astonishing* amount of archaeological evidence for the characters and events of the Hebrew Bible. For example, Joseph, Moses, Joshua, Saul, David, and Solomon return from their assigned realm of myth to historically verifiable characters.

Rohl identifies the four anchor-points upon which the absolute dating of the conventional chronology is based. Pay attention to these, as you may need to refer back to them:

> 1) **The Sacking of Thebes** by Ashurbanipal in 664 BC. This marks the last year of Pharaoh Taharka and the start of the Late Period of Egyptian history. This anchor is supported by a network of interlocking data including the writings of Berosus (260 BC). "We can state without reservation that this crucial anchor point in Egyptian chronology is our first real 'fixed point' in history."[3]

2) **Shoshenk I is the same as the Biblical Shishak** who desecrated Solomon's Temple in 1 Kings 14:25-26 and 2 Chronicles 12:2-9. This anchor is based upon Champollion's 1828 reading of the monumental inscription at Karnak.

3) **The Papyrus Ebers Calendar.** The date for the start of the Egyptian New Kingdom is fixed at circa 1550 BC, using the Sothic date of 1517 BC for year nine of Amenhotep I found in the Papyrus Ebers.

4) **The Lunar Date of Ramesses II.** The date for the beginning of Ramesses II's rule over Egypt in 1279 BC is based upon a lunar date found in the Papyrus Leiden I 350. His fifty-second year fell exactly in 1228 BC.

Of the four anchor-points used to support the currently accepted Egyptian absolute dating chronology, Rohl and his colleagues conclude:

- Only the first – the 664 BC sacking of Thebes by the Assyrians – is sound.
- The Shishak /Shoshenk synchronism proposed by Champollion is historically untenable (their reported campaigns into Canaan/Israel simply do not match up), and is based upon an inaccurate

> **hypocoristicon**
> A shortened form of a name, such as Ted for Theodore.

rendering of what might actually be a hypocoristicon for Ramesses (II or III).[4]
- The Ebers Calendar Sothic date is disputed by many respected Egyptologists, so it can hardly be used as a secure anchor point.

- The year 52 lunar date which supposedly established the start date for Ramesses II rule over Egypt is entirely dependent upon the disputed Papyrus Ebers Calendar.
- "There are therefore no safe fixed points in the chronology of Egypt earlier than 664 BC."[5] Yet we are using this same chronology to condemn the Bible to myth.

Which Pharaoh is Which?

Remember: of the four anchor-points listed above, the revised chronologists contend that only the first (the sacking of Thebes by Ashurbanipal in 664 BC) is solid. So where did the 'zealous intruders' of the nineteenth century go wrong, and how have their errors distorted the conventional chronology? We can find out by looking at the second anchor-point, (Champollion's 1828 claim that Shoshenk I was the Biblical Shishak). But first, we need to look more carefully at another declared link that was based upon Champollion's synchronism.

The Egypt Exploration Fund,[6] established by Amelia Edwards in 1882, linked the store-city of Ramesse in Exodus 1:11 with Pi-Ramesse (the estate of Ramesses) found in Egyptian hieroglyphics, thereby forever welding Ramesses II to the Israelite oppression.

Exodus 1:11 says, "So they put slave masters over them to oppress them with forced labor, and they built Pithom and Rameses as store cities for Pharaoh." At face value this seems like a logical link, even though there are no extant Egyptian records that suggest Ramesses was the oppressor of the Israelites.

This link, made by the Egypt Exploration Fund in the nineteenth century, has become etched in stone. It has become common knowledge . . . taken as fact . . . and found in encyclopedias, textbooks, and Hollywood films . . . from Cecil B. DeMille's 1923 epic *The Ten Commandments* (remade more famously in 1956 with Charlton Heston and Yul Brynner) . . . to DreamWorks SKG's animated *The Prince of Egypt* (1998) (and I have little doubt more may follow). Why, everyone knows that Ramesses was the oppressor of the Israelites![7] Or was he? How can we be so sure? Is it true just because the Egypt Exploration Fund said so?

Here's the first problem encountered with this link between Ramesses and Exodus 1:11. Genesis 47:11 says, "So Joseph settled his father and his brothers in Egypt and gave them property in the best part of the land, the district of Rameses, as Pharaoh directed."

How could Ramesses be the pharaoh of the oppression in Exodus if there was already a district named after him during the time of Joseph? Or how could the Israelite slaves in Exodus build a city that already existed during the Genesis narrative? If Ramesses is in Exodus 1:11, what do we do with the Ramesses back in Genesis 47:11, and vice versa?

This problem was acknowledged . . . and to solve the enigma, scholars concluded that the Ramesses of Genesis 47:11 was an anachronism placed into the Genesis text by a Biblical redactor. A redactor is an editor who brings a text into presentable literary form; in this case, he would have removed an older name for this particular region of Egypt, and replaced it with a name more recognizable to his current readership (the district of Ramesses).

What many people do not realize is that *the name 'Egypt' is itself an anachronism.* Genesis 12:10 reads, "Now there was a famine in the land, and Abram went down to Egypt to live there for a while because the famine was severe." *That's not what the Hebrew says.* The Hebrew says Abram went down to *Mitsrayim,*[8] which we now call Egypt. Egypt is actually a Coptic Christian term. The region of Africa we call Egypt has only been known as 'Egypt' *since the Christian era.*

Plain and simple, anachronisms are used so that contemporary readers will have a reference point to better understand the past. Here's an example:

If I said to you, "It is believed that when the Native Americans crossed over from Russia to the North American continent, there was a land bridge between Russia (or the Soviet Union) and Alaska." This sentence is loaded with anachronisms. If this actually took place *when* it took place . . . the people could not have been called Native Americans, Russia would not have been known as Russia, and Alaska would not have been known as Alaska.

Nor would North America have been a named continent. I have used contemporary names of people and places so you can more readily picture in your mind *what* and *where* I am talking about. That's the job of an anachronism. Obviously, it would be incorrect for someone two thousand years from now to use this sentence as proof that the nation of Russia existed at the time of the intercontinental crossing.

What revised chronologists are suggesting, based on a lifetime of research in Egyptology and ancient history, is that the Ramesses in Exodus 1:11 and Genesis 47:11 are *both* anachronisms. There is no extant evidence apart from the declaration of this supposed link by the Egyptian Exploration Fund in 1891. Further, Rohl adds, there *is* extant evidence within Egyptology that this could *not* have been Ramesses in either verse.

The Shoshenk-Shishak Identity Crisis

With this in mind, I turn your attention to Champollion . . . whose supposed discovery in 1828 became the second anchor-point of the conventional chronology (that Shoshenk I was the Biblical Shishak). Champollion's story goes like this:

During the early nineteenth century, artifacts and treasures from the Near East began arriving in Europe by the shipload. These sensational treasures began making their way back to Europe's wealthy private collectors. Since no one could read hieroglyphics, a frenzy of mystics and occultists began producing extraordinary translations.

Enter French classical scholar, philologist, and orientalist Jean-François Champollion (1790-1832), who became the first to decipher Egyptian hieroglyphs.[9] He translated parts of

hieroglyph
A picture or symbol used in hieroglyphics, a type of writing composed of these.

ideograph
A graphic character used to convey the meaning of something without signifying the sounds used to say it, such as is found in Chinese writing.

cryptogram
A piece of writing in cipher or code.

the Rosetta Stone in 1822 by comparing the written hieroglyphs with the Greek text also on the stone. He learned that the writing system was a combination of phonetic and ideographic signs. (It was actually a phonetic writing form based on an alphabet of twenty-six main cryptograms.) From that moment, the mysterious icons were thrust from the fringe of ignorance into the realm of scholarship.

In 1828, Champollion (together with Professor Rosellini of Pisa University) made his first and only journey to Egypt . . . whereupon he was finally able to stand beneath the walls of the temples and tombs, and record for himself the monumental inscriptions. One day he found himself standing by the triumphal record of Shoshenk I. While deciphering the twenty-year military campaigns of this king, Champollion translated *Yadhamelek*[10] as Judah the Kingdom. Probably very excited by his presumed discovery, he jumped to what seemed a most logical conclusion: since Shoshenk conquered "Judah the Kingdom" . . . and Shoshenk sounded much like Shishak . . . this must be an anchor-point between the narratives of the Bible and this account of Egyptian history.

1 Kings 14:25-26 says:
"In the fifth year of King Rehoboam, Shishak king of Egypt attacked Jerusalem. He carried off the treasures of the temple of the LORD and the treasures of the royal palace. He took everything, including all the gold shields Solomon had made."

2 Chronicles 12:2-9 tells the story this way:
Because they had been unfaithful to the LORD, Shishak king of Egypt attacked Jerusalem in the fifth year of King Rehoboam.

With twelve hundred chariots and sixty thousand horsemen and the innumerable troops of Libyans, Sukkites and Cushites that came with him from Egypt, he captured the fortified cities of Judah and came as far as Jerusalem.
Then the prophet Shemaiah came to Rehoboam and to the leaders of Judah who had assembled in Jerusalem for fear of Shishak, and he said to them, "This is what the LORD says,

'You have abandoned me; therefore, I now abandon you to Shishak.'"

The leaders of Israel and the king humbled themselves and said, "The LORD is just."

When the LORD saw that they humbled themselves, this word of the LORD came to Shemaiah: "Since they have humbled themselves, I will not destroy them but will soon give them deliverance. My wrath will not be poured out on Jerusalem through Shishak.

"They will, however, become subject to him, so that they may learn the difference between serving me and serving the kings of other lands."

When Shishak king of Egypt attacked Jerusalem, he carried off the treasures of the temple of the LORD and the treasures of the royal palace. He took everything, including the gold shields Solomon had made.

Pay close attention here:

Based upon his translation of *Yadhamelek* in the triumphal record of Shoshenk I, Champollion *assumed* Shoshenk raided Jerusalem, *assumed* Shoshenk sounded enough like the Shishak in the two Biblical passages above, thereby *assuming* Shoshenk and Shishak were one in the same person. Now . . . since it was *known* from Assyrian synchronisms in the ninth century BC that the fifth year of King Rehoboam *would have to be* circa 925 BC . . . *assuming* the Egyptian Shoshenk was to be equated with the Biblical Shishak . . . we *assume* Jerusalem was raided in 925 BC (1 Kings 14:25-26 and 2 Chronicles 12:2-9).

Perhaps you feel I have overplayed the 'assume' game here, but I want you to see and clearly understand that we are looking at the most critical and pivotal anchor-point of the entire conventional chronology as it relates to dating the narratives of the Hebrew Bible.

Pay attention here, too:

It is *known* that *Yadhamelek* was mistranslated by Champollion. It is *known* that *Yadhamelek* means MONUMENT/HAND OF THE KING –

not "Judah the Kingdom" (as mistranslated by Champollion in 1828). Scholars acknowledged this error in 1888.

It is *known* that Shoshenk I only conquered one (possibly two) out of fifteen fortified cities in Judah (mentioned in 2 Chronicles 11:5-10; 12:4). He *never* marched on Jerusalem – let alone conquered it (the foremost target of Shishak's campaign as described in both 1 Kings and 2 Chronicles). Shoshenk also widely campaigned in the northern part of Israel (in the territory of the Kingdom of Israel), the area ruled in the Bible by Shishak's ally Jeroboam I. No raid by Shishak into the Kingdom of Jeroboam is reported by the Biblical writers. And we *know* this by the correct rendering of his twenty-year military campaign. Yet *scholars still refuse to correct this critical and pivotal anchor-point* dating the raiding of Jerusalem at 925 BC as correct.

Both John Bimson and David Rohl have repeatedly emphasized that this critical anchor-point is wrong . . . and, as such, the conventional chronology for this time period is wrong. Several proponents of the revised chronology (i.e. in both revised models, i.e. the 300-year-plus and 200-year-plus reductions known as the 'new chronology' and 'CoD' models) conclude that the name Shishak of 1 Kings 14:25-26 is a hypocoristicon for none other than either Ramesses II or III.

The Name Game

But how do they go from *Shishak* to *Ramesses*? Follow along slowly and carefully here. Ramesses II was called Ri'amashesha in cuneiform Hittite documents.[11] But ancient kings often carried shortened versions of their names (hypocoristicons). An example of the use of 'nicknames' in the ancient world would be 'Pul' which was used for Tiglath-pileser III of Assyria. Another example would be the hypocoristicon used for Ramesses III (the most powerful ruler of the Twentieth Dynasty): 'Ss' or 'Sese.' This was a common personal nickname used for people named Ramessu or Ramesse, and took many forms: 'Ssw,' 'Ssy,' and 'Sysw' are among the examples Rohl documents in his book. The Hebrew language also sometimes renders the Egyptian 's' as 'sh.'[12] This brings us from 'Ramesses' to 'Ss,' or to 'Shsh.' Now . . . the last part of the name, the 'k' (actually a *qoph*, in Hebrew), may derive from a Biblical play on words. An English reader would never pick up on this, but a Hebrew reader would. This is all quite clever and gives incredible insight into the humor of the chroniclers of ancient Israel.

Such name games must have been rather common in Biblical Hebrew (as Moshe Garsiel has documented in great detail in his book *Biblical Names – A Literary Study of Midrashic Derivations and Puns*).[13] A good example of this type of 'name game' is the name 'Jezebel' in the Hebrew Bible. Although its original version *Yezebul* meant something like '(Baal) is prince,' the Hebrew writer prefixed the original name with the initial Hebrew letter *aleph* (reading '**A**yzebel' in Hebrew), by which the meaning of the name was radically changed. The name now reads as question: 'Is (Baal) a prince?' – a question which needs to be answered in Hebrew with a definite *No, he isn't!* – simply because Baal is a dead deity and could never pretend to be a true prince.

There's more. The writer also added an additional pun to the second element of name (zebel), which came to mean 'dung' rather than 'prince.' In other words, the Biblical writer was arguing that if Baal was anything at all, he surely was nothing more than 'a mere piece of dung!'[14] This is an example of Hebrew apologetics hidden right in the text.

In the same manner, 'k/q' (found at the end of the name Shisha**k/q**) could have been added to Ramesses' hypocoristicon 'Shsh' for 'Ramesses' . . . to allude to the Hebrew name *Shashak,* with the meaning 'the one who plunges on the spoils of war' (or simply 'the plunderer') – a good description of Shishak's plundering of the Temple and palace treasures in Jerusalem.[15] More detail can also be found in Rohl's *Pharaohs and Kings* . . . where you will also find Rohl's position on anchor-points three and four, the Papyrus Ebers Calendar (which is shrouded in academic debate) and the lunar date of Ramesses II (which is based upon anchor-point three).[16]

Three Anomalies

In addition to casting considerable doubt upon the accuracy of the anchor-points that support the conventional chronology, the revised chronologists also present three anomalies as further evidence that the conventional chronology is in error[17]:

1. The Apis Bulls

The years represented by the Apis bulls buried at Saqqara do not add up using the conventional chronology. The Apis bull was worshipped in Egypt from earliest times[18] and was the physical embodiment of Ptah, the chief deity of Memphis. (Saqqara was the burial area for Memphis. You can find further discussion of Memphis at *www.MyProfessorSays.com*.) The Apis bull was also the manifestation of the River Nile and Hapy, the flood god. The Apis bulls were thus equated with kingship; they were symbols of fertility and strength.

As such, the Apis bull ran alongside the pharaohs during the great Heb Sed jubilee of the king, when he performed his running ceremony to demonstrate his strength. The bull represented one of the living embodiments of the Egyptian king in the animal world. Accordingly, they were given royal burials.

Apis Stele number 31 ("Pasenhor Stela," at the Louvre Museum in Paris) makes it clear that only one bull was used for each pharaoh. There is archaeological evidence for a maximum of twenty-three bulls having been buried in the Lesser Vaults of the Serapeum at Saqqara. The original excavation by Mariette found no evidence for Apis bulls for the Twenty-first and early Twenty-second Dynasties. In order to match the conventional chronology, the bulls at Saqqara need to represent around six hundred years. However . . . with an average lifespan of eighteen years, these bulls represent only around four hundred-plus years, at best . . . which is a much closer match to both the

Apis bull calf from Saqqara (Louvre Museum) Photo Courtesy of © David Rohl

revised models discussed here (the new chronology and CoD models). Thus, it appears there are eight to eleven bulls unaccounted for . . . around 150 to 200 years of bulls missing, if the conventional chronology is correct. Rohl concludes:

> If this anomaly stood alone, then perhaps we might be able to dismiss it. But when I undertook my pilgrimage to the Serapeum in 1986, my other research had already led me to realize that an unexpected solution to the riddle of the missing Apis was at hand . . .. The archeological evidence from the Lesser Vaults of the Serapeum suggests that the length of the Third Intermediate Period may have been artificially over-extended by historians.[19]

2. The Coffin of Seti I

The second proposed anomaly takes us south from Saqqara to the Valley of the Kings. After the death of Ramesses III, the last of the great pharaohs, law and order broke down in ancient Egypt . . . and the very workers that built the tombs commenced to rob their treasures. The officials in Thebes decided action had to be taken to safeguard the mummies. In a top secret mission, the mummies of the pharaohs were moved out of the valley over a steep mountain pass to a secluded shafted tomb known as the Royal Cache. There, the mummies *did* remain safe for nearly 3,000 years – that is, until villagers looking to sell antique relicts to the zealous intruders of the Victorian era came across the shafted tomb. Fortunately, government officials in Cairo got wind of the mummies and had them moved to the Cairo Museum of Antiquities (where they can be viewed today).

The coffin of Seti I was placed at the top of the deep shaft. On the coffin is an inscription dating precisely the time when the coffin was placed and the Royal Cache *sealed*. According to the conventional chronology, Seti I's coffin was placed and the cache sealed in year 10 of Pharaoh Siamun, which is dated to 968 BC in the conventional chronology.

Here's the anomaly. When they were unwrapping the mummy of Djedptahefankh (who was only a minor official from Karnak, and whose mummy was also found in the Royal Cache), the curators at the Cairo Museum discovered his bandages were dated to year 11 of Pharaoh Shoshenk I, dated to 934 BC using the conventional chronology. Do you see the problem? How could Djedptahefankh's coffin be placed at the very bottom of the shaft some 34 years *after* Seti I's coffin was placed at the very top of the shaft, and the cache sealed? To dismiss this anomaly, scholars have suggested the cache must have been reopened at the later date to add Djedptahefankh. But the coffin of Seti I was too large to allow passage.

Valley of the Kings, Egypt

How could they bypass Seti I's coffin and the other thirty-nine coffins? There were forty-one coffins in the shaft, Djedptahefankh being number forty-one at the very bottom. This obvious evidence does not support the standard chronologists' worldview – so *it is dismissed with some rather deficient excuses. And yet, this is the chronology being used to declare the Bible a myth!*

"The burial of Djedptahefankh in the Royal Cache indicates that the 21st and 22nd Dynasties were not chronologically sequential," as believed by those who hold to the conventional chronology. This is yet a further indicator that the conventional chronology is inaccurate.[20]

3. The Tanite Royal Tombs

The third anomaly can be evidenced at the Tanite Royal Tombs. The primary problem is in the way the two tombs were constructed. The Tomb of Osorkon of the Twenty-second Dynasty on the right should have been built *after* the Tomb of Psusennes of the Twenty-first Dynasty on the left. But when we examine the two tombs, it is clear that the builders of the Psusennes Tomb on the left had to cut *into* the Osorkon Tomb on the right to make enough room for the Psusennes floor plan. If the conventional chronology is correct, the tomb on the left would have been constructed over 100 years *before* the tomb on the right. How, then, did the builders of the tomb on the left *cut into* the tomb on the right . . . that presumably had *not yet been built?*

Rohl concludes:

> The evidence seems to be incontrovertible: Osorkon II of the 22nd Dynasty built his tomb and added to the Temple of Amun before Psusennes I of the 21st Dynasty began the construction of his own tomb within the sacred enclosure at Tanis. Therefore King Osorkon II could not have died one hundred and forty-one years after King Psusennes I as is currently believed. The implication of this is that the chronology of the Third Intermediate Period is in error by at least this number of years.[21]

Having made my own pilgrimages to Egypt, I find it extremely slipshod of those who try to frivolously dismiss Rohl's anomalies outlined above. Dismiss them if you like, but as for me . . . after investigating Rohl's anomalies for myself . . . I have returned from Egypt convinced that *scholars see what they want to see and dismiss what they don't want to see.* Truth be told, **those who wish to dismiss the Hebrew Bible as myth are standing on rather shaky ground**.

What If the Revised Chronologists Are Right?

If the revised chronologists are correct,[22] then the second pillar – this critically important anchor-point – is wrong . . . as would be the conventional chronology it supports. Today, when excavated archaeological discoveries on Biblical tells in Israel do not mesh with the conventional chronology, *it is standard practice to immediately assume that the Bible is wrong*. What if it were the other way around? Perhaps the conventional chronology (a discussion of the different revision models is found in Appendix C) has a monumental error of about 200 to 300 years . . . and the Bible's chronology is right! Bizarre as this may seem, we are living in a day when Christian scholars are bending to the prevailing Bible-myth winds . . . while agnostic and secularist scholars are contending for the historicity of the Biblical accounts based on academic merit alone.[23]

Our task in this book is not to try to determine whether the error is 200 or 300-plus years, or who proposed what first. We will leave that for the revised chronology specialists to sort out for themselves. But here's a look at what happens if the revised chronology *is* correct (with noted disagreement amongst the revised chronologists):

The revised chronologists have likely verified the early presence of Israel in the land of Canaan, even though there is some disagreement among them. For example, it is the position of Rohl's new chronology (D. Rohl, B. Newgrosh, B. Porter) that some of the Amarna Letters were written by King Saul, who is called Labayu in the letters. Other revisionists (BICANE and CoD) disagree with this, stating that the Amarna Letters may be a century earlier. The letters would then date to the lesser known period of the later Judges at the time of Jephtah, around 1100 BC.

To date, the Israel Stele contains the only certain mention of Israel of surviving Egyptian texts. Chronology revisionists from BICANE and CoD believe there may be yet an earlier reference to Israel (in a more archaic form spelled *Yish3/rel*), mentioned alongside Ascalon and Canaan (Gaza?) on a block at the Berlin Museum.[24] In Middle Egyptian a "3" can be read as an "a" or "r" . . . hence reading *Yisha'el* or *Yishar'el* or *Yishra'el*. Stylistically it appears to date to the early Nineteenth Dynasty. The archaic spelling suggests that is was copied from an earlier Eighteenth Dynasty topographic list. If the reading is correct (and the original block was studied by several German Egyptologists, as well as by Peter van der Veen and Uwe Zerbst), this would mean that a geographical entity called Israel already lived in Canaan long before Ramesses II, who is believed to the Pharaoh of the Exodus within the conventional chronology.[25] This evidence is exciting – but the public will likely not hear much about it from those whose worldview doesn't support it.

Now . . . here's a summary of things that happen if the revised chronology is correct (*regardless* of whether or not the traditional chronology is shortened by 200 or 300-plus years[26]):

- The palace and tomb are revealed that may tentatively be assigned to the Vizier Joseph. They would have been there all along, but were dated incorrectly.[27]
- The Pharaohs of the Oppression and Exodus are correctly identified, and the Biblical date (early date) for the Exodus is correct after all.[28]
- The city of the Israelite bondage at Tell ed Daba (Avaris, later to be renamed Pi-Ramesse at the time of Ramesses II) is unearthed and becomes historically verifiable.[29]
- Joshua's conquest of Jericho (Tell al-Sultan) is properly located and becomes historically verifiable.[30]
- The wealth, grandeur, and high culture of King Solomon's Jerusalem become historically verifiable.[31]

In an oversimplified nutshell, it is being argued by revised chronologists that the time period allowed for ancient Egyptian history is too long and that the Twenty-first through Twenty-fifth dynasties – rather than ruling one after the other – ruled simultaneously (at least for an extensive period of time) from different locations in Egypt. As a result, the so-called ancient Egyptian Third Intermediate Period (which falls within the field of expertise of Rohl, Robert Morkot, and Ad Thijs[32]) has to be reduced by 200-plus years, while further shortening comes from overlapping the reigns of the later pharaohs of the Twentieth Dynasty (Ramesses IX-XI), or even of the entire Twentieth Dynasty (an oral suggestion made by Rohl).[33] As an unexpected consequence, it is then discovered that the shortened (corrected) Egyptian timeline correlates more closely with the Biblical timeline. The synchronisms between the Old Testament and the ancient Egyptian sources become overwhelming, and **the Bible – dismissed as myth – is suddenly restored as an accurate credible historical record of real Near Eastern history!**

What If the Revised Chronology is Wrong?

If it should turn out that the revised chronologists are entirely mistaken,[34] we will still have them (and the early scholars of the Glasgow Conference) to thank for exposing the vulnerabilities, instabilities, implicit and hidden assumptions, and the probability of mistakes within the ancient dating system now being used by new-generation archaeologists and others to mythologize and discredit the historicity of the narratives of the Hebrew Bible. The ancient world is relative-dated . . . and, as such, will *always* be subject to interpretation and reinterpretation (and *mis*interpretation). Because of the very nature of antiquity, archaeology will never be an exact science. The revised chronologists have documented the indisputable fact that *any* scholarly attempt to produce an ironclad chronology of ancient Egypt – especially prior to 664 BC – is impossible, and fraught with problems. They will have exposed to a broad scholarly and non-scholarly audience the truthful *aide-memoire* that any and all studies of the ancients are always going to be inconclusive works in progress.

So before you give up on your Bible . . . reassess the broader game plan, and remember that our limited resources and knowledge of the ancients will *always* engender a dynamic of uncertainty with any ancient dating scheme, including the Assyrian chronology.

9

'The Facts on the Ground Are Speaking'

New-generation archaeologists and revisionist historians – who have been debunking the Biblical historical record concerning the grandeur of kings David and Solomon – were recently dealt some bad news. Archaeologist Eilat Mazar, a world authority on Jerusalem's ancient past, has placed King David of the Bible squarely back on the charts of living history. Mazar's latest excavation in the City of David is located south of the Temple Mount on the hill called 'the City of David.' Her findings have forced the archaeological world to rethink their new-generation views on David and Solomon. Mazar has just discovered something that has been lying totally undisturbed for more than 3,000 years. What is it? A massive building which Mazar says is King David's palace. That's right . . . King David's grand and luxurious palace. New-generation archaeologists have claimed that, since there was no evidence of such a majestic palace such as described in the Bible, David's monarchy never really existed. Mazar has likely just changed all that – and she is delighted at her discovery.

Mazar is the granddaughter of the renowned archaeologist Benjamin Mazar. Her grandfather was the archaeologist who conducted the southern wall excavations next to the Western Wall. She, like her grandfather, is one of the world's leading authorities on the archaeology of ancient Jerusalem . . . and serves as the head archaeologist of the Institute of Archaeology at Hebrew University, working for the Shalem Center. Her discoveries of the last three seasons since 2005 are the culmination of years and years of hard work and archaeological speculation. From her teenage years onward, she always had her head in archaeology books . . . and, every chance she got, worked closely with her beloved grandfather. Mazar holds a doctorate in archaeology from Hebrew University. She is the author of *The Complete Guide to the Temple Mount Excavations* and two preliminary reports on her City of David excavations.[1]

Here's what's fascinating: *Mazar determined the location of the palace using the Biblical account.* The Bible says that when David heard about the Philistines coming to attack and apprehend him, he "*descended* to the fortress (2-Samuel 5:17)." This clearly implies that the palace was higher in elevation than the city below. David went *down* from his palace, so it would have had to have been higher *up* on the mountain than the citadel/city.

> I am a scientist, not a philosopher. My focus is on how magnificent and enduring these complex structures are, that they were preserved and protected for so many generations. In truth, when I began to excavate, I had to be prepared for any result. I even had to be prepared to accept Finkelstein's hypothesis if that's what the facts indicated. Still, I am a Jew and an Israeli, and I feel great joy when the details on the ground match the descriptions in the Bible. Today it's become fashionable to say there was no David, no Solomon, no Temple, no prophets. But suddenly the facts on the ground are speaking, and those outspoken voices are stammering.[2]

Ginsberg reports that it was more than ten years ago since Mazar first proposed her thesis as to the location of David's palace. She argued her position in Biblical Archaeological Review. Despite her sound thesis and her impeccable academic credentials, she couldn't find any financial backers for her excavations. Why? As Stein's film clearly documented, starving scholars of grants is part of the game plan. Might it have been that no one behind the academic machine's 'Berlin Wall' really *wanted* to find King David's palace?

Kenneth Kitchen (who has spent a lifetime in the field of Biblical archaeology) has stated, "In the increasingly erratic world of Old Testament studies . . . there is still too often *a stubborn refusal* to pay proper attention to the firm factual framework of reference that the ancient Near Eastern world offers us in assessing the nature and worth of the Biblical writings."[3] [Emphasis mine.]

As I have said, the study of the ancients will always be a work in progress, so any current discussion of the Bible's relationship to archaeology (or lack thereof) encompasses a wide variety of agendas and often disparate approaches. Kitchen paints a rather dismal picture of the current scholarly thinking and its environment:

> In the last few years increasingly extreme views about the Old Testament writings have been trumpeted and proclaimed ever more widely and stridently; in the service of these views, all manner of gross misinterpretations of original, firsthand documentary data from the ancient Near East itself are now being shot forth in turn, to prop up these extreme stances on the Old Testament, regardless of the real facts of the case. Ideological claptrap has also interfered with the present-day situation. It has been said that "political correctness" has decreed *a priori* that the Old Testament writings are historically unreliable and of negligible value. Even if this judgment were proved correct, it is no business whatsoever of the politically correct to say so, merely as ideology. Such matters can *only* be assessed by expert examination of the available facts, and not by the ignorant pronouncements of some species of neo-Nazi "thought police." It has also been rumored that, in turn, such things as hard facts, objective fact, and (above all) absolute truth have been discarded by resort to the dictates of "postmodernism."[4]

As you read Kitchen's book, you cannot help but notice that he does not think too highly about current scholarship. This is obvious from the comments he makes about current scholars who think scholarship is "a kind of speculative theorizing," "a 'flavor of the month' fashion, or . . . simple indulgence in academic ego massage ('Look how clever I can be!')" Kitchen justifiably challenges today's so-called clever scholarship (that typically sells a ton of books) by asking, "But can it claim any respectable, independent basis?[5]

Today's battle for the historicity of the Bible, for the most part, has two fronts:

1) The liberal academic machine that has erected an ideological 'Berlin Wall' to protect its postmodern worldviews.
2) The adversaries of modern Israel and Zionism who seek to discredit the Bible's historicity in order to delegitimize all Jewish ties to the land.

Tampering with the Evidence

Toyota Motor Corporation faced a public relations and legal debacle in 2009, over claims it had sold automotive vehicles it knew to be unsafe. In an appearance before the U.S. House Oversight and Government Reform Committee, corporate officials were chastised for withholding documents in order to prevent existing lawsuits against the company (the total of which could cost the automaker billions of dollars) to go forward.

How many times have we heard of someone being convicted of a crime . . . only to find out later that the prosecutor intentionally withheld evidence from the jury – evidence that might have allowed for (or, sometimes, *proven*) the innocence of the accused – in order to win the case. In the legal world, it's called 'spoliation of evidence' . . . defined as the intentional or negligent withholding, hiding, alteration or destruction of evidence. Because it demolishes a person's ability to prove a claim, it's considered a serious crime. After all, how can jurors come to a right and just decision about a case if they're not presented with all the necessary facts? Well . . . guess what. In the world of Biblical archaeology, spoliation of evidence has become standard practice in many circles. Here are two ways in which it occurs, with specific examples:

Arbitrary dismissal

The arbitrary dismissal of evidence is troubling. Consider that, in order to make the conventional chronology work certain evidence has been arbitrarily dismissed and is now ignored:

1) The foundations of the conventional chronology of ancient Egypt used to include the framework of astronomical dates, but no more. Egyptologists gradually chose to abandon Sothic dating . . . until, in the 1990s, most of them discarded all the remaining astronomical dates, including the Middle Kingdom lunar observations (the el-Lahun texts). They focused more and more of their attention on the Assyrian chronology, and a crucial synchronism involving a king by the name of Ashur-uballit. Is it possible to dismiss an entire set of astronomical evidence in favor of another set of evidence – and still be objective in our research? I think not.

2) Many Egyptologists have now ceased using radiocarbon dating as a valid dating tool because it created a major discrepancy for them with the conventional chronology. (This is especially true for the third and early second millennium BC, where the discrepancy between the radiocarbon dates and conventional historical dates surmount to more than two centuries. Hmm . . . a two-century discrepancy. That sounds familiar). Granted, radiocarbon dating has its issues – but should it be discarded entirely?

3) It is important for us to note that some mainstream scholars[6] have recently stressed that the Assyrian King List (AKL) also contains portions of *concurrent* dynasties operating in and around the capital, which is one of the things that revised chronologists such as Peter James and David Rohl have been suggesting all

along.[7] In so doing, mainstream scholars have also acknowledged that the AKL has its own problems, and therefore can no longer be taken at face value. It is therefore hardly different from any other king list in the Mesopotamian tradition. Oddly enough, the AKL is still treated as a literal linear account. Why are scholars so unwilling to discuss this possibility and seriously question the AKL's reliability? May I suggest to you it is because such a discussion would open Pandora's box . . . for if the AKL were correctly treated as a concurrent rather than a literal linear account, one of the main chronological pillars for the conventional chronology would immediately crumble, and the door would be opened to new interpretations . . . let alone to a more drastic revision of Mesopotamian chronology!

Scholars cannot entertain two sets of rules and expect to be objective in their research – yet this is precisely what is happening. This broaches the question: do we want to be objective, or are we more interested in hiding behind the 'Berlin Wall' in order to preserve the sacred-cow, politically correct assumptions of the conventional chronology?

Deliberate destruction

The deliberate destruction of evidence is lamentable . . . even though it has been going on throughout human history. Several of my recent study groups to Israel have observed firsthand the amount of bulldozing that has been going on at the Temple Mount. In a hotly contested case, Israel's Supreme Court has held that the Waqf[8] – the Muslim religious trust – damaged and destroyed important archaeological remains on the Temple Mount in Jerusalem (which the Bible tells us was the location of the First and Second Temples). The court nevertheless declined to issue any order against the Waqf or the government authorities, apparently because of the extreme religious and political sensitivity of the Temple Mount and the need to pre-serve public order.[9]

This story goes back to at least 1994 . . . and can be clearly observed that the bulldozing work continues. Tons and tons of dirt have been re-moved from the site without archaeolo-gists being given the right to study the material on site and in archaeological context. Bulldozing and backhoeing are damaging precious Temple Mount arti-facts.

Ongoing construction destroying evidence at the Temple Mount

Israeli archaeol-ogists were angered at the Waqf's use of bulldozers to reopen a twelfth-century crusader entrance for use as an emer-gency exit for the mosque:

> While the Israel Antiquities Authority has expressed concern over damage to Muslim-period structures within the Temple Mount, other archaeologists have charged that archaeological material dating to the First Temple Period (ca. 960-586 B.C.) was being destroyed. A group of archaeology students examined Temple Mount fill dumped by the Waqf in the nearby Kidron Valley and recovered ce-ramic material and architectural fragments dating to this period and later. According to Seligman and former Jerusalem District archae-ologist Gideon Avni, while the material recovered from the Kidron Valley contained pottery sherds dating from the First Temple to the Crusader (twelfth-thirteenth centuries) periods, it was originally un-stratified fill and lacked any serious archaeological value . . ..

Sources in the Israeli government have told Archaeology that what was originally intended as a simple emergency exit has become more of a 'refurbishment,' with two large entrances under construction.[10]

Bulldozers have been carting away huge mounds of earth from underneath the Temple Mount in Jerusalem, one of the most revered sacred sites in the world, drawing the ire of Israeli archaeologists who say Muslim authorities are damaging the inside of the Mount's eastern retaining wall and destroying possibly priceless historical information in the process . . ..

The huge underground mosque at times attracts thousands of worshipers, so there was no question that a second entryway was needed for safety reasons. But the Waqf's decision to simply haul material from the area and to dump it, in the dead of night, in the nearby Kidron Valley has been attacked as irresponsible destruction of an archaeological site. Israeli archaeologists say the area should first have been subjected to a controlled excavation. Now personnel from the Israel Antiquities Authority (IAA) can only sift through the dump in the Kidron Valley in hopes of gaining some raw, but contextless, data about ancient Jerusalem.[11]

Could some of the items dumped into the Kidron Valley be from the Temple of Solomon? Yes, this might well be the case . . . and indeed some slight evidence of that has come to light. Professor Gabriel Barkay was eventually given the permission to move the piles of dirt from the Kidron Valley dumps to another and safer place in Jerusalem, in order to sift through the material taken from the Temple Mount. There is so much rubble to be checked that Barkay's team will have work for many more years to come.[12] Besides many arrowheads from the late Judean monarchy period down to the time of the crusaders, many other artifacts have come to light, that testify to the importance of this place during the last three thousand years, including thousands of coins (from Persian to modern times) . . . fragments of statuettes and figurines from the Judean monarchy, Roman, Byzantine and Islamic era . . . and pieces of mosaic from the floors of the Herodian Temple. Very little has been found, however, that could directly be related to the Solomonic Temple, except perhaps for a broken clay seal impression (bulla), which mentions a certain "Gaalyahu the son of Immer." The style of the letters suggests a date close to 600 BC, the time of the prophet Jeremiah. It has been proposed that Gaalyahu's father, Immer, may be one and the same person as the priest Immer mentioned in Jeremiah 20:1. There can be no doubt whatsoever that important evidence relating to the Temple has been destroyed forever by the bulldozing described above.[13] It is Mazar's firm belief that Waqf intends to deliberately destroy any and all evidence of a Jewish presence on the Temple Mount. She says their goal is to eradicate all remnants of proof of Jewish sovereignty in Jerusalem. She has also pointed out that Waqf consistently denies there ever was a First or Second Temple. "Who controls the past controls the future: who controls the present controls the past."

> **polemics**
>
> The art or practice of argumentation or controversy. In religious history, with the inception of each new religious group, there often came the need to try to eliminate the antecedent, in order to justify and defend their own existence. This is unfortunately still happening today.

Here's another modern example. The Taliban Islamic rulers of Afghanistan destroyed two monumental Buddhas carved out of limestone during the week I was writing this chapter. The two Buddhas of Bamiyan had stood along the great Silk Road to China for at least 1,500 years. In an effort to eradicate Buddhism (or any memory of same) in this now Islamic territory, they destroyed the Buddhas. However . . . just because there is no longer any physical evidence of the two Buddhas does not prove they did not stand there for 1,500 years.

Human nature, such as it is, suggests to us that some degree of polemics – which, at times, includes the destruction of evidence – has been practiced throughout human history. This is why archaeology, by nature, is such a non-exacting science. As Kitchen points out, "Much has been destroyed beyond recall across the centuries; thus we shall never recover, and never learn of its significance."[14] There should be no surprise that we have not found

Solomon's Temple in light of the "thorough destruction of Jerusalem's official buildings by the Babylonians in 586."[15]

Because we have been unable to find the evidence for Solomon's Temple . . . the absence of what we would like to find does not suggest it was never built. If the grand Temple of 1 Kings 6 was never built, what were the older priests so upset about in Ezra 3:12?[16]

Maximalists Are Speaking Up

As we have seen, new-generation archaeologists and revisionist historians have cast a dark and long shadow of suspicion over Judaism's intrinsic connection to Jerusalem and the land of Israel as portrayed in the Bible. Additionally, Waqf (which oversees the Temple Mount) has for years been claiming there was never a Jewish temple on that site. What has been saddening to me is that respected Jewish scholars (including Israel's own Finkelstein) are now also claiming that Israel is not the historic homeland of the Jewish people, and Jerusalem is not its holy capital.

But this is not the end of the story. Maximalists are speaking up. There is a positive side to this ongoing debate. With every study group I have led to Israel, without fail, there have always been some new and exciting archaeologically related discoveries to share with them. The artifacts and written materials from antiquity being discovered in Israel through ongoing archaeological investigations are indeed speaking, and continue to revolutionize the way we interpret the ancient world.

Great Finds . . . No Fanfare?

Back in 1983 when I was living in Israel, archaeologist Adam Zertal discovered an enormous sacrificial altar on Mount Ebal. This is the mountain where Joshua built an altar after the Israelites had conquered and destroyed Ai. "Then Joshua built on Mount Ebal an altar to the LORD, the God of Israel, as Moses the servant of the LORD had commanded the Israelites. He built it according to what is written in the Book of the Law of Moses – an altar of uncut stones, on which no iron tool had been used. On it they offered to the LORD burnt offerings and sacrificed fellowship offerings. There, in the presence of the Israelites, Joshua copied on stones the law of Moses, which he had written (Joshua 8:30-32)."

One would think that the discovery of an altar mentioned in both Biblical and rabbinic texts would have been accompanied by much excitement and fanfare. After all, this was a monumental find that linked the Biblical record with history. But what happened?

Zertal's academic colleagues virtually ignored him and his discovery. I couldn't believe it. Of course, they said it was because the find *didn't fit the chronology*. I didn't understand it then, but now I think I understand much better. Could it be that Zertal's discovery was ignored – not just because it didn't fit the chronology, but because it didn't fit the *agenda* of a non-theistic worldview? I now believe that to be the more likely reason.

There is no doubt: we are living in exciting times. But as we discussed earlier, due to new-generation archaeology's reinterpretations of past archaeologically related data, together with the analysis of new finds, many sites previously thought to have verified the Biblical text are now suspect, or have been dismissed as Biblically irrelevant altogether. This has raised challenging new questions for students of the Bible, who must now either ignore these new fascinating findings and the interpretations of same, or take them into consideration.

With the advent of infrared technology came the long-awaited ability to make out and decipher previously illegible ancient manuscripts and fragments. Using DNA technology, scholars were finally able to restore the Dead Sea Scrolls by patching together thousands of parchment fragments found in and around Khirbet Qumran in Israel. Because we can now decipher Egyptian hieroglyphics and the ancient languages of Sumer, Akkad, and Canaan, we are able to read texts composed before the time of Abram, as well as texts written during the lifetime of the Biblical writers. From this

> ***Hot Topic***
>
> One major area of controversy today is Bryant Wood's approach to the timing of Joshua's attack on Jericho. What makes Wood significant is that he is an evangelical trying to reconcile the event to fit the standard chronology. For an overview of this issue, see Appendix D.

new research, we know that *our Bible is 95 percent accurate to these most ancient Biblical manuscripts.*

Jerusalem's City of David and Area G digs (also known as Jebus, the Eastern Hill) continue to unearth fascinating vestiges of antiquity.[17] For example, archaeologists unearthed a typical Israelite four-room house (the house of Ahiel) that has an outside stairway that probably led to the flat roof. Inside the house were found cosmetics and housewares, all from the ruins of 586 BC. Was the Ahiel family taken captive by the Babylonians? It is likely they were. Today we can visit this house from Old Testament times.

City of David dig, Jerusalem, Israel

Excavations by Reich and Shukrun have revealed a lower city wall (perhaps from the time of Hezekiah and his son Manasseh) which ran along the eastern slope of the City of David near the bottom of the Kidron Valley. It is fascinating to stand on location in Jerusalem and try to take it all in. For example, in the spring of 2009 a limestone fragment of a plaque with several ancient Hebrew letters was discovered. It dates from the eighth century BC, the period of the kings of Judah. The plaque was discovered broken, with two lines of writing on it. The name preserved on the first line of the plaque could either refer to the Biblical King Hezekiah, or simply a common name used in Jerusalem at the time. Regardless, the plaque demonstrates the fact that ancient Hebrew was used long before liberal scholars dated the Hebrew Bible. Further, it is indicative of a commemorative inscription that may have been meant to celebrate some sort of water building project, Hezekiah's tunnel perhaps, or the Pool of Siloam.[18]

On 11 September 2009, Israeli archaeologists announced they had unearthed a Second Temple period synagogue in Migdal near the Sea of Galilee

in Northern Israel. This synagogue is one of only six synagogues from the Second Temple
period in the world.[19]

In the middle of the synagogue's 1,291 square foot (120
square meter) main hall, archaeologists found an unusual stone
carved with a seven-branched
menorah. "We are dealing with
an exciting and unique find," said
excavation director and Israeli
Antiquities Authority archaeologist Dina Avshalom-Gorni. The
menorah engraving is the first of
its kind to be discovered from the
Early Roman period.[20]

Here's the latest just before we
go to press: Mazar and her colleagues[21] have now unearthed a
small fragment of a Late Bronze
Age letter in Akkadian. It was discovered in the Ophel excavations
in Jerusalem. As to age, based
upon its sign-forms, it is likely a
rough contemporary of the
Amarna letters. It is considered to
be a local product of Jerusalem
scribes, not only because it was
found in Jerusalem, but because
the analysis of the tablet by opti-
cal mineralogy (supported by
XRF spectrometry) reveals that
the raw material of which it was

Ophel

Hebrew name given to a certain
part of a settlement or city that is elevated and/or fortified from its sur-
roundings.

Akkadian

The extinct Semitic language
of Mesopotamia, written in
cuneiform.

Cuneiform

Any ancient script can be called
cuneiform as long as individual
signs are composed of wedges.

Amarna letters

Clay tablets, mostly diplomatic letters, between the Egyptian administration and its representatives in
Canaan.

XRF spectrometry

Identifies basic elements by measuring the energies of the inner elec-
trons of an atom by knocking them
off with X-rays; good for about 35
elements.

Acropolis

Means "highest city" in Greek and
is usually translated Citadel – a
raised (fortified) area holding a
building or cluster of buildings.

made is typical of the *Terra Rossa* soils of the Central Hill Country of Jerusalem. Further, the fact that it was unearthed close to the acropolis of Late Bronze Jerusalem, suggests it is likely a fragment from a letter of a king of Jerusalem possibly to a Pharaoh. The bottom line? This small fragment shows us that Late Bronze Age Jerusalem (possibly the time of David and Solomon in terms of the revised chronology) did indeed exist, and was connected to the international state of politics.

As we close this chapter I would like to take this opportunity to thank Israeli archaeologist Eilat Mazar and her collegues at Hebrew University for allowing the evidence on the ground to speak for itself and for sharing her find with us. Thank you for your transperancy as you excavate this site . . . prepared for any result . . . even the possibility of having to accept Finkelstein's hypothesis if that's what the evidence on the ground indicated. Thank you that in an age when the prevailing worldviews make it fashionable to say there was no David, no Solomon, no Temple, no prophets, no truth to the Bible's history . . . you have the valor as a first-class archaeologist to allow the facts on the ground to speak. Thank you!

You see, my readers, what your professor may not want you to know is that great finds supporting the historicity of the Bible are still being made. The evidence on the ground continues to cry out. But there's little fanfare because the finds do not support the anti-Bible worldviews protected by liberal academia's 'Berlin Wall.'

Ophel tablet: a) obverse; b) reverse; c) tablet's surviving left edge obverse (photos by Mimi Lavi, Head of the Conservation Laboratory of the Institute of Archaeology of the Hebrew University of Jerusalem) Courtesy of ©Eilat Mazar.[22]

10

New Possibilities, New Questions

The Fall of Troy is a universal reference point, an anchor-point (very similar to the Egyptian anchor-points we discussed in chapter eight) used to absolute-date antiquity. As far as ancient chronologies go, this is a *critically pivotal* anchor-point. British scholar Nikos Kokkinos,[1] has recently demonstrated that, by close examination of the surviving fragments of ancient chronography, it is possible to determine the way Eratosthenes, in his lost *Chronographiai* (circa 220 BC), arrived at his date of 1183 BC for the Fall of Troy (which is now used by scholars as a fixed anchor-point in ancient chronologies).

What Kokkinos has exposed is amazing (but then again it shouldn't surprise us, now that we know what we know about the anchor-points used to construct the conventional chronology). He discovered that when Eratosthenes sat in Alexandria to construct a chronology of the ancient world, he combined new information from Manetho with Timaeus, Ctesias, Herodotus, and other sources. Long story short: we now understand that his chronology dating of the Fall of Troy was an *assumed compromise;* that is, it was a date high enough to satisfy the 'politically correct' views of the Hellenists, and a low enough date to satisfy the 'politically correct' views of the Alexandrians. Kokkinos also points out that, prior to Eratosthenes's dating, the Fall of Troy had always been considered a tenth century BC event.

After objectively examining all the data, Kokkinos painstakingly reassigns the date for the Fall of Troy from the twelfth century to the tenth century BC, where he is confident it belongs. As a byproduct of his research, some fascinating details unfold Biblically. For example, the beginning of the Kingdom of Judah falls to the tenth century (just as the revised chronology claims), which is also supported by the Tyrian Annals (now linked to the Mesopotamian chronology). King Solomon had to have been alive during the Trojan War as dated by Hecataeus . . . which, in turn, justifies church father Clement of Alexandria's claim (in *Stromateis*, 1.21/114.2; 117.6; 130.2) that Hiram gave his daughter to King Solomon about the time of the arrival of Menelaus in Phoenicia *just after the fall of Troy*. Clement of Alexandria had used Phoenician sources to back his claim (Menander of Pergamus and Laitus in *The Phoenicia*). Do you find this fascinating or what? The historicity of the Bible can also be linked to the Trojan War.

This, my friend, is exciting new research! It raises new questions – new challenges to the way we try to absolute-date the ancient world. And it is good news for the revised chronology position. The absolute date assigned by Eratosthenes to the Fall of Troy (1183 BC) simply reflects the 'politically correct' *assumptions* of his day (220 BC) and nothing more, calling into question *all* the ancient chronologies that use this date as an anchor-point. This latest research should make us think long and hard when these so-called anchor-points are used to declare our Bibles a myth. Kokkinos's findings may not be in the headlines, but his research strongly supports a revised chronology and puts another significant crack in the 'Berlin Wall' – even if the consensus chooses to ignore it.

The Bible-as-myth worldview is primarily built upon a faulty conventional chronology that has flawed and unstable anchor-points. Kokkinos's research now confirms the ancient Greek chronology is also faulty; it, too, is built upon a flawed anchor-point (the Fall of Troy). I would strongly suggest to you that it is beyond the realm of 'coincidence' that both ancient chronologies are thought faulty by (give or take) two centuries. More significantly, when the necessary corrections are made to both chronologies, there opens before us an expressway leading from ancient Greece to Egypt to Babylon to Tyre – right back to the historicity of the Bible! Kokkinos's research opens new and exciting possibilities. I would encourage you to think long and hard about such possibilities before you give up on God.

The Limits of Archaeology

We must always keep in the forefront of the discussion the nature of archaeological study. One of the many things that Peter van der Veen has successfully drilled into my thinking over the years is that, indeed, archaeology is hardly ever exacting, telling us 'black on white' what has actually happened. As a respected epigraphist, van der Veen admits that, while the mute chronology of ancient Israel lacks sufficient inscribed evidence (especially when it comes down to the earlier history of ancient Israel), we nonetheless possess many provenanced and unprovenanced seals and bullae – even of known Biblical personages – and inscribed sherds as well as a few inscribed monumental inscriptions from the time of the Israelite and Judean monarchy periods. The further we move back in time, he has often reminded me, we are confronted by a striking lack of inscribed material. That doesn't mean such material never existed (Peter indeed believes that it did); either it has not yet been found, or (more likely) has been lost, as only a small amount of material that once existed has actually survived through the ages. In other words, what we do find often lacks inscribed evidence which perhaps *could* have told us more precisely 'who was where' at a given time in history and 'what had happened' at a particular time. We simply do not possess ancient inscriptions that mention Abraham, Moses, or Joshua. It is already remarkable to see that we actually *do* have in-

provenance
An artifact's place and time of origin.

bullae
A seal affixed to an official document.

sherds
A potsherd, or piece of broken pottery typically found at an archaeological dig.

133

scriptions which mention Biblical personages such as King David, Kings Omri and Ahab, and many other kings and officials known from the time of Biblical kings and prophets. We also do have some (not many!) Egyptian inscriptions from ancient Israel (for instance, from Beth Shean) that relate to Egyptian military and political activities . . . and some cuneiform tablets (for instance, from Hebron, Taanach, and Hazor). Many of these are administrative texts or small letters relating to the life at the town or in the area where a given scribe was working. But mind you, all these finds (and they are not numerous) are 'chance' finds in archaeology.

In order to find out about what has happened, we must primarily rely on less instructive material finds and destruction levels. Finds such as pottery sherds and other small finds such as beads, scarabs, toggle pins, spindle whorls, etc. may tell us the story of the local people who lived within the walls of the town. They can also tell us whether or not there was a city or a village at a given archaeological period, whether the people who lived there were rich or poor, or what deities they had worshiped. But they *cannot* tell us precisely in BC and AD chronological terms 'when it happened' or 'who would have destroyed' the site. Could it have been destroyed in 1600 or 1400 BC? How can we tell? Was it destroyed by the Egyptians, the Amorites, or the Israelites? How can we know if we lack inscriptions telling us 'black on white' who had been responsible? Maybe the site was not destroyed by a foreign enemy at all. Maybe there had been civil war in the city . . . or an earthquake had destroyed the site, after which the citizens decided to leave the place. These are the sort of questions archaeologists are asking when they encounter evidence of destruction, when they ask themselves how one stratum terminated, and if the same people built the next stratum or if others took their place. Often there are no easy answers. Often the answers we come up with are hardly ever final. Often our answers are determined by our personal interpretation of history. Sometimes our conclusions are based on nothing more than wishful thinking, on both sides of the argument.

That being understood, I have tried to emphasize over and over again that our worldview determines the questions we ask – and the answers we find. For example, the historical reconstructions we use will determine our conclusions about the historicity of the Bible. I can hear van der Veen saying, "None of us has lived at the time of Abraham, Moses, and Joshua. None of us has been able to go and speak with their contemporaries to find out about them. None of us [including Finkelstein and Silberman!] have ever seen what reality was like then. So do we allow the Bible to direct our interpretations, or do we judge the Bible by using an inadequate yardstick based on many false presumptions?"[2]

The study of the ancient world will always be open-ended . . . and, therefore, always subject to interpretation. It's not the conflict between archaeology and the Bible; it's the conflict between worldviews. The conflict is more the interpretation of the evidence rather than with the evidence itself. **There exists no sure underpinning from which to attack the Bible as a legitimate historical ancient document**. Not only is the jury still out, there's still considerable missing evidence to make such a bold proclamation! The new evidence being exposed by revised chronologists exposes the erroneous academic assaults to Biblical faith for what they are – and the bias from which they have come.

The Limits of History

The overwhelming majority of Egyptologists agree on the fundamental outline of the conventional chronology. However, it is important for you to know that – although there is the appearance of a united front on their part – there are in-house disagreements amongst some conventional chronologists that have resulted in a variety of dates offered for rulers and events. Truth be known, it's not just revised chronologists who have problems with the conventional chronology. This disagreement typically starts with only a few years in the Late Period, but then expands into a decade by the beginning of the New Kingdom. By the time we come to the Old Kingdom period, there is disagreement by as much as a century even amongst some who endorse the conventional chronology.

For example, when did the Hittite king Mursilis I sack Babylon? You would think that we should be able to figure this one out, since – according to the ancient records – a solar *and* a lunar eclipse are said to have occurred in the month of Sivan that year. The date of the fall of Babylon is needed as a fixed point . . . but, quite frankly, we do not know for sure when that fixed point is. Even though the dating of this event is considered a crucial pillar date for calculating the early chronology of the ancient Near East, the suggested 'fixed' dates vary by as much as 150 years. Why? Using everything we have to work with, there remains a significant cloud of uncertainty regarding the length of the 'Dark Age' of the ensuing Bronze Age collapse, resulting in the shift of the entire Bronze Age chronology of Mesopotamia with regard to the chronology of Ancient Egypt and the historical record of the Bible. There are actually at least four possible dates for the sacking of Babylon:

1. Ultra-short chronology: 1499 BC.
2. Short chronology: 1531 BC.
3. Middle chronology: 1595 BC.
4. Long chronology: 1651 BC.

Thus, we do not know precisely *when* the Hittite King Mursilis I sacked Babylon. Estimates vary by as much as 150 years, yet we are willing to declare the historical record of the Bible invalid because it does not match the conventional chronology by 200 years? Do you see a double standard here?

Simple common sense tells us that *with the slightest amount of objectivity*, the Bible's narratives and timeline are *just as legitimate* as any of the other ancient records. As a Bible-believing Christian, you can hold your head high in the academic arena . . . again, because it is not the evidence, but the *interpretation* of the evidence that is at the core of the issue. This is not an archeology or history issue in the same way it is not a science versus the Bible issue. *It is a worldview issue.*

History is not necessarily the past; it is the interpretation of the past. Because the ancients did not absolute-date their historical records, western scholarship has superimposed its interpreted absolute dating over the relative dating of the ancient world like an overhead transparency. The conventional chronology of the ancient world, Rohl's new chronology, or anyone else's revised chronology will never surmount to the past etched in stone. They are all interpretive modern syntheses of the past, flexible tools to help determine the *when*. Historians and archaeologists of modern times have sought to put together an ancient puzzle that still has several missing pieces – and other pieces which we haven't a clue where they fit. If only *one* of the anchor-points is wrong, then the puzzle has been assembled incorrectly, and the resultant dating scheme it portrays is misaligned with the real past. Such a chronology which is merely a modern interpretive synthesis of the real past is not sufficient grounds for declaring the Bible a myth, even if Rohl is wrong about his new chronology, or the BICANE group about their revised models.[3] This side of eternity, studying the ancients will always be a work in progress! When all is said and done, there is no reason to doubt the historicity and truthfulness of your Bible.

Three Admonitions

Revised chronologies admittedly introduce a whole new set of questions – and I would be breaking my promise to leave no stone unturned if I didn't address this new conundrum. David Rohl's new chronology model is still relatively young (as are the other versions of the revised chronology). They are all works in progress. It is going to take some time and additional research before the revised chronology is able to adequately define itself in a generally fixed revised chronology.

Rohl's new chronology model is surely not the end-all solution for the multiple dilemmas encountered when attempting to reconcile the ancient chronologies. Rohl has openly stated this, most recently during his television documentary aired in the UK. Likewise, the scholars who are members of BICANE agree that their models are not end-all solutions to the conundrums between the Bible's historical chronology and other ancient chronologies. To the contrary, the revised chronology models have opened entirely new areas of debate.

Having said this . . . as one who has spent several years climbing the Biblical archaeological sites in Israel as well as numerous sites in Jordan and Egypt (sometimes alone, sometimes with a few, and sometimes when leading a study group) . . . and as a seminary professor who has spent decades contemplating the subject matter . . . I am convinced, on the whole, that the revised chronology is the way to go. I endorse (as you may have gathered) the revised chronology concept.

But be aware that as exciting as the revised chronologies are, they come with their own complexities of which you should be aware. If you are inclined to get involved in the discussion, that's great; however, here are three admonitions:

Admonition no. 1

When entering the arena of debate, remember that the conventional chronology still reigns supreme in the academic world at large, and that the consensus position (right or wrong) remains firmly fixed. In general, books (and individuals) espousing revised chronology positions are typically not well received by scholars entrenched on the other side of the 'Berlin Wall.' I can tell you this: you may be undeservedly intellectually belittled (in much the same way Rohl and others who support a revised chronology have). Do you recall our brief treatment of Sturgis in the first chapter? Well, Rohl is mentioned in Sturgis . . . and the remarks are quite typical:

> In an effort to overcome this difficulty some popular publications on the topic have prescribed a resort to drastic measures. In his book <u>A Test of Time</u> David Rohl, for instance, has recently suggested that the currently accepted Egyptian chronology needs to be drastically revised by almost 350 years. Not the least significant effect of his proposal would be to place Joshua once more amid the ruins of Jericho – at least in theory. Such hypotheses hold little sway with academics in the field.[4]

Rohl *is* an academic in the field – but he is quickly labeled and dismissed. This is basically where things are at. The battle is far from over; it has hardly been launched.

Admonition no. 2

While it is true the revised chronology helps close the door to attacks debunking the historicity of the Bible, it opens a new – perhaps an even more dangerous – door to the unsuspecting. The Bible, it is being asserted, is not revelation from God; it is simply the Israelites' version or interpretation of an ancient history experienced, shared, and also independently interpreted by all the peoples of the earth. This is the supposition in Rohl's *The Lost Testament*:

> The people of the Bible did not live in an archaeological and historical vacuum. They existed and interacted with many ancient Near Eastern civilisations and their renowned leaders. What I hope this reworking of the biblical story has achieved is to explain and illuminate many of its events by setting them in an historical world reconstructed from the archaeological remains of our ancestral past. It is a world which is tangible, giving the biblical narrative a credible background in which to set the lives of its people.[5]

Rohl is an agnostic, and writes from that platform. The Bible, its historical credibility restored, becomes just another of the many historical records of our ancestral past. Citing the amazing number of references in the literature of Israel's neighboring civilizations that synchronize with the Bible, Rohl systematically rules out any possibility of divine revelation without even raising the issue. (We will address the linguistic and other similarities in the chapters that follow this one.)

Admonition no. 3

Beware that while Rohl's new chronology seeks to restore the historicity of the Bible, it simultaneously opens Pandora's Box to new assaults on the Biblical narratives . . . one of them being the supposed likelihood of Egypt maintaining autonomy over Canaan at the time of the conquests of Joshua, and then over Israel when David and Solomon ruled. This is becoming an increasingly hot topic in both conventional and revised chronology spheres. Depending upon how much you are into archaeology, the details of some of these ongoing arguments may or may not make sense to you. (If you're interested, I have included a sample of correspondence between Peter van der Veen and myself on one of the pressing issues in Appendix B.)

As another example of this ongoing discussion, one of Rohl's major critics has been evangelical scholar Kenneth Kitchen. In 2004, speaking at Reading University, Kitchen told the audience that Rohl's proposal was impossible – not because of the Egyptian evidence, but because of the Assyrian evidence. Kitchen says Rohl's new chronology raises more questions than it answers[6]; therefore, he is holding firmly to the conventional chronology. True, the new chronology raises new questions. Yet Rohl's chronology is not the only model . . . and since the conventional chronology can clearly be shown to be mistaken, I would think – in the interest of finding the truth – we will simply need to acknowledge the new questions, rather than hold on to a faulty conventional chronology.

Kitchen's Assyrian chronology concerns have been addressed by a 2004 conference attendee, Bernard Newgrosh, in his 710 page book, *Chronology at the Crossroads: the Late Bronze Age in Western Asia* (see Appendix A). This is a carefully researched and considered response based on many years of research. Newgrosh, a medical doctor who has been fascinated with ancient chronologies all his life, believes Rohl is correct in his research, and accepts his 300- to 350-year adjustment proposal. Although he only finds evidence for a shortening of the Mesopotamian chronology by over a century (suggesting a major overlap within the Middle Babylonian Period), Newgrosh finds evidence for uncanonical rulers, who hadn't been recognized so far, who would now have to be identified with like-named contemporaries of the Amarna pharaohs.[7] And the debate goes on.

The Bottom Line

As a result of liberal academia's 'Berlin Wall,' Christian students today face formidable challenges when they need to critically evaluate what they are reading in their textbooks and hearing from their professors. Since it is obviously beyond the scope of this book to speak to every part of the current ideological 'Berlin Wall,' my goal has been to provide you with an overview of some basic issues, terms, concepts, and arguments that will help you understand the tone (which can get quite passionate and heated) and atmosphere of the current challenges to the Bible's historicity and the various revised chronology models.

Within the past few years I have found myself sharing platforms with revised chronologists, many of whom are agnostic and secularist scholars, yet who are contending *for* the historicity of the Biblical record on academic merit alone. This will again be the case shortly after this book's release, when I will be speaking at a Bible and archaeology conference in Germany. Remember this: ongoing credible academic opposition to the prevailing Bible-as-myth position subsists – has even been gaining momentum – even though no one ever seems to hear about it.

My wife and I were in Berlin the week the border between the east and west was reopened. Our passports have two of the last East German stamps ever to be issued. We have a chunk of the wall to remind us that Berlin Walls do crumble. Although many didn't believe it possible, we watched it happen. There is always hope. When all is said and done, in the end, the integrity of Word of God will prevail.

"As the rain and the snow come down from heaven, and do not return to it without watering the earth and making it bud and flourish, so that it yields seed for the sower and bread for the eater, so is my word that goes out from my mouth: It will not return to me empty, but will accomplish what I desire and achieve the purpose for which I sent it. You will go out in joy and be led forth in peace; the mountains and hills will burst into song before you, and all the trees of the field will clap their hands (Isaiah 55:10-12)."

11

Fact or Fiction?

Is the Israelite religion nothing more than an adaptation of the surrounding pagan religions? Is the Old Testament just an Israelite version of a shared account of a communal past devoid of divine revelation? As we have seen in the previous chapters, the one side of the Bible-as-myth coin says there's no archaeological evidence for the Bible's historicity – including the claim that *the Israelites were never in Egypt*. When we flip this coin, we discover that the other side says the temple, worship rituals, and linguistic similarities *verify* that the Israelite religion of the Old Testament – rather than being the product of divine guidance – was an adaptation of ancient pagan religious practices such as those the Israelites learned while in Egypt.

Prior to the nineteenth century, the Old Testament of the Bible was the extant source for any study of the ancient world. It ruled, for the most part, without challenge. As noted in previous chapters, this changed dramatically after Napoleon reopened the Near East to the West. Champollion's decipherment of Egyptian hieroglyphics opened the ancient Egyptian world to scholars . . . which in turn opened the door to the study of Egypt's ancient religious beliefs and practices. The subsequent and numerous discoveries by archaeologists of extra-Biblical ancient pagan literary texts opened the door even farther . . . by revealing what seems to have been a very close re-lationship between the Israelite religious practices and the religious milieu of the ancient world. As a result, the question of the uniqueness of the Is-raelite religion as depicted in the Old Testament has become an extremely important – and sometimes emotionally loaded – subject.

Depending upon your professor, you may be assigned readings from books such as those by Gary Greenberg, and most likely from *The Moses Mystery: The African Origins of the Jewish People*[1] or *101 Myths of the Bible: How Ancient Scribes Invented Biblical History*.[2] Here's an excerpt from *101 Myths* that pretty well summarizes much of the mind-set that you will en-counter today.

> From these collections of Egyptian myths and traditions, *which Israel not only learned in Egypt*, but which were current, influential, and well-known throughout Canaan after Israel established itself there, Hebrews produced a new theology. Because Israel was monotheistic and the Egyptian myths were polytheistic, the Hebrew scribes had to rework the stories to reflect their own religious viewpoint, and it is in the results that we see some of the great genius of the Hebrew authors. [From page 5, Emphasis mine.]

> This, however, was only part of the story. After Israel moved into Canaan, Hebrew writers were exposed to new traditions from Baby-lon, the other great influence in the Near East. In 587 B.C., the rem-nants of the Hebrew kingdom were captured by the Babylonians and the educated elite were forcibly removed to the homeland of their captors, where they immersed in the local culture. Because of the great respect for Babylonian wisdom, the Hebrews found it necessary to further refine their earlier ideas, which by this time had become divorced from their original Egyptian roots. [From page 6][3]

Your professor may tell you that reading assignments from books such as these will, in theory, assist you in separating historical fact from Biblical fiction. However . . . when you read them, do so with a critical and astute eye. Scrutinize them and ask yourself how much of the so-called historical 'facts' are based upon irrefutable evidence . . . and how much of the content is based upon hypothesis, theory, and wishful thinking. Your initial assignment from your professor was to help you separate historical fact from Biblical fiction; don't forget to separate this so-called historical fact from hypothesis, theory, wishful thinking, scholarly assumptions, and the agendas of non-Biblical post-Christian worldviews.

Gary Greenberg (a trial attorney and president of the Biblical Archaeology Society of New York) theorizes that the monotheistic religion of ancient Israel actually originated in the Aten cult of ancient Egypt. I would concur that Yahwism, in some ways, might resemble Atenism . . . but the assertion that Israelite monotheistic Yahwism comes directly from Atenism is a very speculative proposal filled with assumptions. The general notion that the Israelites originated in Egypt – rather than Ur, as recorded in the Biblical account of Abraham's migration from Ur of the Chaldeans to Canaan (Genesis 11 and 12) – can be traced to the current global scholarly consensus that all modern people are the descendents of one woman ('Mitochondrial Eve') who lived in East Africa tens of thousands of years ago. The 'Out of Africa,' 'African Eve,' or 'Mitochondrial Eve' theory was proposed in 1987 by biochemist Allan Charles Wilson (University of California, Berkeley), Rebecca Cann, and Mark Stoneking.[4] Since the Out-of-Africa theory is the current scientific consensus, most of you have likely been shown the convincing genetic data that comes with the package.

But what you most likely *haven't* been shown is that, supporting this convincing genetic data, are more than a few assumptions and estimates.[5] As we have seen in previous chapters, when the assumptions are not provable, neither are the conclusions; when the assumptions are flawed, so are the conclusions. Henry Gee of *Nature* recognized the faulty conclusions of this theory when he called the entire mtDNA genetic study statistically flawed "garbage."[6] Even one of the original researchers, Mark Stoneking, has recognized the inherent flaws of the African Eve study, calling it an invalidated theory.[7] . . . yet the Out-of-Africa train keeps roaring down the tracks. Why? Might it have something to do with the fact that it supports prevailing worldviews?

Some scientists, confronted by the flaws of the mtDNA study, are now suggesting we do not need mtDNA to prove the East Africa origins of modern man . . . asserting that the fossils support the African Eve theory. But the fossil evidence says otherwise.[8] Moreover, this claim is an antithesis to the proposition of the original researchers who insisted that *only* mtDNA research was "complete and objective," and that "fossils cannot, in principle, be interpreted objectively"[9] [NOTE: In my next book, *My Professor Says Jesus Was a Fraud*, we will speak to the Out-of-Africa theory in more detail . . . when we reflect on the argument that the Jesus narratives of the Gospels were plagiarized from the narratives of ancient Egyptian mythology. For our immediate study, we shall continue our discussion of pagan influences on the Israelite religion and the Biblical text.]

Pagan Practices

The Bible itself does not deny, hide, or play down the influence of pagan religious practices on the Israelites. If anything, it confirms it, talking about it openly and continuously. The Israelite religion did not drop from heaven in a vacuum-sealed bag. The Bible reveals a constant tension between the Israelites and the ancient pagan cultures that enveloped them. God called the Israelites to himself in the midst of that pagan environment. So would we expect to find similarities? Absolutely! We *should* expect to find similarities around every corner.

Abram was called out of paganism and set out from Haran to Canaan. Joseph became a ruler in Pharaoh's court. Moses was born and raised in Egypt. The Israelites sojourned in Egypt and were slaves to Pharaoh. In the wilderness they wanted to go back to Egypt. Even after they had entered the long awaited Promised Land, Joshua had to plead with them:

> "Now fear the LORD and serve him with all faithfulness. Throw away *the gods your forefathers worshiped beyond the River and in Egypt, and serve the LORD.* But if serving the LORD seems undesirable to you, then choose for yourselves this day whom you will serve, whether the gods your forefathers served beyond the River, or the

gods of the Amorites, in whose land you are living. But as for me and my household, we will serve the LORD (Joshua 24:14-15)."

Was not the period of the Judges filled with pagan contaminations? How can we forget the Mount Carmel challenge?

Elijah went before the people and said, "How long will you waver between two opinions? If the LORD is God, follow him; but if Baal is God, follow him." But the people said nothing. Then Elijah said to them, "I am the only one of the LORD's prophets left, but Baal has four hundred and fifty prophets (1 Kings 18:21-22ff)."

The question as to the origin of Baal worship among the Israelites can only be established by tracing it back to the Semites in general. The supernatural powers of the gods most valued to the primitive Semites were those they believed would supply their most pressing needs, such as food and drink. The Israelites most likely learned to worship Baal from the agricultural Canaanites.

The Israelites 'mingled' themselves with the Ammonite worship of Molech, taking on the syncretistic pagan worship practices. They "learned their works and sacrificed their sons and daughters" to this demon of darkness (2 Kings 17:27-31; Psalm 106:35-37).

Consider King Solomon's demise:

King Solomon, however, loved many foreign women besides Pharaoh's daughter – Moabites, Ammonites, Edomites, Sidonians and Hittites.

They were from nations about which the LORD had told the Israelites, "You must not intermarry with them, because they will surely turn your hearts after their gods."

Nevertheless, Solomon held fast to them in love. He had seven hundred wives of royal birth and three hundred concubines, and his wives led him astray. As Solomon grew old, his wives turned his heart after other gods, and his heart was not fully devoted to the LORD his God, as the heart of David his father had been.

He followed Ashtoreth the goddess of the Sidonians, and Molech the detestable god of the Ammonites. So Solomon did evil in the eyes of the LORD; he did not follow the LORD completely, as David his father had done (1 Kings 11:1-6).

syncretism
The attempt to reconcile contrary beliefs, often while melding practices of various religions or schools of thought.

The degradation of worship in Israel in the time of Solomon (I Kings xi. 1 *et seq.*) and of Ahab (I Kings xvi. 31 *et seq.*) illustrate the danger of mixing the rites of the false gods and the true God. It was the return to the syncretism of their ancient culture that contributed more than anything else to the religious and moral decline of Israel.

Isaiah had to speak out against pagan religious practices:

"Some pour out gold from their bags and weigh out silver on the scales; they hire a goldsmith to make it into a god, and they bow down and worship it. They lift it to their shoulders and carry it; they set it up in its place, and there it stands. From that spot it cannot move. Though one cries out to it, it does not answer; it cannot save him from his troubles.

"Remember this, fix it in mind, take it to heart, you rebels. Remember the former things, those of long ago; I am God, and there is no other; I am God, and there is none like me. I make known the end from the beginning, from ancient times, what is still to come. I say: My purpose will stand, and I will do all that I please (Isaiah 46:6-10)."

Indeed, Hosea spoke powerfully and pathetically of the moral and religious ruin created by the people's return to pagan religious practices in the days just before the fall of the monarchy.

Similarities – and Differences

The mixing of pagan practices with the Israelite religion is not the only time we find similarities. Even several of the God-prescribed Israelite rites have similarities with the religious rites of the pagan world of antiquity. But, again, we should expect to find similarities in most places we research.

As regards the temple, for example, we should anticipate similarities between the Israelites and the pagan cultic practices. Think about it. The ancient world believed in divine beings. Belief in divine beings leads to worship. Worship leads to the need for a place to worship, and for an organized system of worship. An organized system of worship leads to the necessity of worship leaders. Temples were, therefore, very common in the ancient world, even temples with sacrificial altars similar to the one in the Jerusalem temple. Sacrifice (while we're on the subject) was a universal religious practice in the ancient world, as best we can tell. We will talk about the temples more specifically in the next chapter. In the meantime, we acknowledge there are abundant similarities.

The discovery of ancient pagan literary texts and their similarities to the Biblical text have provided additional ammunition for those whose objective is to relegate the Bible to ancient pagan myth. While it is true philologists have identified linguistic similarities between the extra-Biblical and Biblical texts, do those similarities necessarily lead to the foregone conclusion that the Israelite religion – rather than being the product of divine guidance – was an adaptation of surrounding pagan religions? I think not.

So how do we approach this topic? First and foremost, it is of utmost importance that, as we recognize the similarities, we train ourselves to focus our attention not just on the similarities, but on that which is distinctive.[10] Not doing so can lead to the grave danger of misinterpretation and misrepresentation. The differences may not always be apparent at the beginning . . . but you will soon discover that, ultimately, they are of much more importance than the similarities.

For example, sacrifice was a universal practice in the ancient world. That's a similarity. So what is different about what God prescribed for the Israelites? Another example is a misapplication of the idiom 'Holy of Holies' – which is unique to the Hebrew language – to describe the sacrificial area of a pagan temple in Egypt. (We'll talk more about this in the next chapter.)

Trajan's Kiosk in the Philae Temple Complex, Egypt

I wish I was welcoming you to my classroom . . . because this topic, like the chronology topic discussed in previous chapters, requires a full semester course just to *introduce* it adequately. What I am presenting here is a brief synopsis, a thumbnail sketch, to help you either answer some of your basic questions or encourage you to dig deeper (thus the reason for the copious endnotes at the conclusion of this book). This chapter and the two that follow are in no way a dissertation on the topic of ancient Near Eastern religious similarities.

Before we consider the linguistic parallels, it will be beneficial to first discuss the similarities of the temples and worship practices . . . which seem to reveal a close relationship between Israelite religious practices and the religious milieu of the ancient world. A critical question to ask: did the Israelites simply design their Jerusalem temple by plagiarizing the temples of the ancient pagans? Let's find out.

12

Timing the Temples: Who Copied Whom?

I was leading a tour through Egypt . . . observing the temples that majestically grace the banks of the Nile River . . . when one observant lady in my group stunned me with the first billion-dollar question of our journey: "Dr. Tom, it really bothers me that we are being shown 'holy of holies' in these pagan temples. Would the true God copy from pagan religions to describe his most holy place?"

How do we answer that? What are we to make of the allegation that the Israelites plagiarized the temple floor plan (including the 'Holy of Holies') and rituals from the pagan religions of the Near East . . . that they invented their own religion? Such a question almost seems like the old "Which came first, the chicken or the egg?" Fortunately, there's ample evidence to answer

Temple of Kom Ombo, Egypt

both of these questions, that is, if you are willing to scale the 'Berlin Wall' and search beyond the consensus position.

Temple of Isis in the Philae Temple Complex, Egypt

The simple answer – for now – is that it depends upon your worldview. In order to give you a more complete answer, let's continue our present journey . . . a journey that will not conclude until the last page of chapter fourteen. As a reminder, the limitations placed upon us only permit an extremely brief overview of a very extensive and complicated subject. In this chapter we will make some preliminary observations. (In the next chapter we consider and tour some of the Egyptian temples for ourselves. Then, in the fourteenth chapter, we consider the north Syrian temples.)

The 'Holy of Holies' . . . from Pagan Temples?

Archaeologists and tour guides have only recently been intentionally referring to the inner dwelling places of the pagan gods as a 'holy of holies' . . . aimed at demonstrating how the Israelite religion – rather than being the product of divine guidance – was an adaptation of pagan religious practices in ancient Egypt. In doing so, they are superimposing their *interpretation* of history . . . making it sound like irrefutable fact to the unsuspecting tourist.

First, *Holy of Holies* is the literal translation of an idiom formed by a construction that is *unique* to Hebrew, namely, קֹדֶשׁ הַקֳּדָשִׁים (pronounced qōdhesh haq-qŏdhāshīm). This idiomatic construction is not found in any of the other texts of the ancient world. In Hebrew, this idiom is intended to express the superlative degree of comparison. Accordingly, the KJV translated this 'Most Holy Place' to express the superlative degree in English. We find similar Hebrew constructions when translated literally that would read:

- Servant of servants (Genesis 9:25).
- Sabbath of Sabbaths (Exodus 31:15).
- Heaven of heavens (Deuteronomy 10:14).
- God of gods and Lord of lords (Deuteronomy 10:17).
- Vapor of vapors (Ecclesiastes 1:2).
- Song of Songs (Solomon 1:1).
- Prince of princes (Daniel 8:25).

Because this idiomatic structure is unique to the Hebrew language, scholars and translators have reserved this phrase to describe the innermost and most sacred chamber of the Jewish tabernacle and temple – that is, until the turn of the century when the 'Out of Egypt' frenzy starting gaining serious attention. That's when it began showing up as an inappropriate description of the dwelling place of the pagan gods in their respective temples. Applying this unique Hebrew idiom to pagan temples is inaccurate (since the gods and goddesses were not exactly 'holy' in their actions!), and philosophically reflects the evolving view that the Israelite religion – rather than being the product of divine guidance – was an adaptation of pagan religious practices of ancient Egypt. (It is also misleading to the millions of tourists who are visiting these sites.)

The use of Holy of Holies to describe the inner sanctums of pagan temples in Egypt is a misinterpreted similarity . . . and, as such, subtly undermines the uniqueness of the Old Testament for those not aware of the Hebrew distinctive that is being ignored.

• **The similarity here is twofold.** First, all of the pagan temples (like the Jewish tabernacle of the wilderness and the later temple in Jerusalem) had special dwelling places for their gods. Second, sacrifice was a universal practice in the ancient world.

• **The distinctive is also twofold.** First, the Holy of Holies is a uniquely Hebraic descriptor that belongs exclusively to the Jewish tabernacle and temple . . . because God – the true God, the God of the Israelites – is utterly and absolutely holy. That this linguistic descriptor is unique to the Hebrew language speaks volumes. It has been stolen from its rightful owners. There is a similarity in the naos of all temples. That is a given. *But the Holy of Holies, linguistically and theologically, is a distinctive of the naos of the Jerusalem Temple – and should not be applied to the naos of other temples.* Second, the

naos
The inner chamber of an ancient temple.

Bible's instructions concerning the Israelite sacrifices were *quite* dissimilar from pagan sacrificial practices, especially in regards to human sacrifice. The Bible is very consistent in its instructions concerning animal sacrifice in the Jerusalem Temple,[1] and its condemnation of human sacrifice[2] – including Genesis 22, where God instructs Abraham not to lay a hand on Isaac, providing a ram for the sacrifice instead.

Egyptologists do not generally connect human sacrifice with ancient Egypt, because there is little extant evidence of human sacrifice during most of the dynastic period. However, some evidence *does* exist that it may have been practiced in the Nile Valley during the First Dynasty and possibly also Predynastic Egypt.[3] There are two slabs dating to the early First Dynasty – one from Abydos and one from Saqqara – showing one person seated, with a pointed instrument to the throat or chest of another person who is kneeling backwards. The arms are tied behind his back. Some scholars believe this denotes human sacrifice, while others believe it to be some form of a tracheotomy being performed.

The Pyramid Texts have a section commonly referred to as the Cannibal Hymn that suggests human sacrifice in the Predynastic period. The king presumably acquires the magical powers of the gods through human sacrifice. "Pharaoh is he who eats men and lives on gods."[4]

Having done his own study on human sacrifice in ancient Egypt, Peter van der Veen concludes that we are indeed dealing with human sacrifice in the First Dynasty. "Also for later periods I completely disagree with many colleagues that there wasn't human sacrifice and that the Bible is wrong about it. I think there was human sacrifice and this was for instance quite clearly practiced by the Phoenicians who also carried this on in their colonies e.g. in Carthage. There is no doubt about that."[5]

Babylonian Exile: the Untold Story

In 586 BC, the kingdom of Judah fell to the Babylonians. You can read the gruesome details of the fall of Jerusalem in 2 Kings 25. In the aftermath of Nebuchadnezzar's conquest, many Judeans were taken captive to Babylon, where by the rivers of Babylon they sat and wept when they remembered Zion. "There on the poplars we hung our harps, for there our captors asked us for songs, our tormentors demanded songs of joy; they said, 'Sing us one of the songs of Zion!' How can we sing the songs of the LORD while in a foreign land (Psalm 137:1-5)?"

This is the story that is familiar to most of us. But the Babylonian exile is not the whole story . . . for in this same aftermath of Nebuchadnezzar's conquest of Jerusalem, Jeremiah tells the story about a migration of Jews to Egypt. If we look at the 2 Kings account again, and link what we are told there with Jeremiah's account, we discover the rest of the story.

The Babylonian conquerors appointed a Judean by the name of Gedaliah as the new governor of Judah over those Jews who remained in the land (2 Kings 25:22; Jeremiah 39:14; and 40:5-12).

"When all the Jews in Moab, Ammon, Edom and all the other countries heard that the king of Babylon had left a remnant in Judah and had appointed Gedaliah son of Ahikam, the son of Shaphan, as governor over them, they all came back to the land of Judah, to Gedaliah at Mizpah, from all the countries where they had been scattered. And they harvested an abundance of wine and summer fruit."

But in 582 BC, Gedaliah is assassinated (2 Kings 25:25; Jeremiah 40:13-41:10). The assassins were then defeated and driven out of the country by another group of Jews avenging the death of Gedaliah. Afterward, they all became afraid that the Babylonians would punish all of them for the death of the governor they had appointed. So, "at this, all the people from the least to the greatest, together with the army officers, fled to Egypt for fear of the Babylonians."[6]

Jeremiah – who had once boldly refused his invitation to accompany his fellow Jews to the Babylonian exile (Jeremiah 40:1-6), and who had pleaded with his fellow Jews to likewise refuse the Babylonian's invitation and remain in the land with him (Jeremiah 42:7-22) – now found himself in an unpleasant position of being forced to accompany his fellow Jews who were fleeing to Egypt (Jeremiah 43:1-7). We know from Jeremiah's account that there were exiled Jews living in Magdol, Tahpanhes, Memphis, and Pathros . . . and that they had all been enticed into engaging in idolatrous religious practices (Jeremiah 44:1ff). The last prophecy from Jeremiah is concerning the Egyptian Pharaoh Hophra (588-569 BC), who Jeremiah said was going to be handed over to his enemies (Jeremiah 44:30).[7] Jeremiah the prophet, along with a large number of other Jews, apparently ended his days in Egypt (Jeremiah 43:8-44:30). Hophra, by the way, was dethroned by his arch enemy Amasis[8] and was strangled to death by the angry mob.[9]

I trust you now begin to see (after hearing the rest of the exile story) that the Babylonian exile of the sixth century BC relocated a considerable number of Jews – not only to Babylon but also to Egypt. Our sources for the Persian period that followed the Babylonians, as well as later sources, confirm Egypt was a place with a significant Jewish population. And it was a population that grew over the years and became quite large indeed.

But that's not the end of the story, either. There is archaeological evidence that confirms this early Jewish presence in Egypt,[11] which was discovered on Elephantine, an island in the middle of the Nile River across from Aswan. In ancient times this island was an important strategic position both for defense and as a trading route. The excavations and reconstructions that have been done over the past hundred-plus years were done by teams of German archaeologists. Over the centuries, there has been a great deal of building activity on Elephantine, though most of the ancient structures have now vanished. But there was something very important that *did* survive: the Elephantine

Elephantine Passover Letter no. 34[10]

Papyri, a series of texts discovered there in the nineteenth and early twentieth century. These texts were written in Aramaic, and are dated from the late 400s to the early 300s BC. They come from a Jewish military colony that was stationed on the island, which (at the time) was called the island of Yeb. Text no. 34 tells the story of the destruction of the Jewish temple:

> (D)uring the month of June [Aramaic: Tammuz] in year fourteen of Darius [410 BCE], when Arshama, the Persian governor [Aramaic: satrap] of Egypt, was out of the country, the priests of Khnum . . . issued an ultimatum: "The Temple of Yahweh [Aramaic: YHW] on Elephantine Island must be destroyed." So, Vidranga, the governor of Elephantine Island, sent a letter to his son, Nafaina, the commander of Syene, ordering him to destroy the temple. Nafaina responded by leading his soldiers to Elephantine Island with weapons and axes.

> The soldiers forced their way into the temple and completely destroyed it. They smashed its stone pillars, wrecked its five stone gateways, and burned the doors in their bronze pivots, the cedar roof, and all of the fixtures. They looted the temple, taking the gold and silver basins and everything else of value.

> Our ancestors built the temple on Elephantine Island when the pharaohs ruled Egypt. *When Cambyses entered Egypt he found it already there.* Although he destroyed all the Egyptian temples, our temple he left undisturbed.

> After our temple was destroyed, we and our households put on sackcloth, fasted and prayed to Yahweh, Creator of the Heavens."[12] [Emphasis mine.]

The papyri make numerous references to other gods, sadly confirming the fact that the Jews of Yeb were dabbling in religious syncretism and living idolatrous lives . . . in much the same manner as the Jews that Jeremiah had condemned so powerfully some 170 years earlier. More importantly for our immediate study, we learn from these documents that the Jews of Yeb had a temple on the island, and that it was there they worshipped Yahweh. According to these texts, this Jewish temple stood on this island even before the Persian King Cambyses II marched on Egypt in 525 BC.[13] This is fascinating, given what we have just read from 2 Kings and Jeremiah. Here we have evidence of a Jewish temple which must have been built sometime after the Babylonian exile in 586 BC, but before 525 BC.

Cambyses II's reputation as a mad tyrant can be found in the writings of the Greek historian Herodotus (440 BC) and a Jewish document known as 'The Demotic Chronicle' (407 BC), which speaks of Cambyses II destroying all the temples of the Egyptian gods. Thus, we have three sources (the Elephantine Papyri, the historian Herodotus, and the Demotic Chronicle) suggesting that Cambyses destroyed all the ancient temples of the Egyptian gods. Unfortunately, the Jewish temple succumbed as well, and was destroyed in 410 BC, a feat provoked by the priests of the Egyptian creator-god Khnum.[14]

A Logical Conclusion

But what are we to make of this? Modern Egyptologists are now suggesting that many of these accounts are biased, and that Cambyses II was not nearly the tyrant Herodotus made him out to be. It is presumed that Herodotus was writing about the Egyptian tradition of a new Pharaoh marking his territory. If that is the case, it is also assumed that the tradition only refers to pharaonic temples. Further, the destruction of all the temples does not seem to stand up to archaeological scrutiny; there are obviously many that stood throughout the reign of Cambyses. The bottom line is: we are not sure how many temples were destroyed, or to what degree they were destroyed.[15] But this does not negate the fact that there was a Jewish community and a Jewish temple in southern Egypt that could have influenced the floor plans of the Egyptian temples constructed or altered after that time.

After the destruction of their temple in 410 BC, the Jews of Yeb tried to rally support for rebuilding their temple. The papyri record a letter that was written to Jonathan the high priest in Jerusalem, asking for support to rebuild the temple. This would have been the Jonathan mentioned by Ne-hemiah – "The family heads of the Levites in the days of Eliashib, Joiada, Johanan and Jaddua, as well as those of the priests, were recorded in the reign of Darius the Persian (Nehemiah 12:22)." There is no mention of a reply from Jonathan. The papyri also record letters asking for support that were written to Bagoas, then governor of Jerusalem, and to Delaiah, a son of Sanballat of Samaria. Interestingly, it was Sanballat, who had strongly opposed Nehemiah in the Jerusalem temple rebuilding project. At the time, Sanballat was the governor in Samaria.

"When Sanballat heard that we were rebuilding the wall, he became angry and was greatly incensed. He ridiculed the Jews, and in the presence of his associates and the army of Samaria, he said, 'What are those feeble Jews doing? Will they restore their wall? Will they offer sacrifices? Will they finish in a day? Can they bring the stones back to life from those heaps of rubble – burned as they are (Nehemiah 4:1-2)?'"

Apparently the Jewish tem-ple on the island of Yeb (Ele-phantine Island) was eventually rebuilt, but animal sacrifices were forbidden. This being the case, we can safely deduce the floor plan of the earlier temple (the one built sometime after the Babylonian exile and destroyed in 410 BC) would have accom-modated animal sacrifice . . . most likely patterned after Solomon's temple, which had been destroyed by the Babylonians.

Mövenpick Hotel, Elephantine Island, Egypt

Today the island of Elephantine is dominated by a beautiful Swiss-owned, five-star hotel. You can easily pick it out by its tall tower. The north-ern part of the island (under the hotel) was not where the Jewish settlement was located. The ancient Jewish settlement was around the temple area, likely in the remains of the tell on the southwest side. If you ever find your-self there, the Aswan Museum is at the entrance to the island. It has recently been expanded, although the exhibits remain in their old-fashioned, dusty, glass-covered cases. Nevertheless, there are some very interesting items which date right back to pre-dynastic times.

So now you have heard the rest of the story concerning the Babylonian exile that began in 586 BC. Here's what we *know* (not *presume*) from the rest of the story. We know that:

• At the time of the Babylonian exile there was a significant Jewish migration to Egypt.

• There was a Jewish presence; and more importantly, we know that there was a *Jewish temple* on the island of Elephantine that was built sometime after 586 BC but definitely before 525 BC.

• The Jewish temple on Elephantine in the upper region of Egypt *predated* the nearby temple of Philae.

• The Jewish temple on Elephantine *predated* the temple of Kom Ombo.

• The Jewish temple on Elephantine *predated* the Horus temple at Edfu.

• The Jewish temple on Elephantine *predated* the temple of Khnum at Esna.

• The Exodus, the Israelite tabernacle of the wilderness, and Solomon's temple in Jerusalem all *predated* these Egyptian temples.

You caught that, right? The Jewish temple on Elephantine in Egypt *predated* the temples that the Jews presumably stole their ideas from.

So how can you walk unsuspecting people through temples that we know were built *after* Solomon's Temple . . . and *after* the Jewish temple on Elephantine . . . and tell them the Jews copied the 'holy of holies' from these temples? I find this devious, to say the least . . . a rewriting of history to promote a worldview, and insulting to the tourists who typically have no background to judge the truth of what they are being told. This is not an example of sound objective scholarship trying to determine the truth of the past – it's a pseudo-scholarly interpretation of history that is obviously predisposed to disproving the historicity of the Bible and the Israelite/Jewish religion. I remind you again of the words of George Orwell: "Who controls the past controls the future; who controls the present controls the past."

Since several of these temples *post-date* Solomon's Temple and the Jewish temple on Elephantine, we can reasonably eliminate them from further discussion. The logical next question: Did the Israelites copy their ideas from the Egyptian temples that we *presume* predate the Jewish temple on Elephantine, as well as the Exodus, tabernacle, or Solomon's temple? We will address this question as we continue our journey in the next chapter.

Ancient Egyptian Temple	Estimated Date of Construction and Comments
Abu Simbel	• Constructed 1224 BC (conventional chronology). • Revised chronology - 200 to 300 years later (c. 985 BC). • Rediscovered in 1813 by a Swiss orientalist. • Was moved and restored in 1964 to preserve it from the rising waters of Lake Nasser as a result of the High Dam at Aswan.
Seti I and Osireion at Abydos	• Started by Seti I Reigned 1291 - 1279 BC (CC). • Revised Chronology - 200 to 300 years later. (c. 1052-1040 BC). • Most northern of the Theban Temples (Ancient Thebes).
Philae √	• Most ancient remains date to Nectanebo I (380-362 BC). • Other ruins – Ptolemy's (282-145 BC). • Was moved and restored in 1977-1980.
Kom Ombo √	• Construction begun by Ptolemy VI Philometor (180-145 BC). • Ptolemy XIII (47-44 BC) built the inner and outer courts. • Some additions made during Roman Period. • Used as a church by Coptic Christians. • Restored in 1893.
Horus Temple at Edfu √	• Built during the Ptolemaic Period (237-30 BC) and dedicated to Horos-Apollo. • Reflects myth and religion of the Greco-Roman Period.
Temple of Khnum at Esna √	The temple shown to tourists is Greco-Roman – one of the latest temples to be built. Some texts mention it may have been built on the site of an Eighteenth Dynasty temple.[1]
Queen Hatshepsut Site (mortuary temples)	• First monument – mortuary temple of Mentuhotep II built during the Eleventh Dynasty (2081-c. 1940 BC). Revised chronology adjusts dates by c. 150 years at this point. (Joseph died c. 1600 BC.) • Amenhotep I and Queen Hatshepsut built extensively during the Eighteenth Dynasty (1540-1292 BC). Queen Hatshepsut reigned from 1479-1458 BC (CC). (Revised c. 1239-1218).
Karnak Temples Complex Last Constructions only √	The earliest artifact found in the area of the temple is from the Eleventh Dynasty (2081-c. 1940 BC), which mentions Amun-Re.[2] Major construction work in the Precinct of Amun-Re took place during the Eighteenth Dynasty (1540-1292 BC). Last construction was in 380-362 BC – world's largest religious/cult center – later used by Coptic Christians.
Luxor	• Built 1400-1300 BC (CC) and famous for the festival of Opet. (Revised twelfth century BC) • Used as a church by Coptic Christians.

√= Temple Constructed Centuries after Jewish Temple on Elephantine

13

A Tour of Egyptian Temples

To help us navigate Chapter 13, I have created a very general thumbnail of the Egyptian temples of significance, showing when they were constructed along with bits of additional information (see left). We will work from this table. For the temples built centuries after Solomon's Temple, and the Jewish temple on Elephantine, I have inserted a check mark in the box. (This is a process of elimination for the sake of the study at hand. I have also placed check marks in the text that follows as we examine and dismiss each particular temple.)

Setting aside the more recent temples marked by the check mark (√) in the thumbnail above, we now work our way through the remaining temples.

Abu Simbel

Like the temple of Philae, Abu Simbel was relocated in its entirety in the 1960s. The two huge temples are now housed on two artificial hills made from a domed structure in southern Egypt, on the western bank of Lake Nasser southwest of Aswan. The twin temples were originally carved out of a mountainside. David Rohl describes his childhood visit to the original site when he was nine years of age.[3] The temples were built during the reign of Pharaoh Ramesses II. They, like many of Ramesses's projects, were built as an everlasting monument to himself and his queen, Nefertari. Their location was also meant to intimidate his Nubian neighbors.

As you walk up the stairs of the Great Temple . . . and enter between the colossal seated statues of Ramesses II . . . continue straight back through

the main hall with its Osirid columns . . . and straight through the inner hall . . . you will come to an inner chamber. This room is often labeled with the Hebrew descriptor 'holy of holies,' yet when you see it and understand its intended use, you realize this labeling is inappropriate and misleading. There are statues of four gods carved into the rear wall, and an offering

Abu Simbel Façade
Courtesy of © David Rohl

table carved from solid rock sets in front of them. According to Rohl, this suggests there may not have been a portable statue of the principal deity at Abu Simbel.

Over the main entrance to the temple is carved a figure of Ra-Harakhte (the sun god of the dawn horizon). As part of the design of the statue, there are two large hieroglyphs – the User symbol and the goddess Maat. Together with the Re sun-disk on top of the hawk-headed god, the three glyphs spell out *User-Maat-Ra* – the coronation name of Ramesses II. This makes it quite clear that the deity of the Abu Simbel temple was dedicated to none other than the deified Ramesses himself.[4] Building a temple for the glorification of one's self is the absolute antithesis of the purpose and function of the Israelite temple and Holy of Holies. Further, the floor plan is not Levantine/Jerusalemite.

Since this site was built over a twenty-year period during the early reign of Ramesses II, the construction date assigned to it must be directly linked to the date we assign to Ramesses II's early rule. If Rohl is correct concerning the proper historical identity of Shishak as Ramesses II, then the construction date of 1224 BC (typically assigned using the conventional chronology) needs to be reworked. The start of construction of Abu Simbel was in Ramesses II's first decade, somewhere between 960 and 930 BC in the new chronology. If we use the 200-year figure, construction would have begun between 1040 and 1010 BC. In either case, the Exodus and the Israelite tabernacle in the wilderness had long passed before this temple was even built. √

Abu Simbel Colossus
Courtesy of © David Rohl

Temple of Seti I in Abydos

Next, we consider the temple of Seti I in Abydos. Located about 300 miles south of Cairo, it was dedicated to Seti I, Osiris and Isis . . . along with Ptah, Ptah-Sokar, Nefertem, Re-Horakhty, Amun, and Horus. Although not visited as much as the others, it is one of the major archaeological sites in that region. In the shape of an L, this structure was built from white limestone. Its landing quay, ramp, and front terrace are in ruin. Of the two pylons, the outer one is mostly in ruin. The remaining façade is actually quite impressive.

Seti and Re at Abydos
Courtesy of © David Rohl

Abydos is truly one of the most important archaeological sites in Egypt – and it is, therefore, imperative we understand the history of this site before considering the charges that the Israelites were influenced by it:

> **quay**
> A landing place along the edge of the river; like a wharf.
>
> **pylon**
> A gateway to the inner part of an ancient Egyptian temple.

- Originally, the site was a pre-dynastic royal graveyard.
- There are some interesting links between the royal chambers in the Valley Temple in Giza and what we now call the Osireion.
- Archaeologists believe the architecture of the Osireion was copied from the Valley Temple and causeway of Khafre at Giza; thus, the tomb is said to incorporate the elements of Old Kingdom royal tombs.
- By the New Kingdom, the Osireion was buried . . . and, is assumed, would have been still known as the tomb or shrine of Osiris. The temple of Seti I was later built on this site, which we can say confidently dates from an earlier time.
- This is why Seti's temple does a funny dog-leg in its ground plan. As you walk the site, you cannot help but noticing Seti's temple does not extend from front to back down a single axis as do the other temples; it turns left and forms an L-shape.
- Rohl believes the reason for this bizarre floor plan must be because the Osireion was already there – forcing Seti I to build around it.
- Accordingly, it is only the underground chamber we call the Osireion that we know for sure predates the Israelites' sojourn and Exodus.

Now . . . with this background established, we are ready to visit the temple of Seti I at Abydos. To the right of the temple's southern wing, you will see a passage that leads to a cenotaph (false tomb), the top of which is below ground level. Today this is called the Osireion – the mythical tomb of Osiris. The Osireion and the Osiris Suite in the Seti I Temple *must not be confused*; one dates back to pre-dynastic times and was built underground . . . the other dates to the time of Seti I (circa 1291 to 1279 BC using the conventional chronology), and is built above ground as part of the temple proper. (Suggested dates for the Exodus using the conventional chronology range between circa 1350 to 1225 BC, with the consensus leaning toward circa 1225 BC – placing the Exodus after Seti I and suggesting Israelite plagiarism.)

In view of that . . . of particular interest for our study is the Osiris Suite (*not* the Osireion) situated behind the main chapels of the main temple. Unfortunately, this part of the temple is not well lighted, and the relief colors are very faded. The suite itself would have been the dwelling place of the statue of Osiris. In recent years, it has been misleadingly referred to as the 'holy of holies' for the Seti I Temple. But this area of the temple is just another ancient naos and nothing more than that (for reasons discussed in the previous chapter). We can draw one of two conclusions:

1. If the revised chronologists are wrong – and this temple somehow predates the Exodus – we would point to its floor plan, which is *not* Levantine/Jerusalemite. (You will read more about the significance of temple floor plans in chapter fourteen.)

2. If the revised chronologists are correct (as I believe they are) about the ancient chronologies being flawed by (give or take) two centuries, the Exodus would have taken place (circa 1447 BC) – four centuries before Seti I (circa 1052 to 1040 BC) even began construction, suggesting no *possibility* of plagiarism.

The possibilities of influence noted by Kenneth Kitchen include the use of wood interior paneling such as was used in Seti I's temple in Abydos and in some of the tombs at Saqqara. But the use of wood paneling was a common phenomenon; the use of interior wood paneling for the inner walls of royalty and important buildings was a common practice that dates back two thousand years before Solomon.[5]

All things considered, there's really nothing here to establish Israelite plagiarism.√

Queen Hatshepsut Site

That takes us next to the Queen Hatshepsut Site. Mortuary temples were typically constructed next to (or in the general vicinity of) the royal tombs of the pharaohs during the Middle Kingdom and New Kingdom pe-

Queen Hatshepsut Mortuary Temple
(aka Al-Deir Al-Bahari Temple),
West Bank of Luxor, Egypt

riods. They were built to commemorate the reign of the pharaoh by whom they were built, again a self-glorification. They also served as a cult center after the pharaoh's death. The most famous mortuary temples at Deir el-Bahri are Queen Hatshepsut's temple, the Ramesseum constructed by Ramesses II, and the mortuary temple of Mentuhotep II that sits just to the left of Hatshepsut's temple at Deir el-Bahri. The Israelite tabernacle and the temple in Jerusalem were not mortuary in any sense of the word. √

Karnak

The temple complex at Karnak is just as it says, a complex of temples dating over multiple centuries. You can easily spend at least half of a day just walking around, trying to take in Karnak's many areas . . . and it would probably take years of study to come to know the complex well. My group was able to get a good overview by not spending too much time at each stop, and no one seemed to mind when we ran out of time. Safe to say, everyone was feeling tired and wanted to get back to the boat.

Significant to our study is an Eighteenth Dynasty festival parade of graven images of the current royal family that began at Karnak and ended at the temple of Luxor. The festival lasted eleven days. By the late Eighteenth Dynasty the journey was made by barge on the Nile River. Each god or goddess was placed in a separate barge that was then towed by smaller boats. Large crowds walked along the river banks to accompany the gods and goddesses. The crowd would have been made up of soldiers, dancers, musicians and high ranking officials. By the reign of Ramesses III in the Twentieth Dynasty, the festival had expanded to twenty-seven days. Records indicate that, at that time, the festival included the distribution of over 11,000 loaves of bread, eighty-five cakes, and 385 jars of beer. During the festival days, the people were allowed to pray to and ask favors of the statues of the kings or to the graven images of the gods that were on the barges. Once they arrived at the temple, the king and his priests would enter the

Karnak, Ancient Thebes
East Bank of Luxor, Egypt

secret chamber. There, the king and his ka (the divine essence of each king, created at his birth) were merged together, and the king was transformed into a divine being. The ka and the king in a back room hardly constitute a 'holy of holies.'

Kenneth Kitchen mentions the use of storehouses around the worship area found here at Karnak as possibly having influenced Solomon's Temple[6] . . . but for our purposes in this study, walk with me to the Sixth Pylon. The Sixth Pylon, the guides tell you as you walk through it, was built by Thutmose III, and leads into a Hall of Records in which the king recorded his tributes. But what you are looking at today as you walk through this area is *not* what Thutmose III constructed. There is very little of the original that still remains of this archive, with the exception of the two granite pillars. Just beyond these pillars lies what we were told was the 'holy of holies,' the *oldest* part of the temple.

What was not mentioned was that the presumed 'holy of holies' back room in which we were physically standing was built by the brother of Alexander the Great,[7] Philip Arrhidaeus (323-316 BC), who was the king of Macedonia. For the record, the present sanctuary (which is built in two sections) was built *on the site of* the earlier sanctuary built by Thutmose III. True, the present sanctuary contains many of the stone blocks from the original Thutmose sanctuary, and still contains Thutmose's inscriptions . . . but, frankly, we have little idea what the original sanctuary ever looked like, or what may or may not have been kept in it. So I have found nothing extant at Karnak that could convince me the Israelites plagiarized this temple's floor plan or 'holy of holies' from here. Accordingly, using the Israelite descriptor 'holy of holies' on a Hellenistic Age structure is quite misleading.
√

Luxor

Luxor has a fascinating temple complex situated on the east bank of the Nile (ancient Thebes). In ancient times it was known as *ipet resyt* – the southern harem sanctuary or the private sanctuary (Opet) of the south. The temple was dedicated to the Theban Triad of Amun, Mut, and Chons. The temple's focus was the annual Opet Festival, in which a cult statue of Amun was paraded from the nearby Karnak Temple *(ipet-isut)* to stay there for a while, with his consort Mut, in a celebration of fertility – hence the temple's name, which means 'southern harem.' The view from the third-floor dining room of the McDonald's restaurant in Luxor is probably the best view from a McDonald's anywhere in the world. There's an amazing panorama over the city of Luxor and the Luxor Temple . . . and (on a clear day) in the background, you can see the Valley of the Kings.)

We have already described the Eighteenth Dynasty festival parade of graven images that would begin at Karnak and end at the temple of Luxor.

The Bible speaks directly to the graven images used in such pagan rituals: "Some pour out gold from their bags and weigh out silver on the

Luxor Temple, East Bank of Luxor, Egypt

scales; they hire a goldsmith to make it into a god, and they bow down and worship it. *They lift it to their shoulders and carry it; they set it up in its place, and there it stands.* From that spot it cannot move. Though one cries out to it, it does not answer; it cannot save him from his troubles (Isaiah 46:6-7)."

And from the Psalms:

> Why do the nations say, "Where is their God?"
> Our God is in heaven; he does whatever pleases him.
> But their idols are silver and gold, made by the hands of men.
> They have mouths, but cannot speak, eyes, but they cannot see;
> they have ears, but cannot hear, noses, but they cannot smell;
> they have hands, but cannot feel, feet, but they cannot walk; nor can
> they utter a sound with their throats.
> Those who make them will be like them, and so will all who trust in
> them (Psalm 115:2-8).

The temple at Luxor, as you see it today, was built on a mound that has never been excavated, and which may be concealing the original foundations of an earlier edifice. No longer visible, the older structure may date back to the Twelfth Dynasty. Archaeologists have also surmised that the few Middle Kingdom fragments found at this site probably came from elsewhere along the Nile, having been transported to Luxor after some other buildings were dismantled. This is believed to be the case, since neither the cult nor any part of the present temple appears to predate the early Eighteenth Dynasty.

For our present study, I need to walk you to the southern end of the complex. After coming through the main entrance, turn to the right and walk straight back through the Court of Ramesses II, the Colonnade, the Court of Amenhotep, the Hypostyle Hall, and the Portico (which has the Chapel to Mut on the left, and the Chapel to Khonsu on the right). Continuing straight back, you would walk into the Offering Hall. Behind the wall to the immediate left is the Birthing Room of Amenhotep III (to get there you need to go forward in the next room and take a left and a left) . . . and, straight in front of you, is the Hall of the Hours. Just a few steps through the Hall of the Hours, and you are standing in the room often labeled 'holy of holies' in current literature. It is in this most southern small room of the temple complex that the cult statue of Amun would have been placed during the Opet Festival, having been carried in the procession from Karnak.

We can see the similarity in that this was the dwelling place of their god Amun – but there it ends, as it does in all of the Egyptian temples. The Israelite Holy of Holies was not part of a fertility rite. I would reiterate: the maps that label this room 'naos' are much more academically appropriate.[8] A naos is a small shrine, often portable, e.g. the battered-sided Egyptian type, carried in procession by a Naöphorus figure. When studying ancient temples, it is important to pay particular attention to the *differences* and *distinctive features* when considering the possible similarities.

Going back to the Birthing Room, we presume it would have been here that the king and his "ka" (mentioned earlier) would have merged. When you step inside, you will notice the scenes illustrating the myth of the divine birth of Amenhotep III depicted on the west wall. After the scenes of the union of Amun with the king's mother, Mutemwiya, the creator god Khnum can be seen fashioning the baby king Amenhotep III with his ka behind him. Mutemwiya is depicted giving birth to the newborn king, whereupon he is presented to the gods. These interesting scenes were meant to give legitimacy to the king and his divine right to rule.

Hang on – there's more to this story as well. Just beyond the Birthing Room is a side room with three columns. Its walls are covered with poorly preserved reliefs. From this room, there is an arched doorway (obviously cut through at a later date) leading into the granite shrine of Alexander the Great. Four columns that were supporting the roof were moved to make room for the Sanctuary of the Barque of Amun. The walls were redone . . . redecorated inside and out with reliefs placing Alexander in the presence of Amun and his fellow deities. Obviously this was an attempt on Alexander's part to legitimize himself as their new king with the divine right to rule. Alexander the Great is ancient – but not nearly as ancient as Solomon; you are therefore not standing in a room that could have influenced the Israelites (if that's what you have been told).

In summation, the Luxor temple was constructed on an unexcavated mound and may cover the foundation of what would have been the actual Twelfth Dynasty structure. Thus, the temple we see today was built essentially by two kings with some later alterations by Alexander the Great. Amenhotep III (according to Rohl, 1050-1012 BC, 1382-1344 BC conventional, and 1142-1104 BC revised) , built the inner southern part. Ramesses II (according to Rohl, circa 960-930-ish BC, and 1184-1153 BC conventional) built the outer part. Alexander the Great (356-323 BC) largely rebuilt the Sanctuary of the Barque, and made a sanctuary unto himself sometime during his reign . . . and that, my friend, is all you are looking at. √

Some Recent Temple Discoveries

Digging near the ancient northern military highway in the Sinai, Egyptian archaeologists have discovered what they believe to be the remains of a 3,000-year-old ancient fortified city and four ancient temples. According to Zahi Hawass (considered by many to be Egypt's top archaeologist), earlier studies suggested the presence of a fortified city along this route. The digs along the military highway have been ongoing since 1986.

The objective of the digs has been to find fortress remains along the ancient military road, so this discovery is quite exciting. Archaeologist Mohammed Abdel-Maqsoud (who served as chief of the excavation team) said that he believes the fortified city corresponds to the "Way of Horus" inscriptions found on the walls of a temple in Luxor. The Luxor inscriptions show eleven military fortresses strategically placed to defend Egypt's eastern border. Only five fortresses have been discovered to date. It is believed that this city could have served as ancient Egypt's military headquarters from some time in the earlier New Kingdom, until the Ptolemaic era. Abdel-Maqsoud also believes this find could potentially rewrite the historical and military significance of the Sinai for all future studies of ancient Egypt.[9]

Keep in mind, however, that this find is in its infancy and will remain open to challenges, interpretations, and reinterpretations as the site is examined further. As we have already seen, this is the nature of archaeology.

The Old Testament book of Exodus speaks of two ancient highways across the Sinai Peninsula, the northern military route referred to as "the Way of the Philistines" and the more southerly route often referred to as "the Way of the Wilderness." The fastest way across was the military path (Way of the Philistines) because it went north-eastward along the coast of the Mediterranean (a much straighter distance). Many scholars believe the way of the Philistines and the way of Horus are basically the same path. In ancient times, this military highway connected Egypt to Canaan (the Philistines and Israelites). This ancient route corresponds to the present-day Rafah[10] border crossing which connects the Palestinian territory of Gaza and modern Egypt.

What I find exciting is, as a result of this 2009 discovery, we now have confirmation of some type of ancient Egyptian presence along this northern military highway. Might this be connected to the reasons God had the Israelites take the more southerly wilderness highway toward the Red Sea?[11] I think it was . . . making these finds of special Biblical interest.

Of the four ancient temples unearthed, the one that has captured the most attention is located 2.5 miles (4 kilometers) east of the Suez Canal in Al Qantana El Sharqiyya. Al Qantara is basically in the Mediterranean coast region in northern Sinai, about 99 miles northeast of Cairo (160 kilometers), and about 30 miles (50 kilometers) south of Port Said.

This temple is the largest mud brick temple found in the Sinai to date, with an area measuring 80 meters by 70 meters (approximately 87 yards by 76 yards). It is fortified with mud brick walls about 3 meters (about 10 feet thick). The temple contains four hallways and three stone purification bowls. There are colorful inscriptions commemorating Ramsesses I and II. Serving as the eastern gateway to ancient Egypt, archaeologists and historians are suggesting the grandeur and size of this temple and fortification was meant to impress visiting foreign delegations and armies as they entered ancient Egypt.

For our purposes, we make careful note that present studies indicate the unearthed temple was built on top of an Eighteenth Dynasty temple (1539-1215 BC, conventional chronology).[12] Thus, since what has been unearthed is on top of the Eighteenth Dynasty structure, it is *post-Mosaic* . . . and the Exodus rendering the Israelite plagiarism of the 'holy of holies' a moot subject. Additionally, Ramesses I and II in the BICANE revised chronology are both pre-Solomonic *and* post-Exodus. √

In January of 2010 the Supreme Council of Antiquities in Cairo announced that Egyptian archeologists unearthed a 2,000-year-old temple that may have been dedicated to the ancient Egyptian cat goddess, Bastet. For purposes of our study, we note that these ruins, discovered in the heart of the Mediterranean port city of Alexandria,[13] are from the Ptolemaic era – and thus post-Exodus and post-Solomonic,[14] making the possible Israelite plagiarism of the 'holy of holies' a moot subject as well. √

Conclusions

As we close our brief temple tour through Egypt, pause and take in the splendor of the magnificent complexes we have seen. They are all worth seeing. And as you do, also pause and make note of the significant contradiction we have discovered.

On the one hand . . . as we made our way along the Nile and visited these magnificent sites of antiquity . . . we have been told that what we have seen proves the Bible is a myth. After all, it is quite obvious that it wasn't the God of the Jews who told the ancient Israelites how to build their Tabernacle and Temple, as the Bible claims. Instead, the Israelites, while they sojourned in Egypt, collected and then plagiarized all these wonderful ideas from the Egyptians.

On the other hand, we have encountered another group of scholars claiming the Bible is a myth because there is no evidence that the Israelites were ever in Egypt; there is no evidence for an Israelite Exodus from Egypt.

While the two schools of scholars disagree on whether or not the Israelites were ever in Egypt, they both agree the Bible is myth. Are their conflicting views based on the evidence – or on the necessary agendas of their 'Berlin Wall' worldviews? The contradiction we have discovered is proof positive that it is *not the evidence* that is in conflict; it is the *interpretation* of the evidence that's in conflict. The conflict is first and foremost a *conflict of worldviews/agendas* – and, sadly, always will be.

None of the ancient temples in Egypt, including the most recent finds in the northern Sinai, were preserved in a glass bubble or in a time capsule unscathed by degrees of destruction and rebuilding over the centuries; indeed, all the extant temples have been considerably altered over the centuries.[15] There have been few stones left unturned, repositioned, and reused.

"*Sites were sacred in pharaonic times not buildings.* As a result, every temple was added to, remodeled or demolished, from predynastic times on. Thus, it is almost meaningless to talk about an 'original, intact form', perhaps only an earliest structure."[16] [*Emphasis mine.*]

What we have discovered on our tour of the temples of ancient Egypt is that it is impossible to prove the 'Holy of Holies' was plagiarized, as if we could somehow examine the most ancient of Egyptian temples in their original forms. We were told that combining the term 'Biblical' with archaeology was antithetical. Well, as we have seen, combining the term *Holy of Holies* with the Egyptian temples is what's antithetical! We were told that Biblical archaeology is not only dubious but wholly ludicrous. Claiming the Israelites plagiarized their temple ideas from the Egyptians is what's not only dubious but wholly ludicrous. It's just not possible. When you go from temple to temple and examine the evidence, it's just not there. Link this with the proper chronological dating of the ancient temples of Egypt (using the revised chronology), and any remaining charges of Israelite plagiary melt away.

Our tour has confirmed that "there are no obvious links between the Egyptian temples and the state cult in Jerusalem."[17] That the Israelite Tabernacle[18] and Temple were an adaptation of the ancient Egyptian temples is a fastidious unproven hypothesis . . . another *assumption*, and there it ends. The same can be said of the Neo-Assyrian and Neo-Babylonian temples, because none of them resemble the Jerusalemite type (which is very Levantine in its layout).[19] √

So it is logical that we now turn our attention to regions north of Israel in our investigation of the alleged theft charges.

14

Temples to the North and Ritual Similarities

According to research by Lawrence T. Geraty, there is not an exact parallel to Solomon's Temple anywhere in the world. Emphasizing the word "exact," Geraty postulates a very reasonable likelihood that, to date, has not been proven incorrect (not even by those claiming the Israelites plagiarized their temple and its rituals from ancient Egypt). The only known temple that has a strikingly close resemblance to Solomon's Temple is the Tell Tainat temple in northern Syria. But instead of the Israelites copying from it, Geraty concludes that the Tell Tainat temple could have just as likely been influenced by Solomon's temple, given Solomon's fame and influence at that time.[1]

The initial archaeological excavations were conducted by the University of Chicago's Oriental Institute from 1935 to

Tell Tainat Temple, Amuq Valley, Syria
(University of Chicago Oriental Institute)

1938, led by Robert Braidwood. Ever since then, this site has remained one of special interest because it remains the only known temple in the world that has a reminiscent floor plan to King Solomon's Temple in the Old Testament.[2] In addition to the Tell Tainat temple, several large palaces have also been discovered in the architectural style known as *Bit-hilani.*

> **Bit-hilani**
> An ancient architectural type of palace that some archaeologists believe became popular during the ninth century BC in northern ancient Syria. Others feel this type of palace architecture may have originated as early as the Bronze Age.

Although not well preserved, the temple itself had a long room measuring 82 feet by 39 feet (25 by 12 meters) that was divided into a portico, a main hall and an inner sanctum. Just like Solomon's, the portico had two columns on lion bases (at least, that's what is assumed, since only one of them was preserved). The inner sanctum was generally small. Inside was what remained of a platform, most likely to hold a statue of the deity . . . and a square structure that may have served for offerings. And, like Solomon's temple, it stood beside the palace on its southern side. However, much like Garety's position noted above, archaeologist Volkmar Fritz[3] states, "The temple at Tell Tainat could not have been the source of Solomon's Temple . . . because it was built later than Solomon's Temple."[4] Regardless, the Bible itself tells us Solomon had help from his northern neighbors in building the Temple in Jerusalem.

Fritz's position is that Solomon's temple most likely resembles second-millennium BC Syrian temples. Pointing to several of those that have been recently uncovered, Fritz postulates that the architectural source of the long-room temple – like that of Solomon's – is traceable to the Phoenician temples of northern Syria. Again, this should not surprise us, since the Bible itself tells us of the assistance Solomon received from the north . . . from Hiram king of Tyre, his workers, and workers from the Phoenician city of Gebal (one of the principal seaports of Phoenicia):

> When Hiram king of Tyre heard that Solomon had been anointed king to succeed his father David, he sent his envoys to Solomon, be-

cause he had always been on friendly terms with David. Solomon sent back this message to Hiram:

"You know that because of the wars waged against my father David from all sides, he could not build a temple for the Name of the LORD his God until the LORD put his enemies under his feet. But now the LORD my God has given me rest on every side, and there is no adversary or disaster. I intend, therefore, to build a temple for the Name of the LORD my God, as the LORD told my father David, when he said, 'Your son whom I will put on the throne in your place will build the temple for my Name.' So give orders that cedars of Lebanon be cut for me. My men will work with yours, and I will pay you for your men whatever wages you set. You know that we have no one so skilled in felling timber as the Sidonians.
When Hiram heard Solomon's message, he was greatly pleased and said, "Praise be to the LORD today, for he has given David a wise son to rule over this great nation."

So Hiram sent word to Solomon: "I have received the message you sent me and will do all you want in providing the cedar and pine logs. My men will haul them down from Lebanon to the sea, and I will float them in rafts by sea to the place you specify. There I will separate them and you can take them away. And you are to grant my wish by providing food for my royal household."
In this way Hiram kept Solomon supplied with all the cedar and pine logs he wanted, and Solomon gave Hiram twenty thousand cors of wheat as food for his household, in addition to twenty thousand baths of pressed olive oil. Solomon continued to do this for Hiram year after year.

The LORD gave Solomon wisdom, just as he had promised him. There were peaceful relations between Hiram and Solomon, and the two of them made a treaty. King Solomon conscripted laborers from all Israel – thirty thousand men. He sent them off to Lebanon in shifts of ten thousand a month, *so that they spent one month in Lebanon and two months at home.* Adoniram was in charge of the *forced labor.* Solomon had seventy thousand carriers and eighty thousand stonecutters in the hills, as well as thirty-three hundred foremen who supervised the project and directed the workmen. At the king's command they removed from the quarry large blocks of quality stone to provide a foundation of dressed stone for the temple. *The crafts-men of Solomon and Hiram and the men of Gebal* cut and prepared the timber and stone for the building of the temple (1 Kings 5:1-18).

Furthermore, Fritz proposes that the northern Syrian temple-type temples themselves can now be traced back to the megaron type of building in Anatolia of the third millennium BC. The megaron was a private residence consisting of a single long room (what we might call an open floor plan).[5] By the second millennium BC, this basic open floor plan used for residences in Anatolia was being used for temple architecture in northern Syria.

Fritz summarizes his position this way. Architecturally speaking, "when Solomon wanted to build a house for Israel's God on the Temple Mount in Jerusalem, adjacent to his own palace, he looked not to available Israelite prototypes, but to Phoenician exemplars, which in turn we can now trace back to long room temples in northern Syria and eventually back to the megaron house in Anatolia, nearly 2,000 years before Solomon built his House of the Lord."[6]

"Phoenician temples no longer exist, or at least we have not yet found them. But now with the archaeological evidence I have just recounted, we can be sure that these Phoenician temples, which were the inspiration for Solomon's Temple, were themselves descendants of the long-room type, so well preserved in Syria and Canaan. . . . The fact that Solomon's Temple re-lied on exemplars *that have not survived* should hardly be surprising, but *this emphasizes the difficulty of tracing the antecedents of Solomon's Temple.*" [Emphasis mine.][7] Truth be told, there is a considerable amount of infor-mation concerning the actual past of the ancient world that we will never know for certain, such as if and who may have borrowed from whom and when. In many instances, the Biblical narrative is all we have to go on. There is nothing here that should dissuade us from accepting the Biblical record as reliable.

Finding the Distinct

Are there architectural similarities? Of course there are. We should expect them. The Bible itself tells us this in the fifth chapter of 1 Kings. The Bible clearly states that Solomon *had plenty of help from his northern Phoenician friends – including their architecture and materials.* Because the Bible and Solomon's temple belong to this ancient world, it would be foolish to deny that some of the architectural features of Solomon's temple reflect a number of architectural elements common to the time it was built. What is important, however, is this: there were significant differences (and not only the specific dimensions) that made the Jerusalem temple distinct.

"Perhaps the most important distinction," Geraty states, "was the way the temple functioned in Israelite theology; it was not God's palace where His human servants supplied His physical needs, but it was the bearer of His name, and thus the focus of religious attention to which prayer was directed. The Jerusalem temple was an accommodation to God's people."[8] A temple whose purpose is to accommodate the desires of a needy god, and a temple that bears the name of an all-sufficient God whose purpose is to accommodate the needs of His people stand in antithesis to one another.

Second Temple Model
(aka Herod's Temple),
Shrine of the Book Museum,
Jerusalem, Israel

Before we leave this section, I would also point out that God showing Moses by divine revelation the very specific model measurements and floor plan (Exodus 25:8-9) to be followed in the construction of the tabernacle was not unique to the Israelites or the Bible. There are other gods in the ancient world that are said to have given specific instructions as to what their temples were to look like. It is, as they say, something that belongs to the phenomenology of temples in the ancient Near East:

Sumerian, Babylonian, Egyptian, Israelite . . . as well as to Confucian temples in China, Japanese shrines, and Hindustani temples in India.

Angel Manuel Rodríguez concludes, "The idea that specific instructions for the building of earthly temples were given by the gods to humans and that therefore the building itself was a reflection of a transcendental reality seems to belong to the human religious consciousness and transcends cultural and regional boundaries."[9]

Geraty's view is that God "guided its builders (1 Chronicles 28:11-12 et al), not in a cultural vacuum but among current options, to choose an arrangement that already had some meaning but one which could be modified to teach Israel how and why she was different from her neighbors."[10]

The evidence leans toward the position of Fritz: Solomon's Temple relied on exemplars from northern Syria that no longer exist, rather than upon the temples of Egypt. Kitchen presents a useful summary of the temples of the ancient world and the influence they may have had on the Solomonic Temple.[11]

Examples of Temple Ritual Similarities

The ritual of the scapegoat, generally known as an elimination rite, is found in Leviticus 16. Beginning at verse seven we read, "Then he (Aaron) is to take the two goats and present them before the LORD at the entrance to the Tent of Meeting. He is to cast lots for the two goats— one lot for the LORD and the other for the scapegoat. Aaron shall bring the goat whose lot falls to the LORD and sacrifice it for a sin offering. But the goat chosen by lot as the scapegoat shall be presented alive before the LORD to be used for making atonement by sending it into the desert as a scapegoat (Leviticus 16:7-10)."

Here's a quick summary of what's happening in Leviticus 16. After Aaron makes a sin offering to make atonement for himself and his household using the blood of the bull, he then makes a sin offering for the people using the first goat's blood in the same manner, sprinkling the blood on the atonement cover and in front of it. In this way he will make atonement for the Most Holy Place.

Picking up at verse 20, "When Aaron has finished making atonement for the Most Holy Place, the Tent of Meeting and the altar, he shall bring forward the live goat. He is to lay both hands on the head of the live goat and confess over it all the wickedness and rebellion of the Israelites – all their sins – and put them on the goat's head. He shall send the goat away into the desert in the care of a man appointed for the task. The goat will carry on itself all their sins to a solitary place; and the man shall release it in the desert (Leviticus 16:20-22)."

The Hittites and Babylonians had similar elimination rites, but the similarities are more superficial than specific. For example, if a Hittite king and his army returned from war afflicted with

> **censer**
> Instrument used for burning incense.

some type of illness or plague, the king was to select one man, one woman, one bull, and one female sheep from the land of the enemy. They were to be presented to the god or goddess who caused the plague. The Hittite king or his representative transferred the plague to the transporters of the evil back to the enemy land as substitutes for the king and his army. Since it was believed one of the local gods or goddess sent the evil, the purpose of the ritual was to return it to the land of the enemy. This elimination rite was known as the Hittite ritual of Pulisa.[12]

The purification rite for the cleansing of the Babylonian temple serves as another example; however, in Babylon it was not the sin of the people that contaminated the temple, it was demons. Because the demons in the temple were believed to be a threat to the local god or goddess, it was therefore necessary to remove the demons at least once a year. The priest was to wipe the temple with the carcass of a ram while reciting an incantation to exorcise the temple of the demons. The priest would carefully exorcise the inner chamber of all demons, and would then take down the censer. The demons attached to the flesh of the ram, and were returned to the underworld when the carcass was carried to the river and thrown in. In Babylonian mythology, demons only had access to the world of the living through rivers and could only be returned to the underworld through rivers.[13]

We also know that the Hittites had a concept of holiness that could be applied to a deity, or the captured territory of an enemy that was dedicated to a god. The concept was also used in conjunction with temples, cultic utensils, priests, sacrifices, and festivals. [14]

For sure there are similarities, but in every instance we can always find that which makes the Israelite temple and ritual practices distinct. At first, the temple ritual similarities may seem intimidating. My research has led me to conclude that the reason for the similarities may well be found in one of the basic suppositions of comparative philology and glottology; namely, similarities point to a common origin. We'll talk more about that in chapter seventeen. But the fact of the matter is: we are thankful such similarities can be found. Why? The similarities intrinsically and irrevocably weld the Old Testament to the ancient world's family of traditions. This is a good thing! It confirms that the Bible is historically linked to the larger world of the ancient Neat East. Because the evidence exposes a relationship between the ancient Near East and the Bible dismisses the popular notion that the Bible was not written until after the Babylonian Exile. Not only are there temple and ritual similarities, there are fascinating linguistic similarities as well . . . and we shall address this specifically in the next chapter . . . as we examine the linguistic similarities between the Hebrew Bible and other ancient texts.

15

Of Translators and Traitors

The field of linguistics encompasses numerous sub-fields and subdivisions. If you have ever taken an introduction to linguistics course (or linguistics happens to be your field of study), you'll have an appreciation for the complexity of this discipline when it is broken down into its various components. At the most basic level linguistics divides between the study of language structure (grammar) and the study of meaning (semantics). In turn, grammar then encompasses the subfields of morphology (the formation and composition of words), syntax (the rules that determine how words combine into phrases and sentences) and phonology (the study of sound systems and abstract sound units). And this is only the beginning.

Of particular interest to our study is philology . . . more specifically,

> **linguistics**
>
> The "science of language, including phonetics, phonology, morphology, syntax, and semantics: sometimes subdivided into descriptive, historical, comparative, theoretical, and geographical linguistics, often general linguistics."
>
> (Webster's New World College Dictionary, Cleveland, Ohio: Wiley Publishing, Inc., 2005.)

glottology
Glottology is the science of tongues or languages. It is a subset of comparative philology, which is a subset of linguistics proper. The theory of glottology is that all the ancient tongues/languages can be traced back to one common primary source tongue/language.

comparative philology. Comparative philology is directly linked with comparative linguistics, which studies the relationship between languages. The numerous similarities discovered between the ancient languages gave rise to the hypothesis of a common ancestor language from which all languages descended . . . which is the definition of the technical term for this hypothesis, glottology (the study of the origin of language).

The study of the ancient languages and their texts encompasses, among other things, glottology and corpus linguistics – the study of language as expressed in corpora (samples) from 'real world' texts. One of the goals of corpus linguistics is to discover the set of abstract rules by which the ancient language is governed and how it relates to other ancient languages.

Philology's interest in ancient languages peaked in the eighteenth century with the onslaught of the many 'exotic' languages recorded on the ancient texts discovered by archaeologists in the Near East (discussed earlier in this study, e.g. Champollion's decipherment of hieroglyphics). Philologists sought to shed light on the problem of understanding and deciphering the origins and meaning of these older texts.

Comparative linguistics and comparative philology definitely have their limitations. In much the same way we have seen that history is not the past but the interpretation of the past, translations and the resultant linguistic comparisons are also based upon a significant amount of interpretation on the part of the translator. Allow me to explain.

On the subject of translations and translators, you will often find reference to the old (and, ironically, not completely translatable) Italian saying that goes, *traduttore traditore*, which might loosely be translated as *every translator is (a) traitor*. Those who work in the field of linguistics and the translation of ancient texts speak of the tension that exists between maintaining the *form* of the source language/text, while at the same time conveying the *meaning* into the receptor language. Bottom line: *there is no such thing as a pure translation*. No matter how hard a translator tries, something must be sacrificed. The translator must either sacrifice the form or the meaning or (preferably) a little of both. Nonetheless, the translation process leaves much room for the possible prejudices of the translator(s).

> **apograph**
> A perfect copy or exact transcript of another manuscript. Originals are referred to as autographs.

Further, any linguistic comparison between an ancient Near Eastern text and the Hebrew Bible is inherently tainted, in that the extra-Biblical ancient text is typically compared to the Masoretic text of the Hebrew Bible (dated 900 AD). The ancient texts of the Near East are often dated millennia earlier . . . so, linguistically, we are not technically comparing apples to apples, date-wise. Manuscripts dated to the same time would be ideal, and should produce the most accurate linguistic comparisons. However, this is not possible – since there are no extant paleo-Hebrew apographs of the Bible. The Biblical books of the Dead Sea Scrolls provide us with Hebrew texts dating to 125 BC (which are more than 1,000 years older than the Masoretic Texts), but the only paleo-Hebrew discovered were the fragments of Leviticus swept up from the floor of cave four.

The point is this: any linguistic comparisons made between the Bible and the ancient texts of the Near East are subject to the interpretative presuppositions of the translator(s). A translator can make a linguistic similarity between an ancient Near Eastern text and the Hebrew Bible look stronger or weaker . . . more obvious or less obvious . . . depending upon his or her interpretative presuppositions evidenced in the translation produced.

NOTE: I'll tell you ahead of time that this chapter is extraordinarily long compared to the others – but well worth your while. Don't try to take it in all at once; read it in sections if you have to. It deals with a most fascinating and critical subject: how ancient texts are translated, and the effect this can have on the original meaning. So grab a cup of coffee or tea . . . settle in comfortably . . . and let's see how, through erroneous presuppositions, some translators betray the early writers by distorting the very meaning they were trying to convey.

Words Fail Us

A. Leo Oppenheim was surely one of the world's most outstanding philologists. In addition, he was also one of the most distinguished Assyriologists of our time. Oppenheim served as editor-in-charge of the *Assyrian Dictionary* of the Oriental Institute, and was the John A. Wilson Professor of Oriental Studies at the University of Chicago. He devoted more than twenty years of his career to the research and writing of his *Ancient Mesopotamia: Portrait of a Dead Civilization*, where he wrote the following in his introduction:

> (T)ranslated texts tend to speak more of the translator than of their original message. It is not too difficult to render texts written in a dead language as literally as possible and to suggest to the outsider, through the use of quaint and stilted locutions, the alleged awkwardness and archaism of a remote period. Those who know the original language retranslate anyhow, consciously or unconsciously, in order to understand it. *It is nearly impossible to render any but the simplest Akkadian text in a modern language with a satisfactory approximation to the original in content, style, or connotation.*"[1]

Matthews and Benjamin refer to this Oppenheim statement in the foreword to their *Old Testament Parallels: Laws and Stories from the Ancient Near East*,[2] a book I recommend to the graduate students enrolled in one of my Old Testament classes. *Old Testament Parallels* is a very useful resource, well organized and user friendly. Matthews and Benjamin have selected and translated some famous stories, songs, and laws from extra-Biblical texts of the ancient Near East, and present them in chronological order with the Old Testament books.[3]

In the foreword to this book, Matthews and Benjamin note that they have tried to meet Oppenheim's challenge . . . and, indeed, their work is commendable. However, that does not rule out the influence of interpretive presupposition on the part of the translators. I appreciate their statement, "Our readings are not literal or visual text-oriented translations, but responsible, reader-oriented paraphrases. The English vocabulary and idiom *em-*

phasizes the relationship between the ancient Near Eastern tradition and the Bible."[4] [Emphasis mine.] They are telling us that the words and idioms used in their translations were purposefully selected to emphasize, to make obvious any potential similarities between the ancient Near Eastern texts and the traditions of the Israelites as recorded in the Bible. I also appreciate the way they have organized the emphasized similarities in a manner that enables students of the Bible to determine that which is *distinctive* to the Old Testament accounts.

The archaeological discoveries of the ancient Near Eastern texts over the last 150 years or so have revolutionized the way we investigate the Hebrew Bible. Since their discovery, any study on the reliability of the Old Testament text without taking into consideration these findings is no longer complete.

If you have not been exposed to the similarities to the degree most of our students have, I encourage you: don't be shocked by them. We *should* expect linguistic similarities between Israel and the religious milieu of the ancient Near East. Personally, I would be more concerned if there were *no* similarities . . . because we would then have reason to question the authenticity of the ancient dating of the Biblical texts.

Hebrew is a Semitic language and close cousin to the other Northwest Semitic languages. This makes linguistic similarities inevitable. The Biblical writers of the Old Testament used religious expressions, stylistic elements, social institutions such as kingship (requested by the Israelites in 1 Samuel 8:5), common legal forms such as the covenant (vassal vs. Hittite), common practices, and images common to the ancient Near East in much the same way the writers of the New Testament wrote from the cultural framework of first century Judaism.

We will now sample and address some of the linguistic similarities.

The Gilgamesh Epic

The story of Gilgamesh comes to us in the form of a series of ancient epic poems that were written on clay tablets using the cuneiform alphabet. They were discovered in ancient Mesopotamia (modern Iraq) over a century ago. The cuneiform records are *believed* to have been made more than 3,000 years ago.

Because the version of Gilgamesh we possess evolved over a period of time, the tablets give an account of the poem's development from the eighteenth century BC to the first millennium BC. To my knowledge, we have eleven pieces of Old Babylonian versions and eighteen pieces from the late second millennium BC (Middle Babylonia). From just these twenty-nine most ancient fragments, an accurate interpretation of the epic's narrative and plot cannot be constructed. We need the 184 fragments from the first millennium BC from ancient libraries in Assyria in order to do that. These fragments came from the library of seventh-century BC king Ashurbanipal, the slightly later tablets found in Babylon and Uruk.

The most complete version of Gilgamesh is traditionally believed to have been the work of a deliberate editing by the learned scholar Sin-leqi-unninni (circa1100-612 BC). Scholars assume he worked from sources for his version from the ninth or eighth centuries BC. The last dated manuscript comes from about 130 BC, about the same age as the Biblical manuscripts of the Dead Sea Scroll collection.

The earliest poems are *believed* to date back to 2600 BC. In general, the poems deal with beliefs about death and the afterlife and the story of the Flood, which were contemporary among the ancient peoples of the Tigro-Euphrates Valley. The dominant theme that weaves its way through the seventy-two more or less complete poems is man's persistent and hopeless quest for immortality. For this reason many have found the poems depressing examples of dreary hopelessness.

The *Epic of Gilgamesh* tells of the heroic exploits of Gilgamesh, the ancient ruler of the walled city of Uruk, and his companion, Enkidu, who is a wild man of the woods. Together they fight monsters and demonic powers in their quest for honor and lasting fame. Gilgamesh travels to the underworld in search of an answer to his grief, and to tackle the question of mortality after his friend Enkidu was put to death by the rancorous goddess Ishtar.

Of particular interest for our study is the account of the flood that is found in Tablet XI, and the first major work we should consider is that of

Alexander Heidel's *The Gilgamesh Epic and Old Testament Parallels*.[5] In the ninth chapter of this volume, Heidel introduces the flood in the following manner:

> The most remarkable parallels between the Old Testament and the Gilgamesh Epic – in fact, the most remarkable parallels between the Old Testament and the entire corpus of cuneiform inscriptions from Mesopotamia – are found in the deluge accounts of the Babylonians and Assyrians, on the one hand, and the Hebrews, on the other. With the study of this material we therefore enter a field which, a priori, should prove most fruitful in our examination of the genetic relationship between the Mesopotamian records and our Old Testament literature. Here, if anywhere, we should expect to find evidence enabling us to decide the question whether any part of the Old Testament has been derived from Babylonian sources. It is therefore with special interest that we shall make the following inquiry.[6]

It is with the same careful scholarship demonstrated in his previous book, *The Babylonian Genesis*, that Heidel approaches the flood account in the Gilgamesh Epic, comparing the numerous details of that flood account with the corresponding portions of the Old Testament. After his detailed examination of the parallels between the Mesopotamian and Hebrew accounts of the flood, Heidel's conclusion is that "it remains to inquire into their historical or genetic relationship. . . . That the Babylonian and Hebrew versions are genetically related is too obvious to require proof; the only problem that needs to be discussed is the degree of relationship."[7]

According to Heidel, scholars have suggested three main possibilities in order to determine the inherent historical relationship of the Hebrew and Mesopotamian flood accounts:

1. The Babylonians borrowed from the Hebrew account.
2. The Hebrews borrowed from the Babylonian account.
3. Both accounts were descended from a common original.

The first option, he states, is generally unfavorable because the Mesopotamian accounts predate the Biblical version by centuries. Therefore, the most widely held and taught view is that of the second option: the Hebrews borrowed from the Babylonians.

However, the second option assumes the accuracy of the conventional chronology. David Rohl – and the emergent scholars who are now proposing a revised chronology – hold that, given the correct chronology, the entire corpus of deluge accounts "relate the story of the great flood catastrophe."[8] While we may not appreciate the liberties taken by Rohl in meshing the various accounts to tell his version of the story, we would agree that all the ancient texts are basically talking about the same event.

Heidel concludes, "It is obvious from all this that the arguments which have been advanced in support of the contention that the Biblical account rests on Babylonian material are quite inconclusive."[9] The comparative study between the Bible's flood narrative and the flood narrative of the Gilgamesh Epic "proves nothing beyond the point that there is a genetic relationship between the Genesis and Babylonian versions. The skeleton is the same in both cases, but the flesh and blood and, above all, the animating spirit are different. It is here that we meet the most far-reaching divergences between the Hebrew and the Mesopotamian stories."[10]

Another book to consider is the translation of the Gilgamesh Epic by John Gardner, John Maier, and Richard Henshaw, *Gilgamesh: Translated from the Sin-Leqi-Unninni Version*, published by Random House in 1985. Gardner's version restores the poetic style of the epic and the lyricism that was lost in the earlier, more literally rigid translations. This volume is helpful if you are taking into consideration the linguistic similarities and distinctives.[11]

I appreciate the candor of the opening lines of the preface of this work: "This *Gilgamesh* takes what Stephen MacKenna called a 'chased freedom' in presenting a very ancient literary work. The translation *assumes* a number of things about *Gilgamesh* that, *like most things ancient and remote, are subject to question*."[12] [Emphasis mine.]

I'm thankful to these authors for their academic integrity. In case you hadn't noticed, that is one of the main points I have been communicating with you as we have worked our way through this book. Studying the ancients is always a work in progress, and the so-called proofs being used to deprecate the Bible are never as irrefutable as you might be led to think! Whenever you find yourself in a position where the historicity of the Bible is being challenged consider the fact that those challenges are based upon an assumption that the conventional chronology is correct. Most things ancient and remote are always subject to question. When push comes to shove, my worldview says trust the Bible.

If the multiple flood accounts are especially disconcerting to you, consider reading *Flood Legends: Global Clues of a Common Event*[13] by Charles Martin. Martin does an excellent job of exposing the two main ways to interpret myths, and how they both fail when applied to the flood legends. Martin concludes (as does Rohl) that all the flood versions refer to a common event. We will talk more about the 'common event' concept in chapter seventeen.

The Thirty Teachings of Amen-em-Ope[14]

We now turn our attention to a twenty-seven page apograph written in hieratic[15] longhand on a papyrus measuring just over 12 feet in length and 10 inches in width. Archaeologists discovered it inside a wooden statue of Osiris in a tomb in western Thebes. (You will recall we visited Thebes/Karnak in chapter thirteen.)

Just like the much older "Teachings of Ptah-Hotep," the "Teachings of Amen-em-Ope" (which, from now on, I'll refer to simply as Amen-em-Ope) is complete. Small fragments of it were also preserved on a papyrus in Stockholm, Sweden. Three writing tablets in Turin, Paris and Moscow, and an ostracon in the Cairo Museum, also contain portions of Amen-em-Ope. You can examine the Thebes papyrus (acquired for the British Museum by Sir E. A. Wallis Budge in 1888 on his first mission to Egypt) for yourself in the British Museum in London. At first glance, it may seem quite unimpressive until you realize its significance – and the firestorm that has surrounded it.

Its significance stems from the claim that the Hebrew writer of Proverbs borrowed material from Amen-em-Ope. Proverbs 22:17 to 24:22 is said to preserve several of Amen-em-Ope's teachings and imitates its structure. Of course "preserve" and "imitate" translate into plagiarize. Although the battle over whether the Hebrew writer borrowed from the Egyptians was raging by the late 1920s, the general capitulation to the idea that Hebrew wisdom literature in the Bible is the product of ancient Egyptian impetus and persuasion became quite popular toward the end of the 1970s and into the early 1980s.[16] Today the borrowing of Egyptian proverbs is taken for granted by most Biblical scholars. For example, in the introductory remarks for the book of Proverbs in *The New English Bible: Oxford Study Edition,* we read, "Proverbs ignores major religious themes (covenant, patriarchs, Exodus, Sinai) and makes creative use on non-Israelite wisdom traditions, particularly Egyptian."[17]

To get a better handle on this view, we need to take a brief look at the history behind the discovery and exposure of Amen-em-Ope to the public.[18] Although obtained in 1888, it wasn't until 1923 that the document was first published by Budge in his *Facsimiles.*[19] Budge provided an English translation and mentioned two possible parallels with the Book of Proverbs.[20] Budge's mention of parallels went almost unnoticed. It was the subsequent article published by Adolf Erman in 1924 that drew worldwide attention to the similarities between the two documents. Erman concluded that a Hebrew living in Egypt during the Saite or Persian periods translated Amen-em-Ope into Hebrew or Aramaic, and that subsequently portions of this translation were later redacted into the Book of Proverbs. In other words, the portions taken from Amen-em-Ope were not part of the original Book of Proverbs. As a result, Erman then set out to emend[21] the Book of Proverbs to bring it closer to the presumed original Egyptian text. He was followed by many other Biblical scholars (H. Gressmann, E. Sellin, and P. Humbert) who believed emending the Hebrew text was necessary.

An example of such emending that has made its way into our modern English translations can often be demonstrated using Proverbs 22:20: "Have I not written **thirty sayings** for you, sayings of counsel and knowledge." *Thirty* is not actually found in the Hebrew text. Rather, there is a term whose meaning is not certain (which most likely means excellent) that has been retranslated *thirty* in some modern versions. The obscurity of the exact meaning of the term is now *presumed* to be *thirty* since it is also *presumed* that the verses that follow were borrowed from the thirty teachings of Amen-em-Ope. The New American Standard version renders this verse, "Have I not written to you **excellent** **things** of counsels and knowledge (which I believe is the correct translation)."

Back to our historical survey, scholars in the 1920s promoted Erman's explanation for the similarities found in both documents. Some scholars took Erman's position one step further. Hugo Gressmann claimed that parts of Proverbs were taken almost verbatim,[22] while D. C. Simpson[23] and W.O.E. Oesterly[24] argued that both Amen-em-Ope and the Hebrew writer of Proverbs shared an earlier common source.[25]

By around 1930, there were scholars who were out-and-out rejecting the notion of any Hebrew dependence on Amen-em-Ope (namely, D. Herzog[26] and G. Posener[27]). In 1930, R.O. Kevin also published his study, claiming it was the Egyptian author of Amen-em-Ope who had done the borrowing from the Book of Proverbs, and not the other way around.[28]

In 1962, Etienne Drioton published a series of articles contending that Amen-em-Ope was the translation of an original Hebrew work written by Jews living in Egypt, but this theory was shattered by subsequent articles released by Ronald Williams and B. Couroyer.[29]

More recently, it has been proposed that the close relationship between Amen-em-Ope and the Book of Proverbs is due to the two texts being merely copies of one another. "G. Bryce (1980) has moved the discussion away from an issue of 'borrowing,' noting that the Proverbs text 'adapts, assimilates, and/or integrates' the Egyptian material to its own world view."[30]

Clearly the majority of the proposed similarities are vague. J.D. Currid does a nice job comparing and analyzing verse by verse Proverbs 22:17-25 with Amen-en-Ope (1.3.0-16). His work demonstrates that there are "only vague similarities" between Proverbs 22:17-25 and Amen-em-Ope. And, for the most part, there are only shared broad concepts and themes and similarities in linguistics and structure throughout the entire section of

Proverbs 22:17 to 24:22. They are similarities in genre that we would expect to find in all ancient Near Eastern literature.

Having said that, and leaving no stone unturned, there are also a few very striking similarities that cannot be ignored. For example:

> Excerpted from Amen-em-Ope 6:
> *Do not carry off the landmark*
> at the boundaries of the arable land,
> nor disturb the position of the measuring-cord;
> be not greedy after a cubit of land,
> *nor encroach upon the boundaries of a widow.*
> Compared to Proverbs 23:10-11:
> Do not move an ancient boundary stone or encroach on the fields of the fatherless,
> for their Defender is strong; he will take up their case against you.

> Excerpted from Amen-em-Ope, 7-8:
> *Cast not thy heart in pursuit of riches,*
> (for) there is no ignoring Fate and Fortune.
> Place not thy heart upon externals,
> (for) every man belongs to his (appointed) hour . . .
> they *(riches) have made themselves wings like geese*
> *And are flown away to the heavens.*
> Compared to Proverbs 23:4-5:
> *Do not wear yourself out to get rich*; have the wisdom to show restraint.
> Cast but a glance at *riches*, and they are gone, for *they will surely sprout wings and fly off to the sky like an eagle.*

As a consequence, striking similarities such as these have brought into question the revelation and inspiration of the Bible. The question of the uniqueness of the Old Testament becomes a matter of critical importance . . . not only in scholarly circles, but (more significantly) in the lives of those of us who have grounded our lives and entire worldview on the words of the Bible. How then should we deal with this topic?

As with our discussion of the flood narrative of the Gilgamesh Epic in the previous section, we are mainly left with three possibilities:

1. The Hebrew text of Proverbs relied upon the Egyptian text of Amen-em-Ope.
2. The Egyptian text of Amen-em-Ope relied upon the Hebrew text of Proverbs.
3. Both texts relied on an earlier source that is now unknown to us.[31]

Currid's position[32] is that there exists a fourth possibility: namely, that there is *no* connection between Amen-em-Ope and Proverbs.

> The evidence appears to support that view. First of all, the correspondences between the two pieces are, by nature, shallow and vague. And in most places the content is only partially similar. Second, many of the parallel themes are common in the various writings of the ancient Near East. Much of the correspondence could be a mark of universal ideas or universally accepted images. Third, the seemingly parallel passages in the two works are arranged in a different sequence. They are out of order. Fourth, many of the proverbs in Amen-em-Ope are not found in Proverbs 22:17-24:22, and vice versa. If there was dependence, it must have been very selective and fragmented. Lastly, any attempt to divide the Hebrew text into thirty sayings is artificial. Moreover, Proverbs 22:17-24:22 is likely not a single, unitary composition but part of a broader literary structure.[33] Such problems are difficult to overcome when one argues a case for direct dependence, one way or the other.

> Yet the writer of Proverbs obviously did have a general familiarity with the genre of Egyptian wisdom literature. This, however, did not have a direct and detailed influence on the Hebrew writer of Proverbs. The impact was of an indirect nature and of the broadest strokes. The Hebrew writer was not guilty of crass plagiarism – on all accounts Proverbs is a thoroughly Hebrew document.[34]

Back in 1977, J. Ruffle, in support of the first possibility, suggested the observed similarities between Proverbs and Amen-em-Ope are the result of contributions of an Egyptian scribe working in the court of Solomon, and basing his writings upon his memory of an Egyptian text that he had once studied or heard during his scribal training.[35]

What about the second possibility, the Egyptian text relying on the Hebrew text? The Bible itself informs us of a very direct link between Solomon and Egypt, being that one of his wives was the daughter of the pharaoh.[36] The Bible mentions her six times, and we know from the Biblical record that Solomon constructed a small palace for her.[37] While we are here, I cannot resist inserting this bit of information in answer to one of Lindsey's e-mailed questions (chapter one) about the supposed evidence suggesting that Canaan was under control of the Egyptian Empire at the time of Solomon. It is significant (yet often set aside) that Solomon was given pharaoh's daughter – and not the other way around. Make a mental note that it was pharaoh who, in the ancient world, would have been seen by this gesture as trying to appease Solomon, which would be a sign of weakness. King Solomon had power that the pharaoh of Egypt respected and needed to tap by way of his daughter.

Revised chronologists have looked at this from varying perspectives. Even when we use the differing father-in-law scenarios of the revised chronologists,[38] we soon see that the Egyptian pharaoh did not hold sway over hinterland Canaan at this time. The Egyptians endeavored to control the main trade routes (Via Maris and King's Highway), but had a hard time controlling the highlands. Now, with a central figure (son-in-law King Solomon) located in Jerusalem, controlling these areas in Canaan, the Egyptians were able to extend their trade control further inland. Royal son-in-law King Solomon was the allied 'Egyptian' power needed to help control the trade routes. Accordingly, as King Solomon strengthened his own rule through treaties with the Phoenicians, Arameans, etc., this opened many new possibilities for his Egyptian father-in-law as well – especially at times when Egyptian power was waning, which is exactly what is happening in the periods above. The power vacuum was filled by a most loyal son-in-law king. (You can find additional information concerning the supposed sovereignty of Egypt over Israel debate in Appendix B.)

Once again, this is only part of the story. Solomon was not only linked to Egypt by his Egyptian wife, he was linked to many nations . . . for he loved *many* foreign women besides pharaoh's daughter.[39]

> They were from nations about which the LORD had told the Israelites, "You must not intermarry with them, because they will surely turn your hearts after their gods." Nevertheless, Solomon held fast to them in love.
>
> He had seven hundred wives of royal birth and three hundred concubines, and his wives led him astray.
>
> As Solomon grew old, his wives turned his heart after other gods, and his heart was not fully devoted to the LORD his God, as the heart of David his father had been.
>
> He followed Ashtoreth the goddess of the Sidonians, and Molech the detestable god of the Ammonites.
> So Solomon did evil in the eyes of the LORD; he did not follow the LORD completely, as David his father had done.
>
> On a hill east of Jerusalem, Solomon built a high place for Chemosh the detestable god of Moab, and for Molech the detestable god of the Ammonites.
>
> He did the same for all his foreign wives, who burned incense and offered sacrifices to their gods.
>
> The LORD became angry with Solomon because his heart had turned away from the LORD, the God of Israel, who had appeared to him twice.
>
> Although he had forbidden Solomon to follow other gods, Solomon did not keep the LORD's command.

> So the LORD said to Solomon, "Since this is your attitude and you have not kept my covenant and my decrees, which I commanded you, I will most certainly tear the kingdom away from you and give it to one of your subordinates.
>
> Nevertheless, for the sake of David your father, I will not do it during your lifetime. I will tear it out of the hand of your son (1 Kings 11:2-12: 2).

This, of course, was not pleasing to the Lord, and there were consequences for his actions (namely, the end of the Kingdom). There is evidence therefore from the Bible itself that Solomon was influenced by the nations that surrounded him, particularly in his later days.

Thus, in regards to shared proverbs, R. Dillard and T. Longman III point to the international character of the wisdom of the ancient Near East as a partial explanation; but in the end surrender to the first possibility, that the Egyptian text influenced the Biblical text:

> The wise men of Israel knew the writings of Egypt and vice versa. However, there are two reasons why *it is more likely that the Egyptian text influenced the Israelite*: (1) A dominant culture (like the Egyptian) is less likely to be influenced by a subdominant culture (like that of Israel). (2) Though the date of the Amenemope text is uncertain, the evidence leans toward one that is earlier then Solomon.[40] [Emphasis mine.]

The certainty of the *uncertainty* of the date of the Amen-em-Ope text leads us nicely into the position revisionist Rohl posits on this matter. Obviously, all of the options suggested thus far are by those who subscribe to the conventional chronology. Rohl, on the other hand, believes the relationship between Amen-em-Ope and Proverbs can best be explained using his new chronology.[41]

Although we are not certain, Amen-em-Ope appears "to date to the New Kingdom and, more specifically, from the late 18th Dynasty to the 20th Dynasty. We cannot be more accurate than that."[42]

In the conventional chronology, this period of the New Kingdom would match up with the Sojourn, Bondage, Exodus, and early Judges. Thus, the thirty sayings of Amen-em-Ope would have had to have been remembered from this early period down to the Solomonic era in order for them to be borrowed for the Old Testament. In the new chronology, the time of Solomon, according to Rohl, is "the time of Ramesses II and so the two eras – Amen-em-Ope and Proverbs are much closer in time. In this context the borrowing of the Egyptian literature for adaptation/use in the book of Proverbs might make sense, given the marriage alliance between Solomon and Pharaoh (in the NC either Haremheb or Ramesses II himself). In a Solomonic era set at the time of Ramesses II it is easy to envisage the Jerusalem court being influenced by Egyptian New Kingdom literature."[43] Even if we take the most modest position held by the BICANE members, the late Nineteenth Dynasty (including the late years of Ramesses II and kings Merenptah and his lesser successors) or even the early Twentieth Dynasty (with Ramesses III and his feeble successors) would be contemporary with the age of Solomon.

So let's take the position held by the revised chronologists a step further. Using the revised chronology models . . . and given the uncertainty and inaccuracy of the dating of "The Teachings of Amen-em-Ope" . . . and depending upon which way we shift the dating . . . Amen-em-Ope and Solomon could very well have been contemporaries, or Solomon could have actually *predated* Amen-em-Ope. As a result, Kevin's study published in 1930 – arguing that it was *the Egyptian author of Amen-em-Ope who had done the borrowing from the Book of Proverbs* – may after all, be the correct option!

Yet with an overconfident air of certainty and assuredness, you will likely hear or read something resembling this statement: "The influence of Egyptian wisdom teachings on the religious literature of Israel is a significant and important part of the larger context of the interaction between these two civilizations, as evidenced by the Israelites' borrowing from the thirty teachings of Amen-em-Ope."

Biblical archaeologist Peter van der Veen seems to lean toward the third possibility (that both texts relied on an earlier source that is now unknown to us). After consulting the sayings of Amen-em-Ope again, and comparing them with the similar verses written in Proverbs, van der Veen writes, "Of course there are very similar sayings here and there in both works, but that doesn't surprise me as I am quite convinced that wisdom teachers in the Ancient Near East were familiar with many sayings of neighboring peoples. A good number of sayings were in use in the different languages when they were based on long experience of moral behaviour. There is however no need to claim that Proverbs borrowed from Amenemope or vice versa. Both authors were familiar with many sayings that belonged to practical 'Wisdom' (Hochmah) and it is far too simplistic to argue for direct borrowing."[44] Thus, he rules out possibilities one and two (which both suggest a direct borrowing).

As I see it, the second possibility (that the Biblical text influenced the Egyptian text) is just as legitimate an option as the others, perhaps even more so. I'll tell you why. The critical question comes down to this: can we date the thirty sayings of Amen-em-Ope with enough certainty to say for sure who did the borrowing – if, in fact, there was borrowing?

Let's pause here and examine the unstable underpinnings upon which the dating of Amen-em-Ope is founded. I apologize (well not really) for my excessive use of *presume* as a hyperbole in an effort to make my point:

- Since the Budge papyrus of Amen-em-Ope has no absolute date, scholars presume it is no earlier than the Twenty-first Dynasty.
- The fragment of Amen-em-Ope found on the ostracon in Cairo is presumed to be from the Twenty-first Dynasty.
- Because the language on this piece resembles the "Wisdom of Ani" – which is dated to the Eighteenth or Nineteenth Dynasty – Amen-em-Ope is presumed to also be from this period.

- Based on the dating of "Ani," scholars presume the original of Amen-em-Ope also dates to the New Kingdom period.
- The papyrus of Ani is undated. There are no facts given in it whereby it would be possible to fix its exact place in the series of the illustrated papyri of the Theban period to which it is said to belong. Scholars presume it was written in 1240 BC. All the different sections of the papyrus were not originally written for Ani, for his name has been added in several places by a later hand.
- All of the above deliberations and presumptions assume the accuracy of the conventional chronology upon which they rest, and the accuracy of the foundational pillars upon which conventional chronology has been constructed. I trust you get the picture.

Thus, the dating of Amen-em-Ope is *presumed* based upon other *presumptions*. Once again due to the dating uncertainties inherent to the study of antiquity, the study of the ancient world will essentially always be open-ended. This makes the evidence subject to interpretation and reinterpretation based upon the scholar's worldview; therefore, any argument supporting any of the above possibilities (or combinations thereof) might be possible, and *none is certain*. Ultimately, your worldview will interpret the evidence and there's nothing here worth losing your faith over.

The Code of Hammurabi

The Code of Hammurabi was discovered in 1901 by French archaeologists doing excavations in Susa on the border between modern Iraq and Iran. It had been taken there by the Elamites, enemies of Babylon. Our knowledge of Elamite history is largely fragmentary, but historians believe the inhabitants of Susa, during their early history, fluctuated between submission to the Mesopotamians and Elamites. Regardless, the code is Babylonian and reflects the legal climate and moral values of the Babylonians. It was written in cuneiform on an eight-foot pillar of black diorite.[45] (If you ever visit the Louvre Museum in Paris, be sure to put this on your list.[46] It may take a minute to sink in, but then you will come to realize how exciting it is to be able to view this nucleus of the ancient past. My students always appreciated our visits to the museum during the years I taught at the college in France.)

The code begins with a treatise on the great military accomplishments of Hammurabi, great king of Babylon, followed by 282 case laws, and concludes with an essay on the importance and role of law in the state. Each case law begins with a dependent clause introduced by "if" . . . followed by a main clause introduced by "then" . . . and the sentence. For example, "If a wife of the father of a household leaves her husband's house on her own business, and if she neglects the house, and shames her husband, then her husband may either divorce her without paying a divorce settlement, or may marry another woman while his former wife is to live in the house as a slave."[47]

The code identifies distinct social groups: slaves, laborers, fathers of households, and priests. With the distinct social groups came distinct social status and punishments.

There are similarities, mostly generic, between the Code of Hammurabi and:

- The Law of Moses/Covenant in Exodus 21-23.
- The prescribed conventions on holiness in Leviticus 17-26.
- The Deuteronomic regulations in Deuteronomy 12-26.

In several cases, the similarities are far-fetched beyond basic linguistic similarities and a broad definition of similarity. For example, the example previously cited (Hammurabi Code art. 141) above is said to have similarities with Deuteronomy 24:1-4:

> If a man marries a woman who becomes displeasing to him because he finds something indecent about her, and he writes her a certificate of divorce, gives it to her and sends her from his house,

and if after she leaves his house she becomes the wife of another man,
and her second husband dislikes her and writes her a certificate of divorce, gives it to her and sends her from his house, or if he dies,
then her first husband, who divorced her, is not allowed to marry her again after she has been defiled. That would be detestable in the eyes of the LORD. Do not bring sin upon the land the LORD your God is giving you as an inheritance.

As you can see with this passage, the similarities are more general than specific. This is true of the majority of passages where similarities have been noted; the list of distinctives far outnumbers the list of similarities.

Having said this, there are a few passages with stronger similarities, typically noticed in apodictic style laws that are frequently phrased with an imperative. For example, in the Code of Hammurabi we read, "If a man, after his father's death, should lie with his mother, they shall burn them both."[48] Compare this with Leviticus:

Do not dishonor your father by having sexual relations with your mother. She is your mother; do not have relations with her.

Do not have sexual relations with your father's wife; that would dishonor your father.

Everyone who does any of these detestable things – such persons must be cut off from their people.[49]

There are actually several similarities between the Bible and Hittite, Babylonian, and Assyrian laws. The Israelites were not the only ones to respect sexual taboos. But the Egyptians did not share the majority of these sexual taboos with their ancient neighbors. I would therefore like to put forward to you – in opposition to those who are suggesting that the Israelites plagiarized from the Egyptians – that this cannot be the case, especially in regard to law. God told the Israelites:

> You must not do as they do in Egypt, where you used to live, and you must not do as they do in the land of Canaan, where I am bringing you. Do not follow their practices.
>
> You must obey my laws and be careful to follow my decrees. I am the LORD your God (Leviticus 18:3-4; 24-30).

Ancient Egyptian texts confirm the fact that sexuality in ancient Egypt was quite free. "Revel in pleasure while your life endures . . . like the gods anointed be; and never weary grow in eager quest of what your heart desires – Do as it prompts you."[50] Other than adultery (where the woman was punished most severely), open sexuality did not come with any sense of guilt for singles or married couples.

Because of the close family relationships in Egyptian mythology, and Egyptians seemed to have no taboos against incest, many scholars have concluded that incest was rife in ancient Egypt. The royal family had to have incestuous marriages since the royal blood ran through the females, not the males. To become pharaoh, a man had to marry a royal princess who would be his sister or half-sister.

The Egyptians believed that their gods practiced sex. The ancient Egyptians even believed in sex in the afterlife. The ancient Egyptian religion is filled with tales of adultery, incest, homosexuality and masturbation[51] – including hints of necrophilia. Without going into any more detail, it is obvious why God told the Israelites, "You must not do as they do in Egypt, where you used to live." As far as similarities between the laws of the Bible and ancient Egypt . . . this, my friend, is one huge distinction rather than a similarity.

| **necrophilia** |
| The sexual attraction to corpses. |

Getting back to our discussion on stronger similarities between the Bible and the Code of Hammurabi, let us consider this example: "If he destroys the eye of a citizen's slave, or breaks the bone of a citizen's slave, he shall pay half of the purchase price."[52]

Compare this with Exodus 21:26: "If a man hits a manservant or maidservant in the eye and destroys it, he must let the servant go free to compensate for the eye." There is indeed a similarity in the dependent clause introduced by the "if." There is a distinction made in the punishment. In the Code of Hammurabi, the slave remains a slave with payment. In the Bible, the slave is set free. Over and over again, the Bible upholds the sacredness of human life. Human life is more valuable than property or money. This slave in the Bible is set free. The death penalty is prescribed as punishment in several of the ancient Near Eastern codes for damage to, or theft of, property. The Bible flatly rejects the death penalty as punishment relating to these transgressions.

How, then, do we explain the similarities between the Bible and the Hammurabi Code? Rohl believes the explanation is quite simple and straightforward. "You will note from the dates that the Orthodox Chronology (OC) has Moses writing his laws several centuries after Hammurabi's Law Code was composed, whilst the New Chronology (NC) has Moses following soon after Hammurabi, thus explaining the similarities in common law within the two documents."[52]

Rohl's explanation may well be all or part of the explanation . . . or there may be another reason for the similarities that appear between the two documents other than chronologies and *relative* versus *absolute* dating. We will discuss this other reason in detail in chapter seventeen. In the meantime we need to keep moving.

The Hittite Code

The Hittite Code was found in the late 1800s. Of the approximately 10,000 baked clay tablets excavated by archaeologists from the Hittite capital in what is now Turkey, only two baked clay tablets in Neshili Hittite written in cuneiform script are of particular interest to our study. On these two tablets are found 200 case laws (Hittite Code). They were first translated in 1915 by Bedřich, who was also the first to fully publish them in 1922. It was not until 1959 that Johannes Friedrich published a new edition. The most recent critical edition was published by Harry Hoffner in 1997.

Similarities between the Hittite Code and the Bible can be found in Leviticus 17-26 and Deuteronomy 12-16, especially in the sharing of technical terms. The Hittite Code gives preference to compensating victims over punishing the offender. In several cases it replaces the death sentence found in other Near Eastern codes with a form of corporal punishment, and frequently reduces sentences from corporal punishment to fines. The Hittites, a people of Indo-European connection, were presumed to have entered Cappadocia around 1800 BC. The spirit of the Hittite Code appears to be more humane than that of the Babylonian or Assyrian legal codes.

While there are similarities between the Hittite Code and the Bible, there are also significant differences . . . the main one being that it is not attributed to a god. The similarities that are found tend to be more general than specific. For example:

> "If the father of a household sets fire to the house of another, then he must rebuild the house and compensate the household for every person or animal killed by the fire."[54]

Compare that to:
> "If a fire breaks out and spreads into thorn bushes so that it burns shocks of grain or standing grain or the whole field, the one who started the fire must make restitution (Exodus 22:6)."

Here's another example:
> "The father of a household may not have sexual intercourse with his brother's wife while his brother is still alive. The father of a household may not have sexual intercourse with the daughter of his wife or with his mother-in-law or his sister-in-law."[55]

And in the Bible:
> "No one is to approach any close relative to have sexual relations. I am the LORD (Leviticus 18:6ff)."

The Hittite Code reserved the right of the royal court to determine the punishment in difficult cases. This concept is paralleled in Deuteronomy 17:8-10:

> If cases come before your courts that are too difficult for you to judge— whether bloodshed, lawsuits or assaults— take them to the place the LORD your God will choose.

> Go to the priests, who are Levites, and to the judge who is in office at that time. Inquire of them and they will give you the verdict.

> You must act according to the decisions they give you at the place the LORD will choose. Be careful to do everything they direct you to do.

Before moving on, we should also make note of the importance of the covenant concept in the ancient Near East and ancient Israel. In the Hammurabi Code, the covenant was in the main between two equal parties (known as a *parity* treaty). In the Hittite Code, the two parties in the main are of unequal status with the lesser party acting almost exclusively as the recipient (called a *suzerainty* treaty).

We see in the most basic covenant expression of the Bible great similarities between Exodus 20ff and the covenant expression found in the Hittite archives at Boghazköy. In the Hittite treaties, we see the vassal entering into a covenant of loyalty to the king out of gratefulness for the benefits that had already been received. The similarities are limited to the pattern of treaties compared, not content.

Because copies have been found written in Old Hittite as well as in Middle and Late Hittite, scholars generally embrace the idea that the laws had authority throughout the duration of the Hittite Empire (circa 1650–1100 BC), which would need to be adjusted by 200 to 300 years if using the revised or new chronology. Using Rohl's 300-year adjustment would place the beginning of the Hittite Empire at 1250 BC; using the 200-plus-year adjustment would place the beginning of the Hittite Empire roughly around 1400-1450 BC. The shared technical terms and the similarity of the Bible's covenant pattern to the Hittite treaty pattern suggest a generic relationship, but to advance any arguments beyond this would be quite indecisive.

A Break in Our Journey

OK . . . it's been a long haul through this chapter . . . but the material we covered is critical to correctly understanding the connection between related Biblical and non-Biblical texts. If this were a bus tour through the sites in the Holy Land, this is where I'd tell my group to take a short break before we move on. So don't be afraid to take a few minutes (or even re-read portions of the chapter) to soak it all in.

Scholars have often stated the simple solutions that are offered for the similarities are the misleading ones. *Not necessarily.* As we demonstrated in earlier chapters, if the *assumptions* that support the conventional chronology are wrong, then the conventional chronology is wrong – and so is our understanding of the relationship between related Biblical and non-Biblical texts here. I hope you are leaving this chapter with a strong impression of how much is *presumed* and *assumed* in dealing with these texts. We will build on this in the next chapter as we briefly consider Zoroastrianism. Ready to go?

16

Zoroastrianism . . . Old or New?

Zoroastrianism, the argument goes, influenced the belief systems of the Bible. If you've heard that one before, you may be wondering where it fits into this picture, and what connection Zoroastrianism may or may not have to the Bible. In my view, Zoroastrianism is not as ancient at it has been made out to be . . . and therefore has little if anything directly to do with our present study. It very well may have been a medieval cult. Nevertheless, since certain scholars are using Zoroastrianism as another means to try to dethrone the Hebrew Bible, we must include it.

We have just left a chapter where we learned how much has been *presumed* and *assumed* by scholars when dealing with non-Biblical ancient texts. Well, as the colloquialism goes, you ain't seen nothing yet. As you will see, to make Zoroastrianism *ancient* takes a whole *lot* of presuming.

Zoroastrianism is *presumed* to have started as an early monotheist religion founded by Zarathushtra (aka Zoroaster to Greece and Zarthosht to India and Persia), and is based on the *Zend Avesta*, their scriptures that were written in Old Iranian. Zoroastrianism is also called Zarathustrism, Mazdaism and Parsism.[1]

As the story is told, Zoroaster received a vision from the god Ahura Mazda. Ahura Mazda chose Zoroaster (after whom the religion is named) to preach the truth, proclaiming to the people that there is only ONE TRUE GOD . . . which, of course, is Ahura Mazda (lord of wisdom). Zoroaster's message told of a cosmic conflict between Ahura Mazda, the god of light, and Ahriman, the principle of evil. Those who followed the teachings of Zoroaster and the one true god were called *asha*, the people of righteousness, and those of the polytheistic majority were referred to as *druj*, the people of the lie. All people have been given the ability and power to choose between good and evil. When the end of the world comes, the forces of light will triumph and the souls that have been saved will rejoice in this great and glorious victory.

In 650 AD, Islamic Arabs invaded Persia. To avoid persecution, many of the Zoroastrian followers fled to India. Then, after Alexander the Great conquered Persia, Zoroastrianism began to die out there, but it survived in India and became the underpinning of the Parsi religion. (Parsism is the term used today among the followers of Zoroastrianism in India.[2])

Because of some obvious similarities in theology, Zoroastrianism is uniquely important in the field of historical theology. Some of the similarities include:[3]

1. Monotheism
There is one god, Ahura Mazda. Ahura Mazda is the uncreated Creator. All worship should be directed ultimately to Ahura Mazda.[4]

2. "Fallen" Creation
The people called *asha* represent truth and order; the people called *druj* represent chaos, falsehood, and disorder.

3. Conflict between Good and Evil
This ultimate conflict involves the entire universe, including spiritual beings and people. Both the spiritual beings and the people have an active role to play in the conflict.

4. Good will overcome Evil
Ahura Mazda will triumph over evil and Angra Mainyu/Ahriman, the leader of all evil.

5. A final Redemption of all things

- At the end of the time, the universe will be redeemed by a celestial restoration, and time will be no more.
- All creation will be resurrected to life and reunited in Ahura Mazda.
- Evil will be purged from the Earth by fire (molten metal) from the heavens by a battle of spiritual forces.
- Every person, asha or druj, will be resurrected into a spiritualized body and soul. People who died as adults will be resurrected into healthy 40-year-olds, and people who died younger will come back everlastingly young, about age 15. In these new spiritual bodies, there will be no need for food. There will be neither hunger nor thirst.
- Everyone will live without weapons or even the possibility of physical injury.
- Everyone will speak the same language.
- Everyone will belong to the same nation without borders.
- Everyone will experience eternal life.
- Everyone will share one purpose and goal, being reunited with the divine for an everlasting adoration and worship of Ahura Mazda's glory.[5]
- A savior figure brings about the above redemptive process.[6]
- The followers of Zoroaster marry only within the extended family, occasionally even with relatives as close as brother and sister.

Scholars debate the connection Zoroastrianism has to the Bible, the development of the three major monotheistic religions (Judaism, Christianity, and Islam), as well as its potential formative links to other Eastern religious traditions. Once more, the debate revolves around how we date Zoroastrianism.

The fact of the matter is we truthfully do not know the birth date of Zoroaster, ergo, the start date of Zoroastrianism. It will remain an enigma, lost in the past. There are many viewpoints on the date of Zoroaster/Zarathustra's birth – and they vary by around 1,000 years. There are two main postulated possibilities.

The Early Date Theories (1500-1200 BC)

It is the view of Mary Boyce that Zoroastrianism is "the oldest of the revealed creedal religions," and that it "probably had more influence on mankind directly or indirectly than any other faith."[7] Boyce believes Zoroastrianism is likely the world's oldest continuing non-pantheistic religion in the world, having its beginnings around 1500 BC. The publication of her book in 1979 popularized this view, and some scholars have concurred with her notion of putting the time-frame for Zoroaster much earlier than what was previously held.

If the early date is correct there indeed would be a stronger case for the possibility of Judaism and Christianity borrowing from Zoroastrianism. Worst case scenario: if Boyce's hypothesis were true, the noted similarities would only give extra credence to our PE (post-Eden) source and/or a PF (post-flood) source (which we'll discuss in the next chapter). The reality is: since we do not in actuality know when Zoroaster lived, any arguments based on the early date theories fall into the realm of pure speculation.

There are at least two logical reasons the early date theories are incorrect. First, the fact that the Greek historian Herodotus never mentions Zoroaster speaks volumes. Herodotus wrote his complete treatise on the Medo-Persian religion in the fifth century BC. Given Zoroaster's presumed level of influence and impact on the Persian religion, Herodotus would have surely included him in such an important work – had Zoroaster's teachings actually existed at the time of writing. French author, orientalist, and antiquarian James Darmesteter (1849 –1894), argued for a date of 100 BC, but his view runs into trouble with the fact that Plato, who founded his famous Academy in his native Athens in 387 BC, does mention Zoroaster in his Alcibiades (however, the authenticity of Plato's Alcibiades is also disputed by scholars).

Second, according to Zoroastrianism's own scriptures (the *Zend Avesta*), Zoroaster was born in Azerbaijan, in northern Persia, probably in the seventh century BC.

The Traditional View (600-500 BC)

The traditionally held dates for the life of Zoroaster are typically circa 630 – circa 550 BC. But even these dates are, at best, speculative.[8] If you were to do an online search for "When did Zoroastrianism begin?" you would receive the following answer from wiki answers: "Zoroastrianism probably began around the 6th century B.C.E. It was founded by Zoroaster or Zarathustra."[9] As noted above, even the *Zend Avesta* supports the traditional dates.

If we suppose the traditional dates are accurate, then Moses, author of the Torah (the first five books of the Old Testament) predates Zoroaster. David, Isaiah, and Jeremiah predate Zoroaster – and all of them talk about the Messiah savior figure, the resurrection, the final judgment, and the redemption-restoration in their writings.

If you find yourself perplexed over the current challenges being leveled against the Bible, Judaism, or Christianity by the presumed age of Zoroastrianism, consider this:

- There is no tangible evidence to determine when Zoroaster lived. The birth date of Zoroaster and Zoroastrianism is speculative at best.
- There is no credible evidence to determine what it was that Zoroaster presumably taught. The fact of the matter is: we are being told by modern Zoroastrianism what Zoroaster taught, but the only source for Zoroaster's teachings is the Zend Avesta . . . the oldest copies of the Zend Avesta being from the thirteenth century AD. Candidly, therefore, we have nothing earlier than a thirteenth century AD document to substantiate the supposed accuracy of these supposed ancient teachings.

- On the merits of textual criticism alone, the late date for this collection of writings should not be used to make such bold declarations against the Bible, Judaism, and Christianity. A thirteenth century AD document does not support the multiple claims being made about the age and teachings of Zoroastrianism.
- On the merits of textual criticism alone, the Bible is the far superior text. We can substantiate that the text of our Bibles is the same (95 percent accuracy) as what was in copies of the Bible 2,000 years ago. The oldest copies that we have of the Old Testament date to the second century BC, from the Khirbet Qumran community on the Dead Sea (Dead Sea Scrolls). The oldest copies of the New Testament date to the fourth century AD.

Consequently, in order for one to accept as true what is being claimed about Zoroastrianism one has to assume that:

(T)he post-Christian form of the religion (which we know about) has remained faithful to the pre-Christian form of the religion (which we know nothing about), and speculating that the similarities between the religion and Christianity are due to Christianity borrowing from the religion in question. *It's a philosophical argument without solid evidence to back it up.*[10] [Emphasis mine.]

An Empty Argument

To claim that the Bible was influenced by Zoroastrianism is a worldview argument void of any solid evidence whatsoever. How thankful we should be that this is not the type of apologetic we have for the Bible. There has never been proven any clear-cut example of influence between the belief systems of Zoroastrianism and the Bible or any of the other monotheistic religions, (nor will there ever be given the *only* source available is a High Middle Age document). Could it be that Zoroastrianism was a cult from the Middle Ages that simply made unsubstantiated claims that its teachings were from antiquity?

> Have we any good reason not to suppose that it was Zoroastrianism which borrowed from Christianity and not vice versa? We know that Zoroastrianism borrowed freely from the polytheistic faiths of the region in which it became popular. Mithra, for example, was a Persian god who found a prominent role in Zoroastrianism. Mithra's Hindu counterpart is the god Mitra.[11]

So let's get back to the study at hand and continue our legitimate examination of comparative linguistics.

Recommended Reading

If you would like to know more about Zoroastrianism, start with:

Walter Martin, *The Kingdom of the Cults, revised and updated edition*, edited by Ravi Zacharias (Minneapolis MN: Bethany, 2003).

You will be amazed. This is a volume worth owning.

17

Exchanging the Truth for a Lie

"For a time is coming when people will no longer listen to sound and wholesome teaching. They will follow their own desires and will look for teachers who will tell them whatever their itching ears want to hear."

– 2 Timothy 4:3 (NLT)

"They exchanged the truth of God for a lie . . .."

– Romans 1:25

Our ability to translate ancient Egyptian hieroglyphics, ancient Sumerian, Akkadian, and Canaanite texts makes it possible for us to explore the writings of authors who wrote before or during the lifetimes of some of the Biblical writers. This wealth of information (much of which is available on the Internet) has given us the ability to better understand the historical, cultural, linguistic, and religious background of the world of the Bible unlike any generations before us. However, with this privilege has come the need to critically sort through all that's out there, primarily to see from which side of the 'Berlin Wall' the information is being interpreted and

221

propagated. Because our postmodern world is aggressively challenging and questioning the uniqueness of the Israelites and the Bible, we must be vigilant as we differentiate between *raw* evidence and the *interpretation* of that evidence – interpretation that is often based upon certain anti-Biblical worldviews and agendas.

To help you homogenize everything we have talked about from the first page until now, I want to introduce you to an important phenomenon that has been referred to as scholarly *parallelomania*. Although I cannot find this term in my *Webster's Unabridged Dictionary*, I do know that Samuel Sandmel (Hebrew Union College – Jewish Institute of Religion) used it for the title of a speech he once gave.[1] Sandmel defined *parallelomania* as "that extravagance among scholars which first overdoes the supposed similarity in passages and then proceeds to describe source and derivation as if implying literary connection flowing in an inevitable or predetermined direction."[2]

Let me explain it more simply.

Extravagance is a pretty strong word to use when describing your scholarly colleagues, but that's what he said. Extravagance is unrestrained excess. (Extravagant behavior was once considered one of the seven deadly sins.) Sandmel was saying that when scholars discover a *supposed* similarity between a non-Biblical text and the Bible, they do so with unrestrained excess – without following any scholarly rules that might restrain them. They overdo the *supposed* similarity making it out to be a whole lot more than it actually is. This is a serious charge, but one with which I fully agree. Scholars, Sandmel charges, first *predetermine* that the *supposed* similarity is in fact an *actual* similarity by ignoring all the restraints of careful scholarship (because their predetermination supports their agenda). Then, he says, scholars have the audacity to interpret the source and derivation (the act of ascertaining relationship of the word or words in relation to their base) to support their predetermined literary connection. In other words, *they first see what it is they want to see* . . . and then proceed to interpret (twist) the evidence to assure the evidence appears to support what it was they saw! With unrestrained excess they overdo the similarity to prove their point. Sandmel lays bare the mindset of the current ideological 'Berlin Wall' – like the man the psychologist stuck with the needle.

It is critically important that you come to appreciate this phenomenon in your journey of faith. When you feel your faith being challenged, be certain you are not turning your back on God based on 'facts' that were *predetermined* to be facts because they supported someone's anti-Biblical worldview.

Alas, Babylon

You might have noticed that in this study I have spent very little time on the ancient Babylonian temples and their ritual practices. Yet we did spend considerable time walking through the ancient Egyptian temples. If someone had written this book seventy or so years ago, they would have done the opposite; they would have spent very little time on the Egyptian temples and concentrated on the ancient Babylonian temples. Let me explain why.

Pan-Babylonialism was the view that Babylonian culture dominated the ancient Fertile Crescent . . . *all* ancient cultures and religions sprang from one common source: Babylon. This view arose around 1900 among German cuneiformists – and the rest of the scholarly world bought into it hook, line, and sinker. Look at it this way. This was the 'Out of Babylon' scholarly craze of that day . . . much like we are experiencing the 'Out of Egypt' scholarly craze in our day. During the 'Out of Babylon' craze, scholars used the then-newly discovered ancient Babylonian texts (which included numerous religio-mythological writings) to assert their predetermined belief that the Hebrew Bible reflected the ancient Israelites' plagiarizing of the Babylonian culture, mythology, and religion. Does this sound familiar to anyone? The 'Out of Babylon' craze eventually faltered and died because its extravagant and predetermined *supposed* facts were found to be nothing more than unsubstantiated and non-defensible claims.[3]

Scholars found a new toy to play with, and have now embraced the 'Out of Egypt' craze with the same fervor they once subscribed to the 'Out of Babylon' craze. They tell us this is so because of the latest discoveries – but I would remind you that the Babylonian evidence is still the same Babylonian evidence. They have reinterpreted that evidence so they could move on to ancient Egypt. Once, not many decades ago, scholars claimed all the evidence pointed to the Israelites having plagiarized the ancient Babylonians. Today scholars claim all the evidence points to the Israelites plagiarizing the ancient Egyptians. What about tomorrow? In my view, when it is finally discovered that the 'Out of Egypt' craze is just as bankrupt as the 'Out of Babylon' craze, the academic machine will next move on to the 'Out of Outer Space' craze, which is starting to peep its head over the academic horizon. (If this seems like an exaggeration, consider this: in Ben Stein's film *Expelled*, some prominent evolutionists – at a loss to explain just how the first simple cells began to mutate into more complex organisms – have considered that such a process was the result of "seeding" by an alien race. No kidding.) I pray all this is making sense to you. Before you give up on God, get the facts. Not the *predetermined supposed* facts that support some anti-Bible, anti-God worldview craze, but the *real* facts.

Now let's move on.

Conceptual and Stylistic Similarities

We need to return to our study of comparative philology as we next explore some important conceptual and stylistic similarities. If you have examined *Old Testament Parallels* by Matthews and Benjamin (recommended earlier), you have seen for yourself that many of the similarities are, at best, obscure. They are more general, broad, and conceptual than literal in nature. However, there are some similarities that are much more striking – and that's what we want to discuss next. Note, for example, the striking stylistic similarities between the Psalms and the Akkadian prayer to Isthar:[4]

> How long, O my lady, are my enemies to look darkly upon me,
> are they to plan evil things against me with lies and deception,
> are my persecutors and those who envy me to rejoice over me?[5]

The words of the above Akkadian prayer are very similar to the words of several of the Psalms, are they not? Consider:

How long, O LORD? Will you forget me forever? How long will you hide your face from me? How long must I wrestle with my thoughts and every day have sorrow in my heart? How long will my enemy triumph over me (Ps 13:1-2)?

My soul is in anguish. How long, O LORD, how long (Psalm 6:3)?

How long must your servant wait? When will you punish my persecutors? The arrogant dig pitfalls for me, contrary to your law. All your commands are trustworthy; help me, for men persecute me without cause (Psalm 119:84 86).

Similarities such as these suggest the existence of a culturally common formula for lament used by most people groups in the ancient Near East. The formula expresses an impatient plea for help in the form of a prayer.[6] The difference, of course, has to do with to whom the prayerful plea was addressed.

The ancient Near Eastern gods and goddesses were said to have providentially cared for their subjects. We find, for example, in the hymn to the Egyptian god Re, that Re "creates the herbs that give life to the cattle, and the fruit trees for mankind. Who makes that on which the fishes in the river may live, and the birds under the heaven."[7]

Compare this to Psalm 104 verses 14, 25, 27 and 28: "He makes grass grow for the cattle, and plants for man to cultivate – bringing forth food from the earth: . . . There is the sea, vast and spacious, teeming with creatures beyond number – living things both large and small. These all look to you to give them their food at the proper time. When you give it to them, they gather it up; when you open your hand, they are satisfied with good things."

Also compare, for example, the Egyptian hymn of Akhenaten to Aten, "How manifold are your works! They are hidden from the face [of man]"[8] to Psalm 104:24: "O LORD, how manifold are thy works! in wisdom hast thou made them all: the earth is full of thy riches (KJV)."[9] The NIV renders this "How many are your works, O LORD! In wisdom you made them all; the earth is full of your creatures."

Psalm 86:7-8 declares, "In the day of my trouble I will call to you, for you will answer me. Among the gods there is none like you, O Lord; no deeds can compare with yours."

Isaiah 45:18 declares, "For this is what the LORD says – he who created the heavens, he is God; he who fashioned and made the earth, he founded it; he did not create it to be empty, but formed it to be inhabited – he says: "I am the LORD, and there is no other."

Isaiah 46:5 and 9 declare, "To whom will you compare me or count me equal? To whom will you liken me that we may be compared? . . . Remember the former things, those of long ago; I am God, and there is no other; I am God, and there is none like me."

Psalm 135:5 says, "I know that the LORD is great, that our Lord is greater than all gods."

Exodus 15:11 declares, "Who among the gods is like you, O LORD? Who is like you – majestic in holiness, awesome in glory, working wonders?"

Declarations such as these are not unique to the Bible. The great hymn to the Babylonian god Marduk[10] declares, "Whatever the gods of all the inhabited world may have done, they cannot be like you, Lord! [There is a fragment of the document missing here, then it continues] of the depth of knowledge, where is your equal?"

In the hymn to Gula (Nintinugga),[11] Babylonian goddess of healing, she declares, "I am sublime in heaven, I am queen in the netherworld, among the gods I have no peer, among the goddesses I have no equal."[12]

No doubt there are numerous similarities, both conceptual and linguistic, to which we could point. However, in a polytheistic system, the declarations of the incomparability of one deity over other deities was interpreted in terms within the sphere over which he or she ruled; that is, the god or goddess was being declared superior in their particular role/realm. The declarations of incomparability used in the Bible are used to declare God's incomparability to all the gods and goddesses in all roles and realms – and herein we find the main *difference*.

Psalm 96:4-5 makes this critical distinction, "For great is the LORD and most worthy of praise; he is to be feared above all gods. For all the gods of the nations are idols, but the LORD made the heavens."

Indeed there is a clear message in the latter chapters of Job. "Where were you when I laid the earth's foundation? Tell me, if you understand (Job 38:4)." "Will the one who contends with the Almighty correct him? Let him who accuses God answer him (Job 40:2)!" "I know that you can do all things; no plan of yours can be thwarted (Job 42:2)."

Likewise Isaiah rhetorically asks, "Did the gods of the nations that were destroyed by my forefathers deliver them?"[13]

Certain passages of Ecclesiastes, as with our last example, also resemble other ancient texts. For example, the Egyptian *Song of the Harper* exhorts the reader to "enjoy life" in terms similar to those found in Ecclesiastes 3:22 and 9:7-9. There are also important parallels between Ecclesiastes and the standard version of Gilgamesh.[14] In the introduction, for example, Gilgamesh is described as one who "saw everything," and who worked hard, including in the construction of buildings (1.1.1-19). It speaks of the limitations of mortals (1.1.8) as they live fleeting existences which achieve for them only "wind" (OB 3.4.3-8). Gilgamesh, like the Egyptian *Song of the Harper* and Ecclesiastes, advises his readers to "enjoy life" (OB 10.3.6-14). He also uses the expression "in quest of wind" to describe the pursuit of immortality (10.1.38, 45; [=10.3.7, 14]). These parallels seem far too precise to be accidental.

We can either interpret the parallels as symptomatic of late Jewish sages forging the Biblical text between 500 and 250 BC by plagiarizing these other texts (as Finkelstein's theory suggests), or we can interpret them as suggesting such precise parallels and styles of writing . . . in effect, securely linking the Biblical text of Ecclesiastes to the ancient world of the Near East. To account for the strong expressionistic parallels between Ecclesiastes, Gilgamesh, and the Egyptian *Song of the Harper* by theorizing that the Biblical text was written by plagiarizing other ancient texts simply reflects the ongoing anti-Bible worldview . . . and takes just as much – if not more – faith than believing the parallels support the integrity of the Biblical text by securing it to its ancient world. For one thing, literary practices and styles had changed significantly between the time of Koheleth (unknown author of Ecclesiastes, but traditionally believed to be Solomon) and the Persian period. It is debatable whether a Jewish scribe of that late a period would have even known, much less used, the ancient Mesopotamian and Egyptian literature to fabricate the Biblical text.

Koheleth was a creative writer – using expressions and sayings in ways that they had never quite been used before – borrowing and stretching the literary forms accessible to him. Because Ecclesiastes shared the ancient world with the texts of Gilgamesh and the Egyptian *Song of the Harper,* the similarities between all three of these texts are the product of a culturally natural occurrence. Worldview determines how we interpret the evidence . . . and the way we have interpreted these similarities (we have every academic right and reason to do so) actually builds a stronger case for the integrity of the Biblical text than any case against it.

It finally dawned on me – after taking my last group to the great tombs and pyramids of Giza and Saqqara – that in its historical-cultural context, the book of Ecclesiastes was nothing less than an intellectual bombshell in its day. Throughout the ancient world that surrounded Israel, rulers were spending their entire lifetimes and worldly possessions building mausoleum temples, monumental structures, and statues in an effort to establish their immortality in the afterlife. The pyramids of ancient Egypt had been designed and engineered to project the "star" of Pharaoh into the eternal heavens. The tombs held much more than caskets with mummified bodies; they were abundantly stocked with material riches – what archaeologists call "grave goods" – in the hope of transferring them to the afterlife. Not only was this practice customary for the ancient Egyptians; it was also a prevalent practice for the ancient Sumerians, Mayans, and Chinese! If you ever visit Epcot at Walt Disney World in Florida, walk through the Chinese Pavilion. There you will view a replica of the Chinese emperor Qin Shi Huang's tomb, which had thousands of life-sized clay soldiers buried near his grave, in order to ensure victory in his battles in the afterworld.

On the very first page of Ecclesiastes, Koheleth says all such practices are utter futility. The Hebrew term is הבל (*hevel*), which means vapor, fleeting, beyond your grasp . . . a theme that is repeated over and over again throughout the twelve chapters of this Old Testament book. This was a bold proclamation to the entire ancient world that it is impossible (like trying to catch the wind) to attain immortality or success in the afterlife by such efforts. "Naked a man comes from his mother's womb, and as he comes, so he departs. He takes nothing from his labor that he can carry in his hand (Ecclesiastes 5:15)." For certain, Israel did not copy this truth from any of its neighbors, for it stands in absolute antithesis to that which was believed about death and the afterlife in the ancient world.

What Similarities Should We Expect to Find?

We have spent the last four chapters considering the spiritual malware threats of historical theology and comparative philology. Examining the relationship of Israel with her neighbors, we have found that there are indeed similarities – most of them obscure, but some more striking and signif-

Guidelines for Similarities

Here are some excellent guidelines available for you to use when considering the similarities (suggested by Professor James R. Davila of St. Andrews University School of Divinity in Scotland)[15]:

• A "parallel" is not necessarily a "borrowing" . . . and, if it is, the direction of borrowing must be demonstrated, not assumed.
• Take into account both similarities and differences.
• The compared elements must be understood in their own cultural and linguistic contexts.
• Patterns of parallels are more important than individual parallels.
• A single parallel between two texts may or may not indicate an important connection between them. As a methodological principle . . . it is good to assume that one or two isolated parallels are insignificant and coincidental unless there are strong reasons to believe otherwise.
• Beware of unfalsifiable parallels. As with all scientific – and . . . historical – theories, it is important to try to formulate our parallels in such a way that they are subject to falsification . . . that is, that new evidence or a better understanding can in principle show them to be wrong. (In other words, beware of assumed or predetermined parallels that when the evidence sticks them with a pin refuse to acknowledge they were wrong.)

icant than others that cannot be denied. But does this mean that the ancient Israelites and the Biblical writers were guilty of crass plagiarism, as claimed by the 'Out of Babylon' and 'Out of Egypt' crazes of the past 110 years?

In 2 Timothy 3:16 the Apostle Paul affirms that all Scripture is given by divine inspiration. The Old Testament – the Scripture at the time of his writing – is thus of divine origin and not the result of human storytellers. None the less, there are similarities between the texts and practices of the Old Testament and the texts and practices of the ancient Near East. It is how we interpret these similarities *after identifying and examining the distinctions* that is of critical importance, especially in light of the Bible-as-myth challenges we face today.

As Bible-believing individuals, how should we address the temple similarities, the similarities in worship practices, and the linguistic similarities in light of the revelation and inspiration of the Bible?

We should expect to find substantial similarities between the Bible and the non-Biblical ancient texts and practices of Israel's neighbors.

This is because the Bible properly belongs to a rich heritage of traditions and linguistic expressions and patterns from a shared ancient Near Eastern cultural milieu. The Bible's narratives are firmly grounded in the ancient Near Eastern economy. This is a good thing! This helps to historically authenticate the text of the Old Testament. But judge the similarities wisely.

We should expect a lucid relationship between the Bible and the ancient Near East.

God did not remove the prophets who wrote the Bible from their own cultural context. This is true of both the Old *and* New Testaments. Given the close proximity of Egypt and Israel, and the major trade routes between and through them, it should be expected that the inspired writers of the Bible would have a familiarity with the literature of their neighbors, especially the wisdom literature. But this is not proof that the "Out of Egypt" craze is any more valid than the "Out of Babylon" craze. What it proves is that God used what was available to the writers of the Bible within their own culture to make known his message to his people.

Our generation has the ability to compare the text of the Old Testament with the ancient Near Eastern texts recovered by archaeologists.

This has dramatically changed the way we view and study the Bible. Typically, these archaeological findings are being dated and interpreted with an agenda to disprove the Bible. But when dated and interpreted without that bias, these archaeological finds are a positive contribution, and open new doors to help us understand Biblical Israel and its culture. We appreciate the work of the revised chronologists (many of whom are agnostics and secularists) who argue the historicity of the Bible on academic merit alone.

Beware of those who set out to use the similarities in an effort to destroy the distinctiveness of the Bible.

They overstate the similarities at the deliberate expense of the distinctiveness of the Bible. The interrelations between Egypt and the Bible, for example, have often been overstated, predetermined, and overdone one way or the other to support the current 'Out of Egypt' craze. I must caution you that some of the writings of my friend David Rohl, while helping to restore the historicity of the Bible, nevertheless fall into this category. Rohl's *The Lost Testament* is actually a classic example of overstating the historical similarities in order to prove the Bible's concretization with the other ancients – but it is done at the expense of the Bible's uniqueness and distinctiveness. Rohl is an avowed agnostic, and is being true to his presuppositions and interpretations. So beware at every junction of neglecting the uniqueness of Israel and the uniqueness of the Bible as the Word of God when studying the historical congruity of the entire ancient world as he presents it. (We still love you, David.)

Glottology! Similarities Point to an Original Source

It has been suggested that the similarities between the Bible and ancient Near Eastern temples, beliefs, and practices might strongly suggest the possibility of a common origin – a primary source of revelation prior to our current Bible. I think we need to at least entertain that possibility. Now don't burn me at the stake just yet. Let me explain. Carl Jung explained the similarities amongst the religions of the world as the "collective unconscious." It was Jung's position that all people are born with certain ideas – no matter where they were born or raised or what they were taught. Belief in God is one of those "collective unconscious" beliefs. Belief in an afterlife is also part of the "collective unconscious." But surely not everyone was born with such elaborate and detailed ideas of temples and cultic worship practices.

I think Jung was on to something, but there is something more. I am not denying Jung's suggestion of a "collective unconscious" . . . for, "since the creation of the world, God's invisible qualities – his eternal power and divine nature – have been clearly seen, being understood from what has been made, so that men are without excuse (Romans 1:20)."

The "something more" is this: the reason there are similarities between the Hebrew and ancient Near Eastern narratives and worship practices (such as the creation and the flood narratives, and temple and worship practices) may be because they all revert back to a common source and understanding of some kind. *In the same vein as the Q source hypothesis*[16] *for the Gospels, there could have been a PE source (Post-Eden Source) and a PF source (Post-Flood Source), both of which were lost in antiquity.*

Each ancient religion, long before the call of Abraham and long before the giving of the law to Moses on Sinai, little by little expressed their own version of the original PE and/or PF source, albeit introducing perversions and defilements. Each group introduced its own differences and preserved some of the similarities of what was once one basic set of beliefs and practices originally shared by all the inhabitants of the earth after the creation and then after the flood. In many cases God refined and restored the distorted ritual practices of the ancient pagan world to properly convey (restore) His truth. In other words, that which God revealed to Moses helped to restore the so-called shared rites and similarities to their correct usage and meaning.

Building a hypothesis on lost sources is *not* preposterous (surely not as preposterous as some of the things being claimed by the 'Out of Egypt' hypothesis). We have examples of lost sources in the Bible itself. For example, Joshua 24:25-27: "On that day Joshua made a covenant for the people, and there at Shechem he drew up for them decrees and laws. And Joshua recorded these things in the Book of the Law of God. Then he took a large stone and set it up there under the oak near the holy place of the LORD. 'See!' he said to all the people. 'This stone will be a witness against us. It has heard all the words the LORD has said to us. It will be a witness against you if you are untrue to your God.' "

Thus we know that Joshua drew up decrees and laws and even recorded the events of the covenant ceremony – yet we no longer have this document. "These things" (the Hebrew text is clear) means *all* these things – not merely the words of the covenant but also the whole ceremony of renewing the covenant. Even though the words have been lost, we know that this source once existed. We do have the covenant stone of Joshua at Shechem, which is now modern Nablus in Israel. It was archaeologist Sellin who first identified the Joshua stone. He was later criticized on the grounds that the stone was too early; however, Rohl's new chronology agrees wholeheartedly with Sellin's identification of this stone.

Another example is found in 1 Samuel 10:25: "Samuel explained to the people the regulations of the kingship. He wrote them down on a scroll and deposited it before the LORD. Then Samuel dismissed the people, each to his own home." We do not know for sure, but to have been "deposited before the Lord," this document was likely placed in the tabernacle where the Law of Moses was also deposited. Thus, we know this source once existed, but we no longer have it. There could just as well have been pre-Biblical sources of revelation that we no longer have. Let's briefly walk through this hypothesis together.

How Did They Know?

Consider first Genesis 4:2b-7:

> Now Abel kept flocks, and Cain worked the soil. In the course of time Cain brought some of the fruits of the soil as an offering to the LORD. But Abel brought fat portions from some of the firstborn of his flock. The LORD looked with favor on Abel and his offering, but on Cain and his offering he did not look with favor. So Cain was very angry, and his face was downcast. Then the LORD said to Cain, "Why are you angry? Why is your face downcast? If you do what is right, will you not be accepted? But if you do not do what is right, sin is crouching at your door; it desires to have you, but you must master it."

It is clear from this passage that God expected Cain to know what the right thing to do was. What Cain chose to do was the wrong way, and was referred to as sin. It is just as clear that there are no extant records of instructions to Cain or anyone else on what was required to make a proper offering in the chapters previous to Genesis 4. Was God being unfair? Or was there some source of revelation (PE Source) that would have told Cain how to prepare his offering the right way?

God judged the people of the earth with the flood. We know that God is a just God. Would He have been just in His judgment if the people of the earth had *not* been given a clue as to what was required of them for right living (PE Source)?

Consider Genesis 6:11-13:

> Now the earth was corrupt in God's sight and was full of violence. God saw how corrupt the earth had become, for all the people on earth had corrupted their ways. (Incidentally, the Hebrew here is דרכו (darkow), which literally means *his way*. I agree wholeheartedly with the KJV here: "all flesh had corrupted his way." Have some translators been traitors in this case?)

So God said to Noah, "I am going to put an end to all people, for the earth is filled with violence because of them. I am surely going to destroy both them and the earth."

God chose Abraham and Israel as His means to accomplish the redemptive process of restoring what had become a defiled, corrupted world of gods and goddesses and pagan worship practices. It was through chosen Israel that God would eventually send His son, Jesus the Messiah, to redeem the world.

Moses wrote about the creation and the Garden of Eden – but he was not there. Moses wrote about the flood – but he was not there. God called Abram out from the peoples of the Earth[17] who had lived from the time of the flood. Moses wrote about the call of Abraham – but he was not there. Moses wrote the first five books of our Old Testament, the Torah. But by the time he wrote them, thousands of years of human history had already elapsed.

Consider Leviticus 18:24-27:

"Do not defile yourselves in any of these ways, because this is how the nations that I am going to drive out before you became defiled.

"Even the land was defiled; so I punished it for its sin, and the land vomited out its inhabitants.

"But you must keep my decrees and my laws. The native-born and the aliens living among you must not do any of these detestable things,

"for all these things were done by the people who lived in the land before you, and the land became defiled."

This text tells us that the nations God drove out from the land had become defiled. To become defiled, there must have been a time when they were not defiled. Paul says, "Indeed I would not have known what sin was except through the law. For I would not have known what coveting really was if the law had not said, 'Do not covet' (Romans 7:7)."

But wait a minute. What Cain did is called sin. The people of the nations had become defiled. Yet God's law given to Moses, that Paul says shows us what sin is, was not revealed until Sinai. How, then, did Cain and the people before the flood and the people of the driven-out nations know righteous living if there was not some type of revelatory law prior to Moses concerning God's expectations for right living?

Job lived and died long before Moses was even born. Since Job is older than Genesis or Exodus, where did Job and his counselors find such theological depth to address Job's plight? Could it not be that the depth of theology in Job is a leftover, a manifestation, of God's original revelation in a PE or PF source?

Does not the Book of Job so much as reference God's post-creation revelation to mankind – a PE source, if you will?

> When he established the force of the wind and measured out the waters, when he made a decree for the rain and a path for the thunderstorm, then he looked at wisdom and appraised it; he confirmed it and tested it.
>
> **And he said to man** (long, long before our Bible), "The fear of the Lord – that is wisdom, and to shun evil is understanding (Job 28:25-28)."

There are at least eight clear references to sin in Job,[18] yet the Law of Moses is still far in the distant future. Job 31:33 says, "Have I covered my transgressions like Adam, by hiding my iniquity in my bosom?"[19] In reference to this verse, H. Morris points out, "The patriarch Job lived long before Moses and the writing of the Pentateuch, yet he knew about Adam and his fall and likewise about God's curse on the world because of Adam's sin." How did Job know this without the Book of Genesis?

In his brief article, "Job and Adam," Morris continues:

> Note the following references in the Book of Job to death and the curse: "Man that is born of a woman is of few days, and full of trouble" (Job 14:1; compare Genesis 3:16). "All flesh shall perish to-

gether, and man shall turn again unto dust" (Job 34:15; note Genesis 3:19). *Evidently Job still had access to the records of primeval history, either by verbal tradition from his ancestors or **perhaps through actual written records of the ancient patriarchs handed down from Adam to Moses.***

There are also a number of references in Job to man's original creation. After speaking first of the beasts, the fowls of the air, and the fishes of the sea, Job asks: "Who knoweth not in all these that the hand of the LORD hath wrought this? In whose hand is the soul of every living thing, and the breath of all mankind" (Job 12:9,10). Note also Elihu's testimony: "The Spirit of God hath made me, and the breath of the Almighty hath given me life" (Job 33:4).

The Book of Job was almost certainly the first written of all the books of the Bible, and it testifies abundantly that the knowledge of the true God and His creation was still *the common heritage of mankind at that time. . . .Quoting what must have been an early revelation from God, he wrote:* "And unto man He said, Behold, the fear of the Lord, that is wisdom; and to depart from evil is understanding" (Job 28:28).[20] [Emphasis mine.]

Such sources are a very distinct possibility (dare I say probability), based upon our discussions above. A PE source and a PF source would not have originated in Canaan. Such sources would have originated perhaps from classical Armenia or the Babylonian region. Rohl presents a strong case for the location of the Garden of Eden in Classical Armenia.[21] Genesis localizes post-flood mankind to the land of Babylonia (the tower of Babel in Genesis 11:1-9) and the call of Abram from Ur in this same general region (Genesis 11:27-12:5).

In summary, this hypothesis *assume*s that the similarities in certain beliefs and practices suggest the possibility of a common primary source that predates our Bible. Each people group, over time, gradually distorted what was originally a pure revelation from the Creator God. In their own particular way, they introduced significant pagan differences. As a result, the similarities that we see between our Bible and the non-Biblical texts simply reflect that which was preserved from God's initial revelation(s).

God calls Abram out from among the pagan mess. Later, Moses, when God gave him the Torah on Mount Sinai (long after Creation and the Flood and Job) purged the pagan distortions. God freed His chosen people, not only from slavery in Egypt but also from the pagan distortions through the gift of the Torah at Mount Sinai. Through Moses (with God's new revelation to His chosen people, the Israelites), God discarded the pagan defilement of His initial revelation(s) and reformulated His truth in the words of Torah.

Whether you agree or disagree with the idea of one or more common origin(s) of revelation is neither here nor there. It is an interesting possibility, though. As to the integrity of the Biblical text, we have more than enough raw evidence (in the light of all we have discussed . . . such as matters of chronology, parallelomania, the 'Out of Babylon' and 'Out of Egypt' crazes) to reaffirm the Bible's integrity. The similarities simply affirm that the Bible belongs to a wonderful family of ancient traditions. Its linguistic links to antiquity reassure us that it was not written after the Babylonian captivity (a leftover idea from the 'Out of Babylon' craze, most likely). The bottom line remains: Do not let yourself be dissuaded by the extravagant parallelomania of the current 'Out of Egypt' craze or any other craze that might happen along in the future. As I said earlier in this chapter: before you give up on God, get the facts — not the *predetermined supposed* facts that support some anti-Bible and anti-God worldview craze, but the *real* facts.

This takes us to our final consideration: *your faith.* Since most things ancient and remote are subject to query,[22] does that mean that evidence should have no part in faith? In the final three chapters, we will address the place of faith in this whole equation. Where does your faith come in . . . and does it really have to be *blind?*

18

Does Biblical Faith Have to be Blind?

Clearly a wide philosophical schism has opened up between those who would accept the biblical narratives at face value and those who would entirely dismiss the historical accuracy of those accounts. This polarization is rapidly becoming an issue of 'blind faith' versus 'scientific skepticism' with little room for compromise. How can an academic then reconcile the two opposing sides?[1]

Is choosing between blind faith and scientific skepticism the *only* option left for Christian students today? Sadly, it has been my experience that many students believe this to be the case. They are often left in a conundrum. On the one hand, like Lindsey (whose e-mail opened chapter one), they want to hold on to the historicity of the Bible and their faith. On the other hand, they sense their faith being slowly but surely eroded by the so-called 'irrefutable evidence' that is being exploited in their textbooks and lecture halls to controvert the historicity of the Bible. Since so much of today's academia is dominated by ideologies and so-called facts which, if not totally false, are alien to the Bible and the Gospel of Christ, keeping the faith can be a challenge. When faced with this conundrum, Paul's instructions to the Philippians – to "continue to work out your salvation with *fear and trembling*, for it is God who works in you to will and to act according to his good purpose (Philippians 2:12c-13)" – seem to take on a whole new meaning.

No Doubt . . . No Faith?

During the decades of her long and successful writing career, Madeleine L'Engle (award-winning author of more than sixty children's books) openly shared insights from her own struggles with doubt and faith. True, her writings and comments were seldom received without controversy; indeed, more often than not she found herself being openly challenged by the more conservative Christian community.[2] Nonetheless, I share with you one of my favorite 'L'Engleisms':

"Those who believe they believe in God but without passion in the heart, without anguish of mind, without uncertainty, without doubt, and even at times without despair, believe only in the idea of God, and not in God himself."[3]

Has not L'Engle encapsulated in this one statement a painfully accurate description of working out your own salvation with *fear and trembling*? Does this not paint a picture of the psalmists' quandaries and struggles to understand God and His ways?[4] L'Engle raised an essential worldview question that cuts right to the heart. Do we believe in the *idea* of God – or do we believe in God *Himself*?

Before we delve further into answering this chapter's main question, we need to establish three preliminary principles:

Doubt that goes unchecked is dangerous.

Like unchecked malware on your computer, doubt will eventually crash your faith. Ken Ham and Stacia Byers tell the story of Charles Templeton in an article titled "The Slippery Slide to Unbelief: A Famous Evangelist Goes from Hope to Hopelessness."[5] Once listed among those best used of God by the National Association of Evangelicals, pastor of the famous Avenue Road Church in Toronto, and the co-founder of Youth for Christ who hired Billy Graham as evangelist for this new movement, Templeton took the slippery slide to unbelief. His doubts began during his years of graduate study at Princeton. After Princeton, he tried to convince Graham that they had been wrong about the trustworthiness of the Bible. Templeton then accepted a position with the National Council of Churches, followed by a position with the Presbyterian Church (USA), and then hosted the popular CBS television series *Look Up and Live.*

During the years just before his death, Templeton wrote his controversial bombshell *Farewell to God . . .* wherein he proclaimed, "I believe that there is no supreme being with human attributes – no God in the biblical sense – but that all life is the result of timeless evolutionary forces . . . over millions of years."[6] Templeton had taken the slippery slide of doubt to unbelief. He had come full circle. Doubt that goes unchecked is dangerous.

Doubt is progressive.

In his book *The Thomas Factor: Using Your Doubts to Draw Closer to God*, Gary Habermas says all Christians experience doubts about God and their faith at one time or another. *It's how we handle them that's important.* Habermas groups all doubts into three basic families and lists them in the specific order of what he views as the progression of doubt:

- **Factual doubt** occurs when we doubt the foundational validity of faith due to a perceived lack of provable historical and/or scientific evidence. If unchecked, factual doubt leads to . . .
- **Emotional doubt**, which is skepticism that surfaces when we base our faith solely on our current emotional state. Unchecked, factual doubt and emotional doubt lead to . . .
- **Volitional doubt**, which is the consequence of a will and attitude that repudiates personal responsibility to repentance, and obedience to Biblical principles. Volitional doubt often includes anger, or a vendetta such as, "I've been lied to and I want revenge," or the "I have a point to prove to the world" attitude. Some of the most

damaging books (some that we have mentioned in this study) and movies have been created by volitional doubters who have acquired volitional agendas.

Handled Biblically, God can use doubt to strengthen faith.

Tucked away in the middle of *The Gift of Doubt: From Crisis to Authentic Faith*, by Gary Parker[7] we find what I perceive as the most significant paragraphs of the entire book:

> (D)oubt does not necessarily lead to the rejection of faith. It certainly didn't for the followers of Jesus. The disciples moved beyond their initial uncertainty in the upper room and stepped into the world armed with renewed faith. Their initial doubt took them not to a graveyard but to a birthplace of stronger commitment. And while our knowledge about the ongoing story of each disciple is sketchy and incomplete, we do know that each had a fulfilling ministry that for the most ended in martyrdom.
>
> Understandably, there will be those who don't accept the idea that doubt can actually strengthen the person of faith. Yet, it seems to me that it takes a braver and wiser traveler to step to the edge of the abyss, look into it, and cross, than it does to sit safely on the side, never to continue the journey. If faith never encounters doubt, if truth never struggles with error, if good never battles with evil, how can faith know its own power? How can it enhance its power if it never exercises its perception? . . .
>
> In my own pilgrimage, if I have to choose between a faith that has stared doubt in the eye and made it blink, or a naïve faith that has never known the firing line of life, I will choose the former every time.[8]

Students of theology in our audience will likely be tempted to argue the point as to whether Parker is being Biblically accurate when he portrays doubt as a gift rather than as a curse or a plague, but that is not our purpose here. Rather, it is to point out that Parker (regardless of what you think of his book's title) clearly touches on an important Biblical principle: the testing of our faith develops perseverance, and perseverance makes us mature and complete.[9] Doubt can be a curse or gift depending upon what we *choose* to do with it. This Biblical principle proves true in the lives of Job, Elijah, David, the disciples as a group at the Last Supper, Thomas, John the Baptist, and Peter, who all went through times of doubt but persevered. As a result, in the end, the doubts that tested their faith made each of them stronger; they each received a greater measure of spiritual fortitude and faith – and thus were able to strengthen others. In Luke 22:30-32, Jesus tells His disciple Simon (called Peter) that he and his fellow disciples are about to endure a great trial . . . but then adds, "But I have prayed for you, Simon, that your faith may not fail. And when you have turned back, strengthen your brothers."

As we shall discover in this chapter, *the notion that faith must be blind is **not** a Biblical teaching.* Rather, it is one of the deceptions of a rationalistic worldview that has infiltrated the western mindset. Spoken as a true rationalist, Bertrand Russell (1872-1970) wrote, "What I wish to maintain is that *all* faiths do harm. We may define 'faith' as the firm belief in something for which there is no evidence. Where there is evidence, no one speaks of 'faith.'"[10]

In a small eighty-page paperback, *Ten Myths About Christianity,* Christian apologist Michael Green[11] shows how defining faith as 'belief not based on evidence' is one of the ten most prevalent myths about Christianity. In Green's view, Biblical faith is not blind faith. Biblical faith is a commitment based on sufficient evidence to warrant belief – even though, in this life, we may never have absolute proof.[12]

The Intellectual Facet of Faith

Biblical faith includes the use of our intellect and reason as part of the equation as well. "That which was from the beginning, which we *have heard,* which *we have seen with our eyes,* which we have *looked at* and *our hands have touched* – this we proclaim concerning the Word of life (1 John

1:1)." In his battle against the growing forms of Gnosticism, John appeals to the physical evidence for Jesus Christ.

Jesus used physical earthly evidence that made use of the intellect and reason as part of his apologetic. Consider John 3:10-12 where Jesus is talking to Nicodemus: "'You are Israel's teacher,' said Jesus, 'and do you not understand these things? I tell you the truth, we speak of *what we know*, and we testify to *what we have seen*, but still you people do not accept our *testimony*. I have spoken to you of earthly things and you do not believe; how then will you believe if I speak of heavenly things?'"

The Greek in these verses is critically important to correct understanding. "we testify to *what we have seen*" The word that is translated "testify" here is μαρτυρουμεν (marturoumen). It literally means "to give evidence." Jesus was saying: we give evidence; we bear record to what we have seen. What is meant by the word translated "testimony" cannot be mistaken. The Greek used here, μαρτυριαν (marturian), is related to the first. But here, in the genitive, it means *evidence in a judiciary sense*. Jesus is saying that He has presented them with evidence, exhibit A if you will, just like in the courtroom, evidence that is presented in a trial. Granted, Nicodemus and the Sanhedrin did not believe even after having seen the evidence firsthand. However, make special note that Jesus presented them with "earthly things." He presented them with physical *evidence* upon which they could make an intellectual judgment, as in a court of law. But He could not talk to them of the heavenly things because they would not believe the evidence for the earthly things. In this instance, physical evidence that appealed to the intellect – and Nicodemus's ability to know and reason – was definitely part of the equation.

The Samaritans believed based upon the testimony of the woman who met Jesus at the well, and upon the evidence of having met Jesus for themselves (John 4:39-42). When the Israelites *saw* the evidence, they feared and put their trust in God (Exodus 14:31). In fact, the Bible tells us that we understand who God is through the *evidence* of what He has created. Such evidence leaves us without excuse (Romans 1:20). Evidence and the intellect are definitely part of the faith equation.

Nevertheless, the intellectual facet of faith *alone*, like the creedal facet of faith *alone*, does not save you; but earthly physical evidence is part of the overall equation. "I have spoken to you of earthly things and you do not believe; how then will you believe if I speak of heavenly things?"

To those who warn that the intellect has no place in faith or apologetics, Ravi Zacharias shares this insight:

> What I did not anticipate was having to give a defense of why I was defending the faith. "You can't argue anybody into the kingdom." "Apologetics only caters to pride, you know." "Conversion is not about the intellect; it is all about the heart." As the litany of questions runs for why we should study apologetics, so the reasons run as to why we should stay out of it.
>
> Apologetics is a subject that ends up defending itself. The one who argues against apologetics ends up using argument to denounce argument. The one who says apologetics is a matter of pride ends up proudly defending one's own impoverishments. The one who says conversion is a matter of the heart and not the intellect ends up presenting intellectual arguments to convince others of this position. So goes the process of self-contradiction.[13]

The intellectual facet of faith and apologetics is something that should never be ignored or brushed aside, and that is precisely what blind faith does. God created us as beings who can examine, think, and reason. Accordingly, the intellect, while it does not establish faith, does play a role in true Biblical faith.

Three decades ago, Inter-Varsity published a tiny paperback by John Stott entitled *Your Mind Matters*. This was a small but powerful book that spoke to those who, at the time, sought to turn Christian faith into raw emotion. Stott says, "God made man in his own image, and one of the noblest features of the divine likeness in man is his ability *to think*."[14] [*Emphasis mine.*]

We are not to conduct ourselves like the horses or mules who cannot reason (Psalm 32:9). The Hebrew here is clear: הבין (haabiyn), meaning *to reason with intelligence.* When we are challenged by intellectual doubts, by the grace of God we must seek answers while doing our best to maintain a Biblically balanced worldview of humanity's intellect. The remedy for an exaggerated view of the intellect is neither to disparage it, nor to neglect it, but to keep it in its God-appointed place, fulfilling its God-appointed role.[15]

"Faith and reason are like two blades on a pair of scissors that cut together toward truth when 'wrought in God.'"[16]

To some degree, true Biblical faith must rest on content (epistemologically). Faith is being sure of what we hope for and certain of what we do not see (Hebrews 11:1). It is not blind. It is not vague. Biblical faith does not require one to believe in an open vacuum, void of any and all substance. True Biblical faith does not require one to believe outside the realm of real understanding. Christianity has its roots in traditional Judaism, and because traditional Judaism and Christianity both claim to be *historical*, they are linked to verifiable time-space history. If not, their claim to being historical faiths is a lie.

Whether you are dealing with archaeology and the Bible . . . or creation versus evolution issues and the Bible . . . evidence and God-given intellect are important. Paul calls faith the shield we use to extinguish all the flaming arrows of the evil one (Ephesians 6:16). That means it needs to have substance and strength. So when you are dealing with the intellectual side of faith ". . . in your hearts set apart Christ as Lord. [In other words, be sure you have the right worldview first – a Biblical faith with Jesus in charge.] Always be prepared to give an answer to everyone who asks you to give the reason for the hope that you have. But do this with gentleness and respect (1 Peter 3:15)."

Room for Doubt

Alfred Lord Tennyson wrote, "There lives more faith in honest doubt, than in half the creeds."[17] If you have gone through times when you have questioned the historicity of the Bible, find encouragement in this accolade. You are likely being far more honest and serious in your spiritual life, working out your salvation with *fear and trembling*, than many who tenaciously attend church every time the doors are open, go through all the motions, and recite all the creeds without even contemplating or exploring their meaning.

There is a *midrash aggadah* that speaks of faith in relation to a mighty oak and a swaying reed. If we were to ask which is stronger, our first response might be the majestic oak. But in a violent storm with strong wind gusts, the oak is often broken or uprooted, while the reed is merely shaken. In such a storm of doubt, the flexible reed often proves stronger than the mighty oak.

> **midrash aggadah**
> In rabbinic literature, this seeks to derive a moral principle, lesson, or theological concept from a Biblical text.

Nevertheless, any degree of faith meltdown can be an agonizing and fearful experience . . . as you contemplate the possibility that all you have believed and based your life upon is nothing more than an illusionary myth. John the Baptist had a major faith meltdown while sitting in prison. When he sent his disciples to ask Jesus if He was truly the Messiah or just another messianic imposter, Jesus did not tell John to "just believe." Rather, Jesus encouraged John to *examine and ponder the evidence.*

> When John heard in prison what Christ was doing, he sent his disciples to ask him, "Are you the one who was to come, or should we expect someone else?"
>
> Jesus replied, "Go back and report to John what you hear and see: The blind receive sight, the lame walk, those who have leprosy are cured, the deaf hear, the dead are raised, and the good news is preached to the poor. Blessed is the man who does not fall away on account of me (Matthew 11:2-6)."

The most infamous case of doubt in the Bible would be that of Jesus's disciple Thomas:

Now Thomas (called Didymus), one of the Twelve, was not with the disciples when Jesus came. So the other disciples told him, "We have seen the Lord!" But he said to them, "Unless I see the nail marks in his hands and put my finger where the nails were, and put my hand into his side, I will not believe it."

A week later his disciples were in the house again, and Thomas was with them. Though the doors were locked, Jesus came and stood among them and said, "Peace be with you!"
Then he said to Thomas, "Put your finger here; see my hands. Reach out your hand and put it into my side. Stop doubting and believe."
Thomas said to him, "My Lord and my God!"

Then Jesus told him, "Because you have seen me, you have believed; blessed are those who have not seen and yet have believed."

Jesus did many other miraculous signs in the presence of his disciples, which are not recorded in this book. But these [evidences] are written that you may believe that Jesus is the Christ, the Son of God, and that by believing you may have life in his name (John 20:24-31).

Jesus told Thomas that he believed because he saw the evidence for himself. Truly blessed are those who can believe without seeing, but Thomas wasn't one of them. Jesus graciously showed His nail-scared hands and His pierced side to Thomas. *Here, Thomas. Look at the evidence. Now, stop doubting and believe.* He did not turn Thomas away during his time of unbelief.

Obviously Thomas had an intellectual problem dealing with someone claiming to have been raised from the dead. I would, too. So I am thankful he saw the evidence some of us need to see. I have lived my entire life wanting to examine everything, take it apart and put it back together again, and see for myself. Think of the time and money that could have been saved if I didn't go to Egypt to see for myself what David Rohl was talking about. But if I didn't have this need to see for myself, I would have missed out on some incredible years of graduate study in Israel. I always told my mother that she named me well. (Then one day she confessed that she hadn't named me after Thomas the disciple, but after Tom Sawyer! Well, the name works for me anyway.)

In all actuality, 'doubting Thomas' is not really a fair description of Thomas. True, he walked away and then refused to believe until he had seen the evidence, but extra-Biblical sources all indicate that once Thomas was convinced by the evidence, he never wavered. There's something to be said for someone like Thomas . . . who checks out the evidence and then finishes well. How sad for those who lunged toward faith in the emotion of the moment . . . and then, years later, drift (or intentionally walk) away rather than confronting their doubt head on.

In the Introduction to this book, I made reference that during my times of doubting and questioning, my friends of the world were more Christian to me than those who professed to be Christians. Think back to Peter van der Veen's Foreword. Remember what he said? "But their exhorting attitude did not draw me closer to God; it drove me away and made me wonder more about the truth of the Bible." The Fuller study we talked about in the first chapter documents the importance of being able to express doubt. Kara Powel, executive director for the center, reported a significant finding from the initial study. "One of the most interesting findings from the pilot project was *the importance of doubt* in a student's faith maturity. *The more college students felt that they had the opportunity to express their doubt while they were in high school, the higher levels of faith maturity and spiritual maturity.*"[18] [Emphasis mine.] That's because Biblical faith leaves room for doubt, as reflected in Jesus's replies to John the Baptist and Thomas, and even His obvious forgiveness of Peter for his outright denial of having ever known Jesus (John 21).

I will leave you with two words of caution before we leave this section. First, there is a difference between 'sincere doubt' and 'doubt so-called' as a pretense or excuse to walk away from God's authority in your life. Sincere doubt is typically an intellectual issue. Are you a skeptic because you no longer want to be under God's authority? Or are you a skeptic under God's authority truly seeking for answers? We will touch on this again in the final chapter. Second, there is also a difference between 'sincere doubt' and those who have left the faith and want to use their doubts so-called to drag others away. Be wise when seeking to help others.

In a broad sense, this is what we have been thrashing out in the previous chapters as we exposed the Bible-as-myth fallacies. As we have discovered, the very nature of antiquity itself precludes absolute proof. As a result, the Bible-as-myth issue is first and foremost a worldview issue, having more to do with the *interpretation* of the evidence rather than the evidence itself. If it sounds as if I'm beating the same old drum, know that I also beat it in my classes . . . with the hope that its rhythm will become fixed in my students' heads and hearts. It is a rhythm that confidently proclaims there is indeed *more than sufficient* evidence for the historicity of the Bible to warrant belief.

19

Who Do You Say I Am?

So what exactly is Biblical faith? In this chapter we will look at certain aspects of faith as described in the New Testament. In Hebrews we read: "Now faith is being sure of what we hope for and certain of what we do not see. This is what the ancients were commended for." The writer adds: "And without faith it is impossible to please God, because anyone who comes to him must believe that he exists and that he rewards those who earnestly seek him (Hebrews 11:1,2 and 6)."

Augustine of Hippo[1] put it this way: "Now it is faith to believe that which you do not see; and the reward of this faith is to see that which you believe."

But . . . let's face it . . . those answers to our question seem a bit nebulous. The vagueness we have encountered is the fault of the English language. Words such as *faith* and *believe* tend to be sloppy, catch-22 words in English. In view of that, our only sure guide to our answer is in the Bible's original languages.

When we work from the Greek and Hebrew, we discover the various facets of faith based upon the term used, its voice (active or passive), and the context in which it is being used. Like so many topics we have surveyed in this book, this one, too, could be a semester study in and of itself; we can only amalgamate the basic facets of faith here. We'll begin in this chapter looking at faith in the New Testament.

Personal Faith

The New Testament uses faith in a creedal sense, to describe a set of maxims to be believed and acted upon such as in Jude 3 (contending for *the faith*). This is **the** *faith*, that which has been handed down from one generation to another. It represents a body of trustworthy teachings – truths that we believe, resulting in a pattern of righteous behavior. 1 Timothy 6:20-21 would serve as another example where Paul talks about those who have wandered from *the faith*, (implying correct doctrine). But faith, as used in the New Testament, has a very personal side, and that's what we're talking about in this study.

Personal faith contains certainty.

It is being sure of what we hope for and certain of what we do not see (Hebrews 11:1). The Greek for personal *faith* and *believe* mainly come from the root πιστιs (pistis). In the passive, this means *trustworthiness* or *faithfulness*. In the active, this means *to rely upon, to trust*. In the New Testament as a whole, the overwhelming majority of time *faith* and *believe* are used is in the active tense.

When we plug this back into our Hebrews passage, we begin to get some clarification. "Now faith (active, meaning *rely upon, trust* – a relationship) is being sure of what we hope for and certain of what we do not see." The active trust implied here is an all-inclusive trust, because it knows it can confidently lean on the passive. We trust (active) because we know that God always keeps His promises; we are confident in the trustworthiness (passive) of God. Our trust is made secure in His trustworthiness. Such a deep relational trust makes it possible for the believer to regard eternity as the present, and the invisible as certain. This is the relational facet of faith – and the essential facet of Biblical faith.

Personal faith is a gift from God.

"For it is by grace you have been saved, through *faith* – and this not from yourselves, it is the gift of God – not by works, so that no one can boast. For we are God's workmanship, created in Christ Jesus to do good works, which God prepared in advance for us to do (Ephesians 2:8-9)." It is by grace through faith. The "it is" is not in the Greek text, so we need not argue whether it's grace or faith that's the gift. The gift is the entire package, including the good works God prepared in the past for us to do.

Personal faith is given in measure.

"For by the grace given me I say to every one of you: Do not think of yourself more highly than you ought, but rather think of yourself with sober judgment, in accordance with *the measure of faith God has given you* (Romans 12:3).

If there's any doubt in your mind about faith being a gift from God in Ephesians 2:8, this verse from Romans makes it clear that faith can only be traced to God as its giver. God has measured to each believer his or her own personal measure of faith. If you have been gifted with abundant faith, keep in mind that measure of faith that is yours is not of your own creation. It is the gift of God in proportion to the life you've been given to live. Your faith will never be tempted with more than you can bear (1 Corinthians 10:13). If the gift of faith given you is strong, rather than being prideful, it should prompt gratitude since it was given by grace. If your faith is weak, seek someone whose faith is stronger to help you. If your faith is strong, use your measure of faith to help someone who is weak. But always remember this: "So, if you think you are standing firm, be careful that you don't fall (1 Corinthians 10:12)!"

Keep what we have talked about here in the back of your mind. When we eventually get to the next chapter I want to show you the beautiful synchronization of faith in the Old Testament and faith in the New Testament.

Beware the Object of Your Faith

On 12 March 2008, Bernard Madoff stood beside his lawyer in federal court and pleaded guilty to all eleven charges against him – including fraud, perjury and money-laundering – for operating the biggest Ponzi scheme in Wall Street history. Madoff's crimes may well serve as a caution for generations to come. From the time of its inception in 1992, the scheme turned into a global empire worth some $65 billion. To accomplish this, Madoff bilked private investors (many of them his personal friends) and some of the largest banks in the world out of billions of dollars.

The letters that his victims sent to the prosecution and the presiding judge were heartrending:

"I falsely believed that Madoff Securities was a conservative and safe place to invest my money, our life savings, along with the belief that the SEC was protecting me against any possible fraud."

"Everything I worked for and all I created over the last 30 years is gone!"

Madoff has ". . . wiped out our savings, our retirement funds, and our son's college fund. I sincerely hope that you spend the remainder of your natural life in a prison."

> **Ponzi scheme**
> A fraudulent investment operation that pays returns to separate investors from their own money or money paid by subsequent investors, rather than from any actual profit earned. Named after Charles Ponzi, who became notorious for using the technique in early 1920.

"The man single-handedly destroyed people's lives . . . forever!"

According to a letter cited by Judge Chin during the trial, Madoff put his arm around one widow and said, "Your money is safe with me."

"I cannot offer you an excuse for my behavior," Madoff told the court. "How do you excuse betraying thousands of investors who entrusted me with their life savings? How do you excuse deceiving 200 employees who spent most of their working life with me? How do you excuse lying to a brother and two sons who spent their entire lives helping to build a successful business? How do you excuse lying to a wife who stood by you for fifty years?"

Madoff – a respected financial advisor, successful pioneer of Wall Street, former chairman of NASDAQ, and a generous philanthropist – had become the object of his investors' faith. But their faith was misplaced; the object of their faith was a fraud. As a result, a Swiss bank lost $1 billion. The Texas treasury lost $19.5 million. The list of those who trusted him is long and impressive.

Lesson learned: the object of your faith is critically important.

The Bible teaches us that the object of our faith should be Jesus Christ . . . from the creation to the cross to the resurrection and beyond. Consider this series of verses:

"In the beginning God created the heavens and the earth (Genesis 1:1)." "He (Jesus Christ) was with God in the beginning. Through him all things were made; without him nothing was made that has been made (John 1:2-3)." "Jesus answered, 'I am the way and the truth and the life. No one comes to the Father except through me (John 14:6).'"

> He is the image of the invisible God, the firstborn over all creation.
>
> For by him all things were created: things in heaven and on earth, visible and invisible, whether thrones or powers or rulers or authorities; all things were created by him and for him. He is before all things, and in him all things hold together. And he is the head of the body, the church; he is the beginning and the firstborn from among the dead, so that in everything he might have the supremacy.
>
> For God was pleased to have all his fullness dwell in him, and through him to reconcile to himself all things, whether things on earth or things in heaven, by making peace through his blood, shed on the cross (Colossians 1:10-20).
>
> In the past God spoke to our forefathers through the prophets at many times and in various ways, but in these last days He has spoken to us by his Son, whom he appointed heir of all things, and through whom he made the universe.

The Son is the radiance of God's glory and the exact representation of his being, sustaining all things by his powerful word. After he had provided purification for sins, he sat down at the right hand of the Majesty in heaven. So he became as much superior to the angels as the name he has inherited is superior to theirs.

For to which of the angels did God ever say, "You are my Son; today I have become your Father"?

Or again, "I will be his Father, and he will be my Son"?

And again, when God brings his firstborn into the world, he says, "Let all God's angels worship him."

In speaking of the angels he says, "He makes his angels winds, his servants flames of fire."

But about the Son he says, "Your throne, O God, will last forever and ever, and righteousness will be the scepter of your kingdom. You have loved righteousness and hated wickedness; therefore God, your God, has set you above your companions by anointing you with the oil of joy."

He also says, "In the beginning, O Lord, you laid the foundations of the earth, and the heavens are the work of your hands. They will perish, but you remain; they will all wear out like a garment. You will roll them up like a robe; like a garment they will be changed. But you remain the same, and your years will never end (Hebrews 1:1-12)."

The Bible is clear and leaves no room for compromise; the object of your faith is critically important.

The Single Most Important Question of Your Life

Of course, the exclusivity of Jesus Christ as the object of our faith does not sit well with our post-Christian, postmodern society obsessed with political correctness. As a result, the Gospels are also being assailed by various scholars.

(We will explore this further in the sequel to this book, *My Professor Says Jesus Was a Fraud* . . . in which we'll return to Egypt to discuss the accusation that several of the details of the Gospel narratives concerning Jesus were lifted from the story of the Egyptian god Horus. We will also address the accusation that the church conspired to cover up the presumed fact that the Jesus of history was actually the Jesus of the Gnostic gospels, rather than the Jesus of the traditional Gospels. Like the Bible-as-myth accusations, these claims are also first and foremost a worldview issue. Here, too, it is the interpretation of the evidence rather than the evidence itself that is at the core of the matter.)

Caesarea-Philippi

For now . . . let me take you back to a recent tour I co-led to the archaeological remains at Caesarea-Philippi (aka Panias/Banias) in northern Israel. I stood before a wonderful group as they sat in a semicircle around me. With the clamor of the other groups passing by, and the sound of the rushing waterfall behind me, we read and pondered together the words of Jesus as recorded in Matthew's gospel:

> When Jesus came to the region of Caesarea Philippi, he asked his disciples, "Who do people say the Son of Man is?"

> They replied, "Some say John the Baptist; others say Elijah; and still others, Jeremiah or one of the prophets."

"But what about you?" he asked. "Who do you say I am?"
Simon Peter answered, "You are the Christ, the Son of the living
God (Matthew 16:13-16)."

I reminded them that the single most important question of their entire
time visiting the archaeological sites – their entire lives, in fact – was first
asked by Jesus in the very proximity of where they sat that day. "But what
about you?" He asked. "Who do you say I am?" This is the ultimate bottom
line. And the answer will determine the direction of your faith – and, by
extension, your life.

20
Moving from Faith to Faith

"We give thanks to God always for all of you, making mention (of you) in our prayers; constantly bearing in mind *your work of faith* and labor of love and steadfastness of hope in our Lord Jesus Christ in the presence of our God and Father.

1 Thessalonians 1:2-3 (NAS)

If we are saved by grace through faith . . . faith being a gift from God that cannot be earned (Ephesians 2:8) . . . what did Paul mean by "your work of faith?" 1 Thessalonians 1:3 must rank in the top ten New Testament verses that have caused the most bewilderment and confusion (particularly since the Protestant Reformation). Much theological ink has flowed trying to explain this one phrase. For generations, theologians and Bible translators have argued (sometimes in an un-Christian-like manner) the meaning of this one phrase. The translators of the NIV solved the dilemma by magically translating the problem away. "We continually remember before our God and Father *your work produced by faith*." This is an example of translators being obvious traitors . . . forcing their own theological presuppositions onto an ancient text.

The Greek could not be clearer. Paul said what he said, and meant what he said. He was commending the Thessalonians for their work of faith. True, the translational change helped solve a perceived contradiction in the Bible for the unsuspecting English reader. It made a theological battle over faith versus works disappear, but it grossly compromised the original text – especially since the Greek is precise and clear. There's not even a textual problem or a variant reading to blame. Paul wrote "your work of faith" and the Greek text *cannot* be mistaken. The incorrectly perceived problem the NIV translators attempted to solve was based upon our misunderstanding of a first century rabbinic expression. (It appears the translators – who are western-oriented theologians – had turned the expression into an unrelated post-Reformation theological debate about the place of *works* in the doctrine of *faith*.) This was most unfortunate; it tarnished an otherwise fairly good translation.

Since Paul would have assumed that the young believers to whom he was writing (some Jews, but mostly Greek God-fearers who attended the Jewish synagogue at Thessalonica) would have understood precisely what he meant by "your work of faith" . . . would not the most reasonable and logical place to look for the meaning of the phrase be within the context of the Old Testament and first-century rabbinic Judaism? Paul, remember, was Jewish.[1] The roots of our Christian faith run deeply into the often-neglected (or ignored) Hebrew soil . . . wherein we can rediscover the Jewish roots and meaning that (trained rabbi) Paul used. The authors of the Bible were virtually all Jewish, and wrote from a profoundly Hebraic perspective. When the church lost touch with its Hebraic roots, Hebraic contextual meaning (including "your work of faith") was often lost as well.

We are also at a loss working from English translations. When the Old Testament writers spoke of faith, they typically used one of two Hebrew terms (that are both translated as *faith* in English) that in Hebrew have distinct meanings. When considering if faith has to be blind (the question we asked in chapter 18), the meaning of these two Hebrew terms becomes indispensable. The first is אמונה *emunah* which is faith as *believing in*; the second is בטחון *bitachon*, which is faith as *trusting in*.[2] I know this is not a seminary class . . . but bear with me as we walk through this. This is so important for any discussion about faith.

The faith of *emunah* (אמונה)

Emunah is related to covenant; faith in/believing that God will keep His covenant. It is knowing that we can rely on God. *Emunah* is faith that believes in the fulfillment of all of God's promises. Of particular interest to our study is the use of *emunah* in the second chapter of Habakkuk, verse 4:

> Then the LORD replied: "Write down the revelation and make it plain on tablets so that a herald may run with it.
>
> For the revelation awaits an appointed time; it speaks of the end and will not prove false. Though it linger, wait for it; it will certainly come and will not delay.
>
> "See, he is puffed up; his desires are not upright – but the righteous will live by his emunah faith (Habakkuk 2:2-4)."

This is the Old Testament verse that Paul quotes in Romans 1:16-17: "For I am not ashamed of the gospel, for it is the power of God for salvation to everyone who believes, to the Jew first and also to the Greek. For in it (the) righteousness of God is revealed *from faith to faith*; as it is written, "But the righteous (man) shall live by faith (*emunah* in Habakkuk)." (NAS) The righteous live by the assurance that God is a covenant keeper. It will not prove false. It will certainly come. When we see connections like this, it establishes a significant standard for how the term is being used. It illustrates an essential truth about faith from the Hebraic perspective . . . but, more importantly, helps us determine what Paul probably had in mind.

Basically, *emunah* says "I believe God keeps His word; God's word is sure because God is trustworthy. God is the perfect promise keeper. He means what He says and says what He means. With His signature on the 'promise check,' I know it will never bounce."

The Bible-as-myth issue is a direct attack on *emunah*; it seeks to reduce the Bible to myth to convince everyone that God's word is not sure. It's the very first thing Satan attacked in the Garden of Eden by moving human reason to the front of the equation. "Now the serpent was more crafty than any of the wild animals the LORD God had made. He said to the woman, '*Did God really say*, 'You must not eat from any tree in the garden (Genesis 3:1)?'" Did God really say? Did God really mean what He said? Can you hold God to His Word?

Emunah is called *simple faith*. There's a saying in Hebrew that goes something like this. *Emunah* is the "simple faith" (*emunah peshutah*) of the "simple Jew" (*yehudi pashut*) that links him to the "simple unity" (*achdut peshutah*) of God's Atzmut (*Heart*). Believing in the simplest terms that God always and forever keeps His promises links me to the very heart of God, the very essence of God. Paul says the righteous will live by *emunah*.

The faith of *bitachon* (בתחון)

Bitachon is faith defined as *absolute trust*. The root of *bitachon* is *batach*, which literally means to lean or rest on someone or something. *Batach b'* means *to trust in* (usually in God) when used in the Bible: "It is better to take refuge in the LORD than *to trust* in princes (Psalm 118:9) . . . or "Let the morning bring me word of your unfailing love, for I have put *my trust* in you. Show me the way I should go, for to you I lift up my soul (Psalm 143:8)."

From this, *bitachon* comes to mean faith. But unlike *emunah*, as we shall see, it means active faith in an applied sense . . . that is, consciously placing the burden of one's concerns and worries on God, and trusting that He will work everything out. It translates into something like this: "I believe that God is faithful in all that He has promised, and because I know that He is the perfect promise keeper *emunah*, I can trust Him completely *bitachon* with every single aspect of my life, indeed, with my entire being."

Bitachon faith gives me the security of knowing I can trust Him totally – no matter what predicament I find myself. *Bitachon* is faith that says God's sovereign plan for me is never wrong. He knows the end from the beginning, and does all for the ultimate benefit of those who are His.

Hence, the Hebrew *bitachon* may best be described as *applied faith. Bitachon* is the outworking of faith that includes:

- The desire for more and more of God.
- Complete trust and total reliance on God.
- A desire to obey God in all areas of life.
- Security in the fortress of strength and nourishment that only God can provide.
- The peace and tranquility that comes from trusting God.
- Ultimate meaning and purpose for life.

Applied faith is personal and emotional. It speaks of trust, reliance, dependence, and hope. I trust God to the extent that I will live by the Word of God and, if need be, die for Him. This is the measure of faith that allows Job to proclaim, "Though he slay me, yet will I hope in him; I will surely defend my ways to his face (Job 13:15)." This is fortitude of faith, the result of the testing.

The Hebrew concept of *bitachon* (applied faith) enables us to treat the future as the present. It enables us to treat the unseen as already seen. This Hebrew concept of *bitachon* faith is clearly reflected in the words of Hebrews 11:1: "being sure of what we hope for and certain of what we do not see." My wife served with a mission on Maui for twelve years (how rough that must have been!) before we were married. One of our Hawaiian friends who had gone to San Diego to visit her son shared this thought with us in an e-mail. After all the passengers were seated and the plane began backing from the gate in San Diego the pre-departure message played on the screen. In the last part of the message they were thanked for flying Hawaiian Airlines and in closing the following words were said, "Hawaii starts here." Not only was this a clever marketing tool, it enabled the passengers to treat the unseen as already seen. Because the passengers had faith that the plane was going to get them to Kahului Airport in Maui, it enabled them to treat the future as the present . . . and that which was unseen as seen. (OK, this may not be the best illustration . . . but you get the idea.)

The 'Work of Faith'

It should come as no surprise that the Hebraic (*emunah/bitachon*) concept of faith in many ways parallels the Greek active/passive voice concept of faith. They are both relational; they both require a relationship with God. In the Greek, the active *leans* on the passive, I trust God (active voice) because God is trustworthy (passive voice). In the Hebrew, *bitachon* – active faith (completely trusting God) – *leans* on *emunah*, because God always keeps His promises.

When his daughter was just a little girl playing by the poolside, a man I know here in Florida used to wait until she was preoccupied with a toy or little pretend adventure, then sneak up behind her, grab her, and hold her out over their swimming pool. For him it was a game; not so for the daughter.

"Please Daddy. Don't drop me," she would squeal.

"OK. I won't drop you."

"No, Daddy. Please, Daddy. Daddy, promise me you won't drop me!"

"OK. OK. I promise. I promise I will not drop you!"

Then he would drop her in the water and roar with laughter.

Daddy never thought much about the little pool game he used to play until his daughter grew up . . . and, in front of a counselor, told her father how he had damaged her – and their – relationship by it. She never felt she could trust her own father because she didn't know when she could believe him. The little pool game had also caused damage with her relationship with her Heavenly Father because, in her mind, daddies (even heavenly ones) make promises they don't keep. The story is heartbreaking, but I can't think of a better illustration to explain the Hebraic concept of faith.

Biblical faith is understood in the Old Testament as a process: *faith to faith*. Paul as you would expect carries this rabbinic concept into the New Testament in Romans 1:17 – literally, faith to faith. It is *faith* that *begets faith*. My faith allows me to have faith. Once again, when the rabbinic cultural background has been lost (or ignored), *faith to faith* has little meaning in our western mindset. Translating "faith to faith" as "by faith from first to last" (NIV) once again superimposes a western interpretation onto a first century Jewish rabbinic idea . . . not to mention being a traitor to the Greek text. Paul is telling us that we move from faith to faith, and his teaching is drawn from the Old Testament. My *emunah* (believing that God always keeps His promises) allows me to *bitachon* (trust Him completely); this is the work of faith, a faith that really works – from faith to faith.

Believing that God keeps His promises (*emunah*) allows me to trust and obey Him in every situation (*bitachon*). When God my Father tells me He will not drop me into the pool I relax completely in His arms trusting He will never drop me, no matter what. This is *faith to faith;* it is faith strengthening faith. This is an applied faith that is personal and emotional. This relationship of trust depends upon a state of contact, the contact of our entire being with the One we trust. It speaks of trust, reliance, dependence, and hope. It assures that we can trust God through the darkness because of what He has shown us in the light. It empowers us to trust and obey God. This is the Hebraic portrayal of faith. I can trust God and obey Him because when He promises He's not going to drop me, He's not going drop me! Because He keeps His promises (*emunah*) I can trust Him completely (*bitachon*).

Paul's use of "your work of faith" in 1 Thessalonians has nothing whatsoever to do with works versus grace; he is quite simply using the Hebraic definition of faith . . . from faith to faith . . . from *emunah* to *bitachon*. He was commending the Thessalonian believers for the way they were moving from faith to faith (maturing in their faith). Alas, if the NIV translators had translated this "your faith produced by faith" they would have hit the nail right on the head. And rest assured, Paul understood and believed without reservation that the "work of faith" in their lives was exclusively by grace.

The "work of faith" can be seen in all of Scripture. The psalmist in the midst of his distress and doubt found new faith and strength as he *remembered* past songs in the night, the past deeds of the Lord, and the Lord's miracles of long ago. In the midst of doubting God's unfailing love, he purposed to meditate on all of God's past works and mighty deeds.[3]

Marking Occasions of Faith

On the day David faced off with Goliath, he proclaimed, "This day the LORD will hand you over to me, and I'll strike you down and cut off your head. Today I will give the carcasses of the Philistine army to the birds of the air and the beasts of the earth, and the whole world will know that there is a God in Israel. All those gathered here will know that it is not by sword or spear that the LORD saves; for the battle is the LORD's, and he will give all of you into our hands (1 Samuel 17:46-47)."

When Max Lucado metaphorically labels David's first stone "the stone of the past," he has actually expressed the work of faith — faith to faith. David's *emunah* (recalling God's faithfulness to him in the past) allowed him to *bitachon* in what seemed to everyone else an impossible situation. "Goliath jogged David's memory. Elah was a déjà vu. While everyone else quivered, David remembered."[4]

God was active not only in David's life, but in the lives of many of the Israelites. God's actions were a testimony to the covenantal relationship He had with them. God's precedent participation in the lives of His people was the evidence, if you will, that He would keep His word in the present and future. The tangible proof that God kept His promises (*emunah*) gave the Israelites, like David and others, the faith (*bitachon*) that would give them the courage and strength for the hard days ahead. God often demonstrated that He was a promise keeper.

Not long after the spies had returned from Rahab in Jericho, and reported to Joshua, he began organizing the Israelites for the crossing. Joshua sent officers among the people to prepare them for the big day. The Ark of the Covenant of the Lord was to lead the way, for it represented the presence of God. Between it and the people, there was to be a space of about a thousand yards. Everything was to be made ready for morning. Before the night came upon them, Joshua himself addressed the people: "Consecrate yourselves, for tomorrow the LORD will do amazing things among you." After forty years of wandering and fighting and misery in the wilderness, they had finally arrived. Can you believe it? Can you feel the excitement and anticipation? They were crossing into the Promised Land. This would be a huge and glorious day.

The next morning God told Joshua, "Today I will begin to exalt you in the eyes of all Israel, so they may know that I am with you as I was with Moses (Joshua 3:7)."

And just as God had promised . . . when they came to the edge of the Jordan that day . . . and the priests who were carrying the ark put their feet in the water . . . the waters stopped – even though it was the rainy season. Many times I have stood on the brink of the Jordan (literally and metaphorically), imagining what that day must have been like.

> That day the LORD exalted Joshua in the sight of all Israel; and they revered him all the days of his life, just as they had revered Moses.
>
> Then the LORD said to Joshua, "Command the priests carrying the ark of the Testimony to come up out of the Jordan."
>
> So Joshua commanded the priests, "Come up out of the Jordan."
>
> And the priests came up out of the river carrying the ark of the covenant of the LORD. No sooner had they set their feet on the dry ground than the waters of the Jordan returned to their place and ran at flood stage as before.
>
> On the tenth day of the first month the people went up from the Jordan and camped at Gilgal on the eastern border of Jericho. And Joshua set up at Gilgal the twelve stones they had taken out of the Jordan.
>
> He said to the Israelites, "In the future when your descendants ask their fathers, 'What do these stones mean?' tell them, 'Israel crossed the Jordan on dry ground.' For the LORD your God dried up the Jordan before you until you had crossed over. The LORD your God did to the Jordan just what he had done to the Red Sea when he dried it up before us until we had crossed over. He did this so that all the peoples of the earth might know that the hand of the LORD is powerful and so that you might always fear the LORD your God (Joshua 4:14-24)."

God showed his people how vitally important it was to set up commemorative markers for the big events in their lives and the life of Israel.[5]
We see in the book of Joshua a classic example of the Hebraic notion of
faith to faith and faith begetting faith. God instructed them to record their
big day with a memorial of twelve stones, so that their faith (*emunah*) and
the faith of future generations would know that God keeps his promises
. . . and that, accordingly, they could always trust God completely (*bitachon*). In the future, God told Joshua, when your descendants ask their fathers, "What do these stones mean?" tell them, "Israel crossed the Jordan
on dry ground." They set up the commemorative marker so that all the peoples of the earth might know that the hand of the LORD is powerful . . .
and so that they and future generations might always fear the LORD their
God.

Recording Acts of Faith

A vital component of the faith equation is to "remember the wonders
he has done, his miracles, and the judgments he pronounced (1 Chronicles
16:12)." If you have never kept records for your faith equation, now would
be an excellent time to start. God wants us to remember the days we cross
the turbulent rivers of this life on dry land. Keep a good record of God's
victories in your life. We should also remember to include thanks for the
days when God has intervened on our behalf that we are not even aware of,
and will never know about until eternity. This is faith that begets faith.

Lucado says, "Write today's worries in sand. Chisel yesterday's victories
in stone."[6] Allow me to make some adjustments for our purposes. "Write
today's *doubts* in the sand. Chisel yesterday's *faith-building* victories in
stone." It is your remembering *emunah* faith that heartens your *bitachon*
faith when you are tempted to doubt. For me, it was remembering the
miraculous ways that God had made my graduate studies in Israel possible
that helped to sustain my belief in Him during many a time of intellectual
doubt. All that I knew was that God did not take me to the Promised Land
to destroy my faith. Over a decade later, I came to find out the reason why
I had been in Israel and walked through that dark tunnel of intellectual

doubt. It was so that, in years to come, I would be able to empathize with my graduate students, and minister to them in their times of doubt in a unique way.

A couple of days after my dad's sudden and unexpected death, I was sitting at his desk in his basement study. My eyes caught a well-used notebook filled with pages of entries. As I looked closer, I found page after page of prayer requests, people's names, dates . . . of immediate family, cousins, work associates, friends. Scattered on every page were stars commemorating answers to very specific requests. The starred items, I soon discovered, were days when he (or someone he had been praying for) had experienced walking across one of life's turbulent rivers on dry land in victory. They were not twelve stone commemorative markers, but page after page of noted victories when God had clearly intervened in some impossible situation . . . events that had God's fingerprints all over them. It was an amazing record of God's grace and love. His old and tattered notebook, that no one in the family ever knew anything about, gave me a cherished glimpse into the *emunah* faith of the man who had fathered and raised me. It was a simple faith that had repeatedly given birth to fortitudinous faith, a *bitachon* faith that gave him the strength and courage to walk his family through some tough times. I believe his record-keeping played a major role in his faith equation.

Is Evidence Really the Issue?

Nablus, an Arab village in Samaria, was Biblical Shechem. (My mom always remembered where Nablus was because she liked to tell the story about the time she watched a boy steal an apple from the grocer's stand, and be chased down the pavement with a broom by the grocer). Just before his death, Joshua gathered the people at Shechem (Joshua 24). Joshua rehearsed with them all the great things God had done for them, beginning with the call of Abraham. He reminded them of the sojourn in Egypt, and Moses and Aaron, and how God had covered Egypt's horsemen with the waters of the Red Sea. He reminded them of the time in the desert, and of their big day when they – together – had crossed the Jordan. He reminisced with them about the conquest, and how the Lord had driven their enemies out from before them. These people had lived the archaeological evidence firsthand. They had helped set up the commemorative markers along the way. They had evidence coming out their ears that God was indeed faithful to His promises. Yet . . . somehow . . . their worldview had become contaminated. Many of them had drifted from God and had returned to the foreign gods of the Amorites.

God had instructed them to build the commemorative markers so they would remember the evidence. They did. Frankly, *they had all the evidence they needed, yet they still chose to follow the gods of the Amorites and walked away.* What does this say to us? Irrespective of the evidence, the worldview you embrace is a choice. Faith is ultimately a choice to receive God's gift of faith and obey Him. Agnosticism is also a choice. Atheism is a choice.

Are you a skeptic because you no longer want to be under God's authority? Or are you a skeptic under God's authority truly seeking answers? There is an enormous difference between sincere doubt and the pretense of doubt as an excuse to walk away. We had raised this question in the "Room for Doubt" section in chapter eighteen.

With all the ironclad evidence in the world, *faith is still a choice* – and it is still a gift from God. It has never really been a conflict of evidence. *The conflict is first and foremost a worldview conflict.* Faith is not blind. Evidence is important. There is an intellectual facet to the faith equation. But when all is said and done, when push comes to shove, we have to choose.

Jesus said in Luke 11:9 that we have to be willing to seek in order to find, and that seeking needs to be under God's authority. Based on what we learned in chapter four, there is a myth of neutrality in modern and postmodern thinking that says Christians, like non-Christians, have to deal with their doubts like everyone else using reason alone. But we saw where using reason alone ended up, in a void of meaninglessness. Go back and review chapter four if you need to. You have to believe that the object of your search is real in order for your search to be real. The Hebraic notion of *emunah/bitachon* faith assumes the existence of God and His authority over all creation.

This Biblical Hebraic notion of faith is expressed clearly in the New Testament book of Hebrews 11:6: "And without faith it is impossible to please God, because anyone who comes to him *must believe that he exists and that he rewards those who earnestly seek him.*" That's a given in the Hebraic notion of *emunah/bitachon* faith. You have to believe that the object of your search is real in order for your search to be real! Faith produces faith. Faith (*emunah*) produces faith (*bitachon*).

What I came to realize through my own intellectual doubting is that you can work out your evidence questions relating to history, textual criticism, archaeology, prophecy, creation versus evolution – you name it – and still find an excuse to walk away. And that is when you know that your doubting has become an issue of pretense.

Even though the Israelites had all the ironclad evidence they needed (they had actually lived the evidence), they still slipped and fell back into their old ways. They did not stop believing in the existence of the true God; they just chose to walk away and go back to following their old gods. It basically came down to not wanting to be under God's authority. They wanted to substitute God's authority with an authority that could provide them no evidence or proof whatsoever! They were willing to settle for the gods of the Amorites, gods (an authority) grounded in human reason. They chose blind and speechless gods whose only foundation for rationality was irrationality. Sound familiar? Be careful that your intellectual doubting is not the pretense of doubt that can only lead you from faith in the Creator God – that is based on evidence and rationality that you can actually seek and find – to a faith in gods grounded in human reason that can offer no evidence, plenty of irrationality, and a first class ticket to meaninglessness and hopelessness. The Israelites made a choice. It was a wrong choice. They chose, for a time, to walk away. So Joshua pled with them:

> "Now fear the LORD and serve him with all faithfulness. Throw away the gods your forefathers worshiped beyond the River and in Egypt, and serve the LORD. But if serving the LORD seems undesirable to you, then choose for yourselves this day whom you will serve, whether the gods your forefathers served beyond the River, or the gods of the Amorites, in whose land you are living. But as for me and my household, we will serve the LORD (Joshua 24:14-15)."

Choosing Faith

Sometimes correcting a wrong turn takes time, and often takes a lot of work . . . in much the same way getting rid of malware on the hard drive of your computer takes a lot of time and work. It's much easier to *get* it than it is to *get rid* of it. It took my friend Rob three long days of scanning, cleaning, and restoring to rid my computer of malware. Finally, the malware was completely gone . . . but then a week later, there were more problems as a result of the damage the malware had done while it was present. So don't be discouraged. It took me years to work out some of the intellectual enigmas encountered in my graduate and post-graduate studies. Malware is tough to find and tough to clean. God did years of scanning, cleaning, and restoring my heart and mind. And then – even after the malware was gone – there was still rebuilding and restoring work to be done. But God was faithful throughout, more than I was to Him.

The people of Israel realized that they had somehow made a wrong turn. After Joshua reviews with them their *emunah* (the record of the evidences of God keeping all of his promises to them), they realize afresh that it all comes down to a choice. And the people said to Joshua, "We will serve the LORD our God and obey him (Joshua 24:21)."

> On that day Joshua made a covenant for the people, and there at Shechem he drew up for them decrees and laws. And Joshua recorded these things in the Book of the Law of God. Then he took a large stone and set it up there under the oak near the holy place of the LORD. "See!" he said to all the people. "This stone will be a witness against us. It has heard all the words the LORD has said to us. It will be a witness against you if you are untrue to your God (Joshua 24:24-27)."

Do you have a stone? I can tell you this. I'm so thankful I do – literally. I picked one up on the beach in Newport, Rhode Island, on a foggy summer night many years ago when I was just out of college. It has traveled with me from state to state and country to country. Currently it sits just to my left on a shelf here in my Florida study. It has served me well as a warm and comforting witness to God's gracious claim on my life even in times of doubting.

As one who has spent his career in the academic world . . . as one who has personally struggled with many of the same issues you may be struggling with . . . let me close by saying the myth is not the Bible. The real myth is the one that claims you can answer the three basic questions of philosophy ("Where did I come from?" – the question of human origins; "Why am I here?" – the question of human purpose; and "Where am I going?" – the question of human destiny) without God and the Bible in the equation. The real myth is the myth of neutral, secular reasoning devoid of all reference to God and His Word. Reliance upon human reasoning alone will only lead to the meaningless void of postmodernism.

We typically read from Mark 2 while standing in the Capernaum synagogue (on the northern shores of the Galilee) when we are in Israel.

> A few days later, when Jesus again entered Capernaum, the people heard that he had come home.

> So many gathered that there was no room left, not even outside the door, and he preached the word to them.

> Some men came, bringing to him a paralytic, carried by four of them.

> Since they could not get him to Jesus because of the crowd, they made an opening in the roof above Jesus and, after digging through it, lowered the mat the paralyzed man was lying on.

> When Jesus saw their faith, he said to the paralytic, "Son, your sins are forgiven."

> Now some teachers of the law were sitting there, thinking to themselves, "Why does this fellow talk like that? He's blaspheming! Who can forgive sins but God alone?"

Immediately Jesus knew in his spirit that this was what they were thinking in their hearts, and he said to them, "Why are you thinking these things?

Which is easier: to say to the paralytic, 'Your sins are forgiven,' or to say, 'Get up, take your mat and walk'?

But that you may know that the Son of Man has authority on earth to forgive sins . . .." He said to the paralytic, "I tell you, get up, take your mat and go home."

He got up, took his mat and walked out in full view of them all.

This amazed everyone and they praised God, saying, "We have never seen anything like this!"

Once again Jesus went out beside the lake. A large crowd came to him, and he began to teach them (Mark 2:1-13).

Try to picture the scene. Jesus had just come home to Capernaum. Such large crowds had gathered to hear His teaching, there was no room left . . . and people were even huddled outside the door trying to listen. Four men arrive carrying a paralytic on a mat and find it impossible to get their friend to Jesus. So they break through the roof and lower the man on his mat to where Jesus is teaching. And then Jesus saw *their* faith. Have you ever noticed that? The text does not say when Jesus saw *his* faith (that is, the paralytic man's faith); it says when Jesus saw *their* faith . . . the faith collectively of the paralytic *and* his four friends. When you find yourself crippled by doubt, it's important to have understanding friends to help carry you back to faith wellness. In the Introduction, I had shared with you the story of our friend in Brazil who had shared with her pastor that she was running out of faith. His answer – "Then it's time for the Body to have faith for you" – was loving and gracious and Biblical.

Never take for granted that our souls have a spiritual enemy. Your intellect is not the primary enemy of your faith, even though that may seem to be the case. Jesus said to Peter, "Simon, Simon, Satan has asked to sift you as wheat. But I have prayed for you, Simon, *that your faith may not fail. And when you have turned back, strengthen your brothers* (Luke 22:31-32)." [Emphasis mine.] What I find especially helpful about this verse is found in the Greek text. Jesus's forecast of Peter's denial is tied to a prediction that *all the apostles* (*you,* plural) would be "sifted like wheat" . . . but that it would be Peter's task (*you,* singular), when he had turned back to his faith, to strengthen his brothers. Could that be what God is saying to *you?*

Thank you every one for your attention and resilience; you have made it to the last page. Although you may want to do some further study on any number of the issues we have discussed before reaching your own verdict (as you should), I trust this introduction has helped you recognize that the so-called 'indisputable facts' being used to declare the Bible a fraudulent myth are an exceedingly long way from being rock-solid. I've made you aware of the interpretive faults, limitations, and worldview prejudices and agendas of new-generation archaeology and our post-Christian postmodern culture. We've noted that there has never been anything proven in support of the postulations that the Israelite religion of the Old Testament was nothing more than an adaptation of surrounding pagan religions. We have talked about philosophy, worldviews, agendas, history, archaeology, conventional chronologies, revised chronologies, historical theology, philology, philosophy, ancient temples, linguistic and ritualistic similarities, the Bible-as-myth allegations . . . and even the place of evidence, intellect, and reason within the overall faith equation.

However, my dear students (I refer to those who have endured my classes over the years . . . who have survived my study tours through Israel, Egypt, or Jordan . . . and *you,* who have mustered the stamina to finish this book) . . . before we part, I must now share with you the real reason I wrote this book. Although all of the things we have talked about are essential and significant, this book is not really about them. It's not about me. It's not even about you. This book is about a Savior, whose name is Yeshua (Jesus) . . . who wants *you* to know that *He will not drop you* as you dangle over doubting waters. He still rewards those who earnestly seek Him.

So take Him at His word. Seek Him. Seek Him with all your heart and soul and intellect. You *will* find Him . . . and you'll love what you find.

An Afterword from Our Editor

After more than two decades as an evangelical Christian, I began to lose my faith. It has taken nearly a decade – and editing this book – to find it again. And what a long, strange trip it has been.

The groundwork was actually laid in the mid 1980s. Upon my conversion to evangelical Christianity in 1979, I became one of those annoying zealots who go from being in the world to being totally committed to the faith. It was zeal, however, without wisdom. I became critical of the complacency and hypocrisy I was seeing in the Church at large. While I loved Christian *books*, visits to Christian book*stores* made me bristle. Commercialism was rampant; the Church had sold out to Mammon. Scripture verses and gospel messages were as ubiquitous as the trinkets that carried them . . . they were even found on ashtrays. The late Christian singer-songwriter Keith Green once called it "the selling of Jesus."

As a result, I ended up joining a church of like-minded people . . . people that – I was convinced (without knowing a thing about early church social or theological history) – really behaved like a New Testament church. We lived close to one another, and became a community as tight-knit as any family, if not more so. In deeming ourselves one of the few churches being truly obedient to God, we became elitist. Instead of being humble, we became more arrogant and assertive in telling others how *they* should live, and what they should believe.

When the church dispersed in tragedy, my world was rocked. I had dedicated four years to this body. My devotion had even cost me my first marriage. (My wife was pregnant when she left me. I saw my son once, when he was three days old, in the hospital nursery. In my pride, I would not submit to my wife's increasingly difficult conditions to see him. Soon after, she spirited him off to another country. I would not see him again until, by the Lord's grace, we were all reconciled here in the United States – my family *and* my ex-wife's family – in 2005, when our son was eighteen.) While the church was not technically a 'cult,' it displayed 'cultic' tendencies . . . some of which I've since witnessed in mainline churches, too (such as the pastor whose board of elders would disagree with him on an issue, and he would overturn their decision by asserting that 'God told him' to do it his way). An account of some of the church's activities can actually be found in chapter seven of Ronald M. Enroth's *Churches That Abuse* (1992, Zondervan Publishing House) . . . where it's called the 'No Name Fellowship.'

Wounded by the experience, I did my best to return to the mainline evangelical churches. I attended denominations from strict Baptist (where one couple was asked to leave for being 'disorderly' by raising their hands to God during a service) to charismatic . . . in sizes from a home church to a large complex complete with its own school. But I was adrift . . . and still carried as ballast some of the erroneous beliefs fostered by the abusive church.

By the mid 1990s – remarried, with two (of what would ultimately be five) children – I began attending the same large Southern Baptist church as my parents. It was there that a Sunday school teacher (who would become a great friend) named Mark Knox helped my worldview take a turn. He taught from a video series by Dr. R.C. Sproul called *Objections Answered*, which outlined reasoned, rational responses to questions commonly asked by skeptics. That class fueled a passion for the study of apologetics. After reading Sproul's *The Holiness of God*, I became a fan of his work . . . and ordered numerous books and seminary-level video and audio courses from his Ligonier Ministries, most of them on apologetics.

I guess I was afraid, to some extent, of my faith being considered stupid. After all, if God is rational and intelligent, He expects His followers to be the same. I was excited to find out the Christian faith could be defended with reason. I *loved* apologetics . . . although, I have to admit, I started having a few minor nagging questions about issues concerning the translation and interpretation of Scripture, and certain beliefs held by evangelicals with certain theological leanings that seemed to defy logic. Nonetheless, I put them on the back burner. Big mistake.

By the time the terror attacks of September 11, 2001, rocked the world, I was an editor at a Southwest Florida regional daily newspaper. One of my duties was unofficial religion editor, a position appointed to me when the executive editor discovered that I (unlike other reporters and editors) enjoyed covering religion stories. One thing you have to realize is that good journalism breeds skepticism. As veteran New York journalist Pete Hamill observes: "I was . . . at the mercy of the people I interviewed. The journalist can prepare well, listen carefully, and, thanks to modern technology, record what he hears with absolute fidelity. But human beings lie. Cops lie. Lawyers lie. Actors lie. Victims lie. Statistics lie. The objective reporter writes down the lies and tries to check them against other sources. But sometimes one lie is merely countered with another lie and the reporter is forced by the standards of objectivity to print both."[1] (Hamill's statement assumes the basic competence and ethical sense of the reporter. In these days of slashed media budgets, newspapers disappearing like dinosaurs, and the rise of untrained members of the public feeding news outlets with the latest drivel (some of it dangerously irresponsible) . . . competence and decency and even the hint of objectivity are getting harder to find. All journalism is not good . . . and sometimes – yes – even reporters lie.)

Like Hamill, I had also come to learn that people lie – and not all of them outside of the Church. Pastors lie. Sunday school teachers lie. Theologians lie. Academics and scholars lie. It is common for people of all faiths to ignore, deny, or dismiss evidence that doesn't support their particular worldview or interpretation of Scripture.

In the aftermath of 9/11, my area's Islamic community began a series of lectures on Islam. Their purpose wasn't conversion, but to foster understanding. The mosque had already suffered some vandalism, and the Muslims wanted their neighbors to know that not all people who espouse their faith are terrorists. As religion editor, I attended. And it blew me away. I thought I had been thoroughly equipped by my studies in apologetics to filter out challenges to my faith. But now I found myself listening to these Muslims defend the Qur'an *using some of the same arguments I would use to defend the Bible.* I began to ask myself: How is it that I can blow *their* arguments away as invalid, yet consider those same arguments valid for *me* when contending for *my* faith? Thus began a downward spiral into doubt.

My journalistic ethos came into play: I had been betrayed! If I hadn't been downright lied to, then at least I had been denied the facts about the origins of Christianity and the transmission of the Scriptures that might have raised questions. The pastors and theologians had provided, at best, simplistic, inadequate – sometimes misleading answers . . . because they were uncomfortable facing certain truths that would force them to alter their worldviews.

My reading tastes switched from Biblical apologetics to Biblical criticisms. I was stunned by the allegations levelled against the New Testament and its translators in *Misquoting Jesus: The Story Behind Who Changed the Bible and Why* by Bart Ehrman. My worldview was equally rocked by his *Lost Christianities*, and a video lecture series of his on the New Testament. Here was a scholar whose investigations into the reliability of the Bible had turned him from a once faithful believer into an avowed agnostic. I soon felt as if someone had pulled the stopper on my faith.

If only I had been alone in my descent. But I had a wife and family who would be adversely affected as I gradually lost my standards of Christian conduct. The best way I can describe it is: the first doubt was like having a callus grow on my heart. With each succeeding doubt over the years, more calluses formed . . . until my entire heart became as a rock. I still attended church (occasionally), prayed (occasionally), had tender feelings toward the Lord (occasionally). But all these positive things did little more than chip away at that rock . . . it was just too big and well-encased.

Then the Lord, in His righteousness, allowed a situation in my life that came straight for my heart – not as a chisel, but as a sledgehammer. For the first time in years, I was able to see clearly my sin – and the extent of its effects on the wife and children I adored. It was clear I had unintentionally gone from being the spiritual leader of my household to its destroyer. Almost immediately, still in the midst of a terrible trial, something wonderful happened. The Lord gave me an undivided heart and put a new spirit in me; He removed from me my heart of stone and gave me a heart of flesh (Ezekiel 11:19).

Part of my rescue was the arrival of another academic who, as with Ehrman and others like him, had wrestled with similar critical doubts – to the point of almost losing his faith. But instead, he arrived at a totally different conclusion. Through the grace of God, that academic – Tom Tribelhorn – threw me a lifeline. We had been friends for years . . . and I would occasionally come to him with some of my doubts. He answered my toughest questions with more honesty than I'd ever witnessed before. He helped me to understand that doubt can become an integral part of faith . . . that a faith that has never experienced and confronted doubt . . . that accepts certain tenets gullibly, with no evidence to support their claims . . . may not be faith at all.

Am I still skeptical? Absolutely – and *glad to be*. Tom helped me also to understand that skepticism is *good* . . . it's what keeps me from blindly accepting every wave of error that may come my way. I remain a *skeptic* – but am no longer a *cynic* – and there's a world of difference. Do I still have some questions and doubts? Again, absolutely. But they're not 'deal breakers.' I'm not naive enough to believe that *all* of my questions will have answers this side of eternity. But there are enough answers to maintain a sound, logical, rational, intellectually defensible faith. I concur with Ralph Waldo Emerson: "All that I have seen teaches me to trust the creator for all I have not seen."

I believe that, if this very book you're holding in your hands now had been available to me in 2001, it would have hampered my descent into faithlessness. Going through the manuscript . . . discovering anew that there are indeed reasoned responses for Christianity . . . has increased my own faith, even as I have been performing my editing work. My hope is that this book will reinforce your faith as well . . . and equip you to fortify the faith of others who may be losing their way. Whether in times of faith or doubt, one of the greatest gifts of God is free will – the power of choice. We can choose faith. In reading this book, you have already chosen wisely. Don't stop now . . . for at the end of the road is God himself.

Bob Massey
Editor
Port Charlotte, Florida

Appendix A: On Ancient Mesopotamia

Additional information on the revised chronology of ancient Mesopotamia as suggested by Bernard Newgrosh

Chronology at the Crossroads contains four parts that are interdependent, designed to be read in conjunction with each other:

Part one is an update of the most recent comprehensive study of geopolitical relations in the Late Bronze Age.

Part two looks at the AKL including a detailed discussion of the editing and construction of the AKL and a review of the many related modern studies.

Part three examines the new chronology solutions. A new chronology must observe all the attested synchronisms of the ancient world, be free of all the anomalies of the old conventional chronology, and present a coherent history. With some differences from David Rohl's proposed chronology, Newgrosh proposes a highly detailed revision– with the stipulation that other revised chronologies may also be possible. Newgrosh believes there are two very different characters that bore the name 'Ashur-uballit' during the Middle Assyrian period. To build his case, he compiles geopolitical, archaeological and linguistic evidence in support of the case. This allows the histories of Assyria and Hatti to realign in a different way from that in the conventional chronology. Such a proposal makes possible an absolute chronology, also supported by the evidence of astronomical dates previously discarded by Egyptologists because they did not fit the conventional chronology.

Part four is dedicated to Babylonian history, treated separately because it has few of the geopolitical problems that cause trouble for the rest of Western Asia in the Late Bronze Age.

About Newgrosh

Who is Bernard Newgrosh? He is actually a medical doctor in the northwest of England. He went to St. Edmund Hall, Oxford, for his studies in physiology before graduating in 1975 from St. Mary's Hospital Medical School, Paddington. It was during his studies at the university that he acquired an interest in ancient history. The possibilities for chronological revision caught his attention, so he attended the Glasgow Conference in 1978. Disappointingly, the conclusion of the conference was that the revised chronology proposals of Immanuel Velikovsky were untenable. But a few years later, Newgrosh was asked to edit a new proposal for a revised chronology, less radical than Velikovsky's. His agreement to help brought him into contact with its authors, Rohl, Peter James (co-author of *Centuries of Darkness*[1]), and Peter van der Veen.

But it wasn't until 1987 that Newgrosh began his own studies in ancient history when Rohl sought his help with an extraordinary assignment: comparing the period of the Amarna Letters with that of the early Israelite monarchy. The resulting article became one of the pillars of the Rohl's new chronology. Later, with major input from Peter van der Veen, this same article was revised and republished in JACF 6 (1992/3).[2]

A first critical review on Newgrosh's research was presented at the BICANE (Bronze to Iron Age Chronology of the Ancient Near East) colloquium in Cambridge in July 2008 by Simon Sherwin (Ph.D. in Assyriology at the Oriental Institute of Cambridge University). The presentation was based upon a review done for the new BICANE research group (with James, van der Veen, John Bimson, Robert Morkot, et al) and was a positive assessment of *Chronology at the Crossroads: the Late Bronze Age in Western Asia.*

In particular, Sherwin said he was rather impressed with Newgrosh's methodology and critical examination of the conventional chronology. Several points raised by Newgrosh appeared valid, but in Sherwin's view they may not lead to such a radical revision as Newgrosh has suggested. Sherwin also argued that the suggestion that the Ashuruballit of Assyria (at the time of Pharaoh Akhenaton) was another, non-canonical king independent of Ashuruballit I, must be taken seriously and cannot be rejected out of hand.

A similar view is held by another BICANE colleague, Pierce Furlong, who completed his Ph.D. at Melbourne University (2007) on a 200-year revision of the Middle Babylonian Period. While Newgrosh suggests a 350-year revision (in line with Rohl), Furlong`s views on Mesopotamia are more compatible with the current views shared by the BICANE group.

Chronology at the Crossroads goes far beyond Egyptology to refute the conventional chronology. Newgrosh sees the conventional chronology as an inaccurate synthesis of the ancient past built on faulty anchor-points, a chronology that conceals a considerable collection of anomalies. Moreover, Newgrosh's research also offers a new set of exact dates for the rulers of Hatti, Assyria, and Babylon in the Late Bronze Age.

Happy reading; it's a long and meticulously detailed (but fascinating) study.

Appendix B: The Sovereignty Debate

Here's a shortened version of a query that I posed to Peter van der Veen in Germany. He worked with David Rohl for many years on the new chronology, but has since changed his position in recent years. Van der Veen now believes that no more than 250 years can be removed from the standard traditional chronology. Hang in there and pay close attention to Peter's answer.

Basically what I had said to him was: if we follow Rohl's new chronology model . . . then, according to my calculations, Seti I would have ascended to the throne in Egypt around the middle of the forty-year reign attributed to King Solomon. Not long after taking the throne, Seti I and the Egyptian army set out to deal with a crisis of some sort in Canaan. The Karnak account says that their chiefs gathered on the hills of Canaan,[1] and that Beth Shan was under attack from a Canaanite king and could not get help.[2] However, the Bible says that Beth Shan was one of Solomon's fortifications, perhaps the most important of Solomonic cities[3] . . . and yet, Seti I is taking action to defend some kind of Egyptian interests there. So was Solomon in charge of Beth Shan or the Egyptians?

Van der Veen's Unedited Response

Dear Tom,

In "New Chronology"[4] it is assumed that due to the peace treaty between Egypt and Israel, Egypt was granted some autonomy over its former trading stations to continue its foreign policies.

I never particularly liked this however. This situation did not exist when I spoke to you first about the revised chronology in Lamorlaye, as we dated Ramesses II much earlier than David Rohl did later on in his book Pharaohs and Kings/Test of Time 1995 (much of which is based on research done by Rohl when I was working as a missionary in Africa). Back in the early 1980s we hadn't even completely decided yet whether or not Shishak was to be equated with Ramesses II (Shisha, Sessu) or Ramesses III, who is also called Sesi by his daughter at the Harem of Medinet Habu. Note also that back then Peter James was still heavily involved with the revised chronology which at that stage was called the 'Rohl-James Chronology,' not 'New Chronology.'

Nevertheless at the time we much preferred Ramesses II as Shishak, but placed his year 1 in c. 985 BC with an extended overlap between him and his father Seti I, who continued to reign until c. 980 BC. As you will notice Seti's interference in Canaan was now placed during the turbulent years of David's reign and some of his claims having fought in Syria were connected with David's battle against Hadad-ezer of Beth Rehob and Zobah. Some of the more local fights could then have related to rebellions within David's own kingdom (at the time of Absalom and Sheba of Benjamin) and Seti's Canaanite wars could be seen as those of an ally to David. Year 18 of Ramesses II (i.e. the 17th reign year in Egyptian terms!) then coincided with year 1 of Solomon and hence there was no real clash between Egypt and Solomon in the mid 10th century BC either. Ramesses II could have taken Gezer in year 1 of Solomon according to this scenario.

Now as David Rohl knows, before I decided more recently that even this scheme is hard to reconcile with the known data for the remaining dynasties as well as for the archaeology of Palestine in the 9th-8th centuries BC, I much preferred our earlier scenario with Ramesses II starting his reign around 985 BC.

But as I just said, things have moved on from there over the last 5-10 years and a mass of new evidence has come to light (especially due to the assembled effort/energy of several revised chronologists within our new international BICANE group)[5] that made me change my mind about the extent of the revision. That's a long story, but it all boils down to early Iron Age archaeology at sites such as 9th and 8th century BC Samaria, Jezreel, Megiddo, but also 10th century Jerusalem (where both the Millo and a palace structure uncovered by Eilat Mazar since 2005 may be directly related to building activities during the reign of Solomon – conventionally these are dated to the 12th century BC), the development of local Canaanite/Phoenician alphabet scripts, but above all also Egyptian Third Intermediate Period chronology, i.e. the impossibility of completely overlapping the 21st and 22nd Dynasties as Rohl suggests. There is important evidence that an independent 21st Dynasty reigned some 30-50 years (there are different opinions on this within BICANE!) before the start of Shoshenk I's reign (now dated independently by lunar dating to either 839 or 835 BC) and that the 20th Dynasty definitely reigned longer than Rohl wishes (he gives only ca. 40 years to the independent 20th Dynasty, which is much too short, anything lower than 80 years seems to be out of the question).

This seems to tip the balance in favour of a "later" Shishak who may be either Ramesses III (as per James and I tend to think that he is right here, though possibly later in the reign than James originally suggested) or an even later Ramesside king (Ramesses VI or IX, different views held within BICANE).

Solomon's reign then either falls within the late years of Dynasty 19 which was typified by national turmoil or largely within the later years of Ramesses III which also was plagued by national upheavals.

The Pharaoh who conquered Gezer may have either been Ramesses II in his late years (when his army was led into Canaan by Merenptah who literally claims to have seized Gezer) or Merenptah in his year 1 or 3 (i.e. after the death of Ramesses II). The military expansions of David's earlier years now fully fall within the "quiet" mid years of Ramesses II when he was no longer active in Palestine. But the stela which he set up near Damascus in his year 56 may now relate to smiting local rebels around 990 or 980 BC at a time when David's kingdom was threatened by several rebellions (Absalom and Sheba). Ramesses/Merenptah could therefore have acted on David's behalf, smiting the Israelite rebels (he mentions "Israel" on his Israel-Stele), securing the via Maris and the King's High Way and establishing a peace treaty with King David and his son Solomon, who then subsequently married Pharaoh's daughter. With year 1 of Ramesses c. 1040 BC (or slightly earlier??) his active years fall within the late years of Samuel's office as Judge and during the early reign of Saul. Seti's reign now belongs to the period of the Eben-Ezer conflict and the years of Samuel as Judge.

Amarna is of course no longer at the time of Saul and David but must now be dated to c. 1100 BC, about the time of Jeftah and Boaz/Ruth. We know extremely little about this particular period so that it is difficult to relate anything at this stage, except that also Jeftah's behaviour has been compared with that of the Amarna Habiru by several scholars.

Now this reply has become much longer than I originally intended but I think this will help you to recognize the general outline of the 200-250 years revision better.

Please keep asking if things remain unclear or if you don't like certain things about this scenario. I will be happy to help out or "think afresh."

Best wishes
Peter

Appendix C:
History of the Revised Chronology

To properly understand and appreciate the tone and atmosphere of the current discussion on the revised versus conventional chronology, I offer this very brief summary of the history and development of the revised chronology.[1] From there we will then address other matters concerning the current discussion ending with an overall assessment of the bottom line.

Summary Background of the Revised Chronology[2]

As you know, I first became aware of the revised chronology through the photocopied pages on the Glasgow and Rohl-James models that then-student Peter van der Veen gave me after class in France. However, it is important to understand that the suggestion that something was seriously off beam with the traditional Egyptian chronology was suggested long before the Glasgow Rohl-James studies during the early days of modern Egyptology. It was the renowned Norwegian Egyptologist Jens Lieblein (1827-1911) who first took to task the standard chronology of ancient Egypt back in the 1860s, in his book *Aegyptische Chronologie* (1863).[3] Much like David Rohl and Peter James suggest today, Lieblein argued that Egypt's Third Intermediate Period (conv. 1070-664 BC) had to be shortened. He suggested that the late New Kingdom (conv. c. 1200-1070 BC) needed to come down in time, and would coincide with the late Judges and the early kings in Israel (c. 1050-920 BC).

During the 1890s, ancient historian Cecil Torr (1857-1928) also queried the accuracy of the standard Egyptian chronology, this time on the basis of Aegean pottery that had been discovered in Egypt. His findings are found in his book *Memphis and Mycenea* (1896). Although his arguments were discussed at length in a long and heated debate between him and the famous Egyptologist Sir William Flinders-Petrie and an ancient historian by the name of John L. Myres during the 1890s, the revised chronology proposed by Torr never received the scholarly attention it deserved, and the issues raised were never finally settled.[4] Both Torr and Lieblein had suggested a maximum but radical reduction of some 200-plus years.

After the Second World War, a Jewish amateur historian of Russian descent, Immanuel Velikovsky, revived the revised chronology debate once again, but this time for completely different reasons. Whereas Lieblein and Torr had been mostly concerned about technical Egyptological and archaeological matters, Velikovsky primarily wished to find better synchronisms between the archaeology and history of his own Jewish people. In a series of books (the first of which is *Ages in Chaos*, published 1952) he suggested removing some 500 to 800 years from the standard chronology of ancient Egypt.[5] His reconstruction, which became more and more arbitrary and unprofessional over the years, was soon to be rejected completely by all serious scholars.

Some scholars, however, still felt that there was a definite need for revision simply because too many unresolved anomalies existed that could not possibly be explained within the conventional chronology. They felt that the standard BC chronology of the ancient world had been artificially overstretched by several centuries, and had caused an implausible archaeological 'Dark Age' of several centuries in many cultures of the eastern Mediterranean world (whose own chronologies were dependent on the master chronology of ancient Egypt).

One of these scholars was John Bimson, who had just recently completed his Ph.D. thesis at Sheffield University on the date of the Exodus and Conquest.[6] Bimson emphasized that only a revised chronology would ultimately solve the problems between archaeology and the early history of ancient Israel (a position adopted later by Rohl). These scholars gathered at the so-called Glasgow Conference in 1978. Many of them had been introduced to revised chronology studies merely through the work of Jewish amateur historian Velikovksy, and were unfamiliar with the earlier works of Lieblein and Torr. At Glasgow they sought to modify Velikovsky's scheme into a more plausible model[7] – an endeavor which quickly was shown to be impossible. Instead of removing 500-plus years from the traditional time scale (as per Velikovsky), it became evident that only a maximum of 250 to 350 years would be feasible. The so-called "Rohl-James Chronology" was born. At first a brief outline was published in April 1983 while I was teaching in France.[8] It was at this point I was introduced to the revised chronology through van der Veen.

The Work Expands

Despite its initial name, several more scholars have been involved in this project over the many years that followed.[9] To enhance the scope and quality of the work in progress, the Institute for the Study of Interdisciplinary Sciences (ISIS) was founded in 1985 . . . along with its own academic journal, the Journal of the Ancient Chronology Forum (JACF), in which the pros and cons of a revised chronology were to be critically debated in an open-minded spirit.[10] (ISIS was chaired by Rohl.)

From 1987 onwards, Rohl and James went their separate ways. Rohl continued to work on a 300-plus year reduction (the so-called 'new chronology') with a group of colleagues within ISIS, while James and a group of colleagues from the University College London worked together on a less radical revision of some 200 to 250 years (the so-called 'Century of Darkness' or 'CoD' chronology).[11] Both groups continued to emphasize that the main crux of the overall discrepancy between ancient world chronology and the archaeology of the eastern Mediterranean (including Biblical archaeology) was to be found in Egypt. Both groups stressed that the main problems were situated within the later part of Egyptian history, where several dynasties had ruled simultaneously over various parts of the Nile Valley. By overlapping these dynasties to a larger extent than in the conventional chronology, the preceding periods would come down by more than two centuries.

While Rohl studied Egyptology and ancient history at University College London during the late 1980s and early 1990s, others working closely with him (such as Bob Porter and van der Veen) were also pursuing their studies in Old Testament and Levantine archaeology. Rohl started his doctoral studies in Egyptology, but decided not to finish his work after he had decided to present the new chronology theory to a much larger audience through his book and documentary series *Pharaohs and Kings*.

The actual debate, however, continued in the pages of JACF. The mass publicity Rohl's bestselling book and documentary series received almost immediately generated many critics. The actual debate, however, continued quietly in the pages of *JACF,* as well as in Peter van der Veen's and Uwe Zerbst's German book, *Biblische Archäologie am Scheideweg?* . . . through which some of the weaker elements within Rohl's new chronology became gradually more apparent. As a result, other revised chronologists found the 350-year revision as presented by Rohl in *Pharaohs and Kings* too difficult to reconcile with the increasing amount of epigraphic and archaeological evidence from Egypt and Mesopotamia, as well as from other cultures within the Ancient Near East (such as Israel). When the ISIS finally decided to 'close its doors' and publish the final issue of JACF,[12] several important things had happened.

It was important that the revised chronology work continue. The focus of the careful reconsideration and reformation of the revision work (a work still in progress) was then shifted to the newly founded research group now called Bronze to Iron Age Chronology of the Ancient Near East Study Group (BICANE). Since 2006 this group has held two colloquia, one in Berlin and the other at Cambridge, and they currently plan to meet regularly in the future. Its principal founders (Bimson, James, van der Veen,

Zerbst, and Robert Morkot) intend to publish the colloquium papers in a series of future proceedings.

Meanwhile, some twenty-five to thirty international scholars from the fields of archaeology, Egyptology, Mesopotamian studies (as well as within the field of scientific dating) now belong to this new group. All of them believe there is a need for substantial chronological revision. Although the individual members of the BICANE group may disagree about the precise number of years that must be ultimately removed from the standard chronology of the ancient world, they have, as a group and as individuals, made their mark in the academic arena. Several of their works have already appeared in print in renowned publications.[13] It is hoped that their work will continue . . . the work once begun by Jens Lieblein and Cecil Torr . . . in a worthy manner, to help to reconstruct the jigsaw puzzle of the chronology of the ancient world – including its synchronism with the Biblical text.

Appendix D: The Jericho Dilemma

Another proposal to reconcile the Jericho dilemma without revising the conventional chronology has also been offered. Bryant Wood[1] claims that the Middle Bronze Age fortification walls which collapsed at Jericho (Tell al-Sultan) fell only at the end of Late Bronze Age I (around 1400 BC, in conventional terms). It is (as might be expected) difficult to find anyone who agrees with him. The city that was destroyed was a Middle Bronze city – not a Late Bronze city. The Conquest took place circa 1400, according to Biblical dating . . . therefore the Middle Bronze city (if that is the one destroyed by Joshua) must be dated to 1400. The problem is that 1400 in the conventional scheme is Late Bronze. Bimson and Rohl argue that when the chronology is corrected and is lowered, the Middle Bronze city is still in existence in 1400. The same argument would be applied for Hazor and all the Middle Bronze cities destroyed circa 1400 according to the Old Testament.

According to the conventional chronology, dates for the transition from Middle Bronze to Late Bronze, the Middle Bronze age came to an end with the expulsion of the Hyksos from Egypt circa 1530 BC. That is more than one hundred years before the Biblical date for the Conquest. As a result, the conventional dating for the archaeological data . . . linked to the conventional chronology . . . linked to the supposed anchor-points from Egyptology . . . do not match the Biblical date for the Conquest. What Bimson, Rohl, and other proponents of the revised chronology are saying is: the only way to reconcile the dating is to correct the anchor-points and the chronology. Wood disagrees, and suggests we fix the dilemma by re-dating the pottery at Jericho rather than the chronology. Wood tries to date the fall of Jericho (via pottery typology) to the Late Bronze rather than the Middle Bronze period, even though everyone else dates the pottery at Jericho as Middle Bronze. His is an upstream swim as well.

Recent excavations at Tell al-Sultan (Jericho) by an Italian-Palestinian[2] expedition have confirmed that the Middle Bronze Age walls at Jericho indeed fell at the end of Middle Bronze, and not later. They firmly disagree with Wood's conclusions. I am indebted to Peter van der Veen for sharing information attained through his personal communications with N. Marchetti (1999, 2005, 2008).[3]

Notes

Chapter 1: Why Students Are Turning Their Backs on God

1. Lindsey's personal e-mail has been used with her permission.
2. The Fuller study was conceived by Cameron Lee, professor of Marriage and Family. Findings of the study are published along the three-year track and can be found at http://cyfm.net.
3. Lillian Kwon, "*Survey: High School Seniors 'Graduating from God,'*" ChristianPost.com, August 10, 2006.
4. Ken Ham and Britt Beemer, with Todd Hillard, *Already Gone: Why your kids will quit church and what you can do to stop it* (Green Forest AR: Master Books, 2009), 31.
5. Ham and Beemer, *Already Gone*, 38-39.
6. Jeff Myers, *Handoff: The Only Way to Win the Race of Life* (Dayton TN: Legacy Worldwide, 2008). Also see www.passingthebaton.org.
7. As quoted in Kwon, ibid.
8. Harold Lindsell, *The Battle for the Bible* (Grand Rapids, MI: Zondervan, 1976).
9. This is not to dismiss or consider less important some of the other reasons why people depart from the faith, such as falling into sin or hurtful experiences at the hands of an abusive pastor, parachurch organizations, church, or fellow Christians. These reasons merit their own consideration in their own right.
10. Victor H. Matthews and Don C. Benjamin, *Old Testament Parallels: Laws and Stories from the Ancient Near East* (Mahwah NJ: Paulist Press, 2006), p. 284.
11. Lloyd M. Graham, *Deceptions and Myths of the Bible* (Secaucus NJ: Carol Publishing Group, 2000), p. 5. This book was originally published in 1975 by University Books.
12. Research authors Gary Tobin and Dennis Ybarra of the Institute for Jewish and Community Research have found some 500 shocking distortions concerning religion in twenty-eight of the most widely used social studies and history textbooks now being used in the United States, which they discuss in their recent book, *The Trouble With Textbooks: Distorting History and Religion* (Rowman & Littlefield Publishers, Inc. 2008). This is a worthwhile read. Ybarra believes part of the problem is that publishers employ or contract with writers who are not experts in their subjects. More importantly, their research documents the fact that textbook publishers are now bowing to the worldviews and agendas of special interest groups. (Also see article by Lilly Fowler, *Institute Uncovers Bias in K-12 History Textbooks*, in *The Jewish Journal*, – www.jewishjournal.com/education.)

Ybarra states, "They're under pressure from all kinds of minority groups, religious groups, and they try to satisfy everyone and that results in content that is dumbed down to the lowest common denominator. And so, in that process, things can be missed. Errors can survive." As quoted by Lauren Green, *Authors Warn That Many Textbooks Distort Religion*, Accessed at www.foxnews.com 7 March 2009
Ybarra also claims that their research clearly documents the unequal way textbooks in the United States treat Christianity, Judaism and Islam. Their research shows that Islam has a privileged position. It is not critiqued, criticized, or qualified in the same way Judaism and Christianity are. For example, in the glossary of *World History: Continuity and Change,* the definition of the Ten Commandments reads, "moral laws Moses *claimed to have received* from the Hebrew God," while the entry for the Qur'an contains no such qualifier in saying it is the "Holy Book of Islam containing revelations *received* by Muhammad from God." [Emphasis mine.] (Holt Rinehart & Winston, 1997).
13. Ham & Beemer, ibid., p. 49.

Chapter 2: What the Experts Say About the Bible

1. William G. Dever, *Recent Archaeological Discoveries and Biblical Research* (University of Washington Press, 1993), p. 47. Dever's book *Did God Have a Wife?: Archaeology and Folk Religion in Ancient Israel*, (Grand Rapids MI: Eerdmans, 2005), was intended as a popular work making available to the general public the long held view held by archaeologists and scholars regarding ancient Israelite folklore that the Israelite god (Yahweh) had a consort, that her name was Asherah, and that she was part of the Canaanite pantheon.
2. He has published with Eerdmans, for example: *What Did the Biblical Writers Know and When Did They Know It?: What Archaeology Can Tell Us about the Reality of Ancient Israel* (2001) and *Who Were the Early Israelites and Where Did They Come From?* (2006).
3. William G. Dever in an article "Contra Davies" http://prophetess.lstc.edu/~rklein/Documents/deverb.htm.
4. William G. Dever quoted in Hershel Shanks, "Losing Faith" *Biblical Archaeological Review* (March, April 2007) 33 (2):54.
5. Silberman, Finkelstein's co-author, is a journalist who has published critical works on the history of archaeology in Israel. He is also a contributing editor to *Archaeology Magazine*.
6. Israel Finkelstein and Neil Asher Silberman, *The Bible Unearthed: Archaeology's New Vision of Ancient Israel and the Origin of Its Sacred Texts* (New York: Simon and Schuster, 2002). *The Bible Unearthed* DVD was released in June of 2009. Also see *David and Solomon: In Search of the Bible's Sacred Kings and Roots of Western Tradition* (New York: Simon and Schuster, 2007).

7. Also commonly mentioned are readings from *The Quest for the Historical Israel: Debating Archaeology and the History of Early Israel: Invited Lectures Delivered at the Sixth Biennial Colloquium of the International Institute for Secular Humanistic Judaism, Detroit, October 2005* edited by Israel Finkelstein, Amihai Mazar, and Brian B. Schmidt (New York: Simon and Schuster, 2007).

8. Kenneth A. Kitchen, *On the Reliability of the Old Testament* (Grand Rapids MI: Eerdmans, 2003).

9. Comments made in a *Jerusalem Post* article: http://www.jpost.com/servlet/Satellite?cid=1167467747621&pagename=JPost%2F JPArticle%2FShowFull.

10. Finkelstein, ibid., p. 79.

11. Ibid., p. 118.

12. Thomas L. Thompson, *Early History of the Israelite People: From the Written & Archaeological Sources* (Leiden and Boston: Brill Academic Publishers, 2000).

13. Thompson, ibid, p. 403.

14. Michael Sturgis, *It Ain't Necessarily So: Investigating the Truth of the Biblical Past* with Introduction by John McCarthy, (Leicester UK: Ulverscroft Large Print Books, 2003, and Bargain Books, 2004).

15. Sturgis, ibid, pp. 55; 57-58.

16. Sturgis, ibid, p. 88.

17. Sturgis, ibid, p. 161.

18. Sturgis, ibid, pp. 5; 6-7.

19. Sturgis, ibid, p. 12.

20. Michael D. Coogan, *The Old Testament: A Historical and Literary Introduction to the Hebrew Scriptures* (Oxford UK: Oxford University Press, 2006), p. 11. For further research on creation versus evolution, see Answers In Genesis, www.answersingenesis.org and Institute For Creation Research, www.icr.org.

21. Coogan, ibid., p. 202.

22. Coogan, ibid., p. 256.

23. "That for the good of the Seminary (Faculty Manual II.4.C.4) Professor Peter Enns be suspended at the close of this school year, that is May 23, 2008 (Constitution Article III, Section 15), and that the Institutional Personnel Committee (IPC) recommend the appropriate process for the Board to consider whether Professor Enns should be terminated from his employment at the Seminary. Further that the IPC present their recommendations to the Board at its meeting in May 2008."

24. Peter Enns, *Inspiration and Incarnation: Evangelicals and the Problem of the Old Testament* (Grand Rapids MI: Baker, 2005).

25. See G. K. Beale, *"Myth, History, and Inspiration: A Review Article of Inspiration and Incarnation by Peter Enns," Journal of the Evangelical Theological Society* (June, 2006). You can access this article online at:

http://findarticles.com/p/articles/mi_qa3817/is_200606/ai_n17176285/?tag=content;col1

Peter Enns, *"Response to G. K. Beale's Review Article of Inspiration and Incarnation," Journal of the Evangelical Theological Society* (June, 2006). You can access this article online at: http://findarticles.com/p/articles/mi_qa3817/is_200606/ai_n17176284.

26. July 23, 2008: The *following statement is being posted per the instruction of Rev. Charles McGowan, Chairman of the Institutional Personnel Committee.*

The administration and Prof. Peter Enns wish to announce that they have arrived at mutually agreeable terms, and that, as of 1 August, 2008, Prof. Enns will discontinue his service to Westminster Theological Seminary after fourteen years.

The administration wishes to acknowledge the valued role Prof. Enns has played in the life of the institution, and that his teaching and writings fall within the purview of Evangelical thought. The Seminary wishes Prof. Enns well in his future endeavors to serve the Lord.

Prof. Enns wishes to acknowledge that the leaders of the Seminary (administration and board) are charged with the responsibility of leading the seminary in ways that are deemed most faithful to the institution's mission as a confessional Reformed Seminary.

Prof. Enns expresses his deep and sincere gratitude to the Lord for his education and years of service at Westminster Theological Seminary.

Chapter 3: What Do You *Really* Believe About the Bible?

1. Ralph Beich earned his Ph.D. in Semitic languages from Brandeis University. He was my Greek professor.

2. "Symantec Internet Security Threat Report: Trends for July-December 2007 (Executive Summary)" (PDF). Symantec Corp.. April 2008. 29. http://eval.symantec.com/mktginfo/enterprise/white_papers/b-hitepaper_exec_summary_internet_security_threat_report_xiii_04-2008.en-us.pdf.

3. F-Secure Corporation (December 4, 2007). F-Secure Reports Amount of Malware Grew by 100% during 2007. Press release. http://www.f-secure.com/f-secure/pressroom/news/fs_news_20071204_1_eng.html.

4. See Mark 9:21-29.

5. See Jean-Francois Lyotard, *The Postmodern Condition: A Report on Knowledge*, translated by Geoff Benington and Brian Massumi (Minneapolis MN: University of Minnesota Press, 1984), p. 82.

6. Peter Adkins, "The Limitless Power of Science," in *Nature's Imagination*, edited by John Cornwell (Oxford UK: Oxford University Press, 1995), p. 132.

7. I believe this to be a false view. True science and the Bible can be reconciled. The Hebrew Bible and archaeology can be reconciled or I wouldn't be writing this book. It is the purpose of this book to present you with the evidence that refutes the skeptics

and re-establishes the firm archaeological and historical evidence for the truth of the Biblical narrative.

8. Edward J. Larson and Larry Wuthan, "Scientists are still Keeping the Faith," *Nature 386* (April, 1997), pp. 435-436.

9. *The American Heritage Dictionary* defines worldview as: "1) The overall perspective from which one sees and interprets the world. 2) A collection of beliefs about life and the universe held by an individual or a group."

The etymology of the word can be traced to the German *Weltanschauung* meaning *world and life view*. It is the framework through which one makes sense of life. Apologists generally recognize seven major worldviews: theism, atheism, deism, finite Godism, panentheism, pantheism, and polytheism. It has become more and more common to use various adjectives to modify worldview and clarify the emanations of the worldviews; for example, the descriptors "Christian worldview" and "Biblical worldview" are emanations of theism. For additional study see Norman L. Geisler, *Baker Encyclopedia of Christian Apologetics* (Grand Rapids MI: Baker Academic, 2005), pp. 785-787. A variety of definitions have also been offered by numerous Christian authors over the past thirty or so years. For example, James Sire asserts that "A world view is a set of presuppositions (or assumptions) which we hold (consciously or subconsciously) about the basic makeup of our world." James W. Sire, *The Universe Next Door* (Downers Grove, Ill.: InterVarsity, 1988), p. 17. Phillips and Brown state that "A worldview is, first of all, *an explanation and interpretation of the world* and second, *an application of this view to life.* In simpler terms, our worldview is a view *of the world* and a view *for the world.*" W. Gary Phillips and William E. Brown, *Making Sense of Your World* (Chicago: Moody Press, 1991), p. 29.

10. CBS Evening News with Katie Couric: http://www.cbsnews.com/stories/2009/12/05/eveningnews/main5908487.shtml.

Chapter 4: Postmodernism's Attack on Biblical Truth

1.http://www.evangelical.edu/index.php?option=com_content&task=view&id=7&Itemid=10.

2. For an excellent discussion see *"Postmodern Challenges to the Bible,"* by Amy Orr-Ewing in Ravi Zacharias, author and editor, *Beyond Opinion: Living the Faith we Defend* (Nashville TN: Thomas Nelson, 2007), pp. 3-20.

3. See Douglas Groothuis, *Truth Decay: Defending Christianity Against the Challenges of Postmodernism* (Inter-Varsity, 2000).

4. Linked to this, you will also find that postmodernism, which is grounded in critical theory in general, may also be viewed as skeptical by degree. Sometimes you will notice a distinction being made between affirmative postmodernists, who say theory needs to be altered, rather than rejected, and skeptical postmodernists, who say

all theory should be rejected – everything needs to be completely rethought and changed.

5. A phrase that was coined by the German philosopher Ludwig Klages in the 1920s referring to the perceived tendency of Westerners to locate the *center* of any text or discourse within the *logos* (a Greek word meaning *word, reason,* or *spirit*). Logo centrism is used as a derogatory term by postmodernists, referring to the tendencies of some works to emphasize language or words to the exclusion or detriment of the matters to which they refer.

6. See E. P. Sanders, "But Did It Happen?" in *The Spectator* Vol. 276 (April 6, 1996).

7. http://www.history.ac.uk/ihr/Focus/Whatishistory/index.html.

8. www.history, ibid.

9. Francis A. Schaeffer, *He Is There and He Is Not Silent* (Wheaton IL: Tyndale House, 1973) p. 71.

10. For further study see Diogenes Allen, *Christian Belief in a Postmodern World: The Full Wealth of Conviction* (Westminster John Knox Press, 1989); David S. Dockery, *The Challenge of Postmodernism* (Baker Book House, 2001); Millard J. Erickson, *Postmodernizing the Faith: Evangelical Responses to the Challenge of Postmodernism* (Baker Book House, 1998); Dennis McCallum, general editor, *The Death of Truth: Responding to Multiculturalism, the Rejection of Reason, and the New Postmodern Diversity* (Baker Book House, 1996); and Timothy R. Phillips, and Dennis Okholm, eds. *Christian Apologetics in the Postmodern World* (Inter-Varsity, 1995).

11. Sartre rejected any eternal verities and stated that meaning can only be created by and for the individual, which he then admits is absurd. As Schaeffer pointed out in his DVD series *How Should We Then Live*, Sartre could not live by his own philosophical principles. He may assert that there is no difference between choosing to help a little a little old lady across the street or choosing to run her down, but he would never live that way. He, like any other modern, would be appalled and would condemn the running down of little old ladies.

12. Frances Schaeffer, *How Should We Then Live: The Rise and Decline of Western Thought and Culture* (Old Tappen NJ: Fleming H. Revell, 1976), p. 121.

13. Schaeffer, ibid, pp. 144ff. We will also discuss the predictions of French existentialist Jean-Paul Sartre (1905-1980) later in this chapter.

14. The International Socialist Tendency is an international group organized around the ideas of Tony Cliff, founder of the Socialist Workers Party in Britain. It has chapters around the world; however, its strongest presence is in Europe, especially in Britain, Greece and Ireland. The politics of the IST are similar to the politics of many Trotskyist Internationals. The IST has generally adopted a position of state capitalism. A state capitalist country is one where the government controls the economy and essentially acts like a single giant corporation.

15. The Protests of 1968 were a worldwide phenomena . . . a series of protests whose leaders were mostly students and workers. The most prevalent of these was May

1968, which occurred in France. It was the largest general workers' strike to ever grind the economy of an advanced industrial country to a halt. In opposition to a modern consumer and technical society, eleven million workers went on strike for two weeks, nearly collapsing the French government. (Even president Charles de Gaulle had to be sheltered in Germany.) A number of universities witnessed a long series of student strikes. The idea was to attach established social values and morality. Nonetheless, the revolutionary generation of 1968 sold out to the very ideology they were protesting against. In my view, modernism left the door cracked open for the meta-narrative – and postmodernism locked the door completely. Therefore, it is something new… something the world has never experienced before . . . a result of modernism, for sure, but not an extension of it.

16. Alex Callinicos, "Against Postmodernism: A Marxist Critique" (University of York, 1990). http://www.polity.co.uk/book.asp?ref=9780745606149.

17. The Levant is a non-political archaeological term used to describe the region between Egypt and Mesopotamia. Today that area would consist of the modern states of Israel (1948), Syria (1946), Lebanon 1943), Jordan (1946), parts of northwestern Iraq (1932/1959), and parts of southeastern Turkey (1923).

18. Naomi Shepherd, *The Zealous Intruders: The Western Rediscovery of Palestine* (London: Collins, 1987), p.13. Raised in London, Shepherd studied at London and Oxford Universities. She moved to Jerusalem in 1963 were she taught at Hebrew University and was political correspondent for New Statesman and the New York Times. Over the years I have recommended this book to many students, friends, and colleagues. It is a fascinating read if you are at all curious about this period of history. "At the end of the 18th century, in the wake of Napoleon's disastrous invasion, Palestine was seen by the West as a barren and neglected country in need of Western enterprise – a belief which led to the greatest rush to the Holy Land since the Crusades." (Book Flap) Used copies can still be found.

19. Schaeffer, Francis A. *How Should We Then Live: The Rise and Decline of Western Thought and Culture* (Old Tappen NJ: Fleming H. Revell, 1976, p. 211.

20. Colin Brown, *Philosophy & the Christian Faith* (Downers Grove IL: Inter-Varsity, 1979), p. 284.

21. See *Do Hard Things: A Teenage Rebellion Against Low Expectations* by Alex and Brett Harris, Multnomah Press, 2008. The Harris twins, the sons of homeschooler pioneers Greg and Sono Harris, and brothers of Joshua Harris, who wrote, *I Kissed Dating Goodbye*, are the founders of www.TheRebolution.com. In *Do Hard Things* they tackle the teenage myth that defines the life of an adolescent as a vacation from responsibility. Using Biblical insights, history, and modern examples they redefine the teen years as the launching pad of life. Also check out *Start Here: Doing Hard Things Right Where You Are* (Multnomah Books, 2010).

Chapter 5: Where Has All the Archaeological Evidence Gone?

1. Raamses, in the Bible, city of the eastern delta of Egypt, believed to have been built by Hebrew slave labor.
2. For the record, the site was not excavated by him, and he was not the first to suggest the identification.
3. Yadin, in fact, found out that the Chicago archaeologists were wrong about the Solomonic dating of the stables. Yadin dated them later to Omri and Ahab.
4. Halley, Henry H. *Halley's Bible Handbook: An Abbreviated Bible Commentary* (Grand Rapids MI: Zondervan, 1962), p. 7. This old treasure still graces my study bookshelf.
5. Halley, Ibid.
6. Halley, ibid, p. 154.
7. Halley, ibid, p. 156.
8. Surely Halley must have been aware of Kenyon's dig at Jericho and her findings (1952-1961). My assumption is that he felt her work too liberal, chose to ignore it, and emphasized the details and conclusions of Garstang's dig.
9. Unger, Merrill F. *Unger's Bible Handbook: An Essential Guide to Understanding the Bible* (Chicago: Moody Press, 1966), p. 160.
10. It is also beyond the scope of this book to argue the merits (or lack thereof) of these two terms. There are those who argue that these terms are helpful and those who say they are not helpful. Nevertheless, they serve as helpful tools for our current discussion.

Chapter 6: A Dutch Student Sets Me on the Journey My Life

1. Hermann Göring was the commander of the German Air Force and Hitler's designated successor. After the war he was convicted of war crimes and crimes against humanity at the Nuremberg Trials and was sentenced to death by hanging. He committed suicide the night before he was due to be hanged. Interestingly, his younger brother, Albert Göring, opposed the Nazi regime and helped Jews and other dissidents escape. It is said that he forged his brother's signature on transit papers to accomplish this, as well as other brave acts.
2. Originally published in the United Kingdom and the rest of the world as, *A Test of Time: The Bible from Myth to History*. In the United States it is known as *Pharaohs and Kings: A Biblical Quest* (New York: Crown Publishers, 1995).
3. I have purposed to avoid the term 'New Chronology' in this book when referring in general to the several revised chronology models (varying between 200-350 years). As we will discover, Rohl uses New Chronology to refer to *his* model which proposes a 300 to 350-year revision and "BICANE chronologies" propose a 200-plus-year revision. The term new chronology will thus only be used when referring to

Rohl's model to avoid confusion (and same will be lowercase to conform more closely to the general rules of capitalization as found in the Chicago Manual of Style). Additionally, this term suggests it is more final than it really is, suggesting that the 'new' has now replaced the 'old chronology.' The use of revised chronology suggests much more realistically that this is all work in progress with differing positions.

4. David Rohl graciously accepted my invitation to come to Florida and present his first workshop in the United States in January 2004, which was filmed by Stretch Productions. The DVD set *The Bible: Myth or Reality?* is available through Stretch Productions, Fort Worth, TX. Go to: www.stretchproductions.com/RohlProducts.html.

5. David M. Rohl, *Pharaohs and Kings: A Biblical Quest*. (New York: Crown Publishers, 1995). Originally published in the United Kingdom and the rest of the world as, *A Test of Time: The Bible from Myth to History*. These books are out of print but used copies are generally available.

Chapter 7: How the Past is Being Controlled

1. English author, Eric Arthur Blair (1903-1950), was better known by his pen name, George Orwell. His writing was marked by a profound consciousness of social injustice and a strong dislike of totalitarianism. Unlike postmodernists, Orwell believed there was meaning in the text and that we had better get that meaning right. He was passionate about the necessity of clarity in language. His most famous works are two novels: *Animal Farm* (written in 1945) a dark satire of Stalinist totalitarianism with its famous quote: "All animals are equal but some animals are more equal than others," and *Nineteen Eighty-Four* (written in 1949), a description of modern dystopia with its famous quote, "Big Brother is watching you."

2. See BBC News: http://news.bbc.co.uk/go/pr/fr/-/2/hi/americas/7878580.stm .

3. See http://www.usnews.com/blogs/mideast-watch/2009/01/30/irans-ahmadinejad-endorses-another-holocaust-denial-conference.html.

4. See *Guardian* article: *"The 'new' anti-Semitism: is Europe in grip of worst bout of hatred since the Holocaust?"* http://www.guardian.co.uk/world/2003/nov/25/thefarright.politics.

5. In India, the world watched in shock on 28 November 2008 as Islamic terrorists singled out the Mumbai Jewish Center in a well-planned and well-coordinated attack.

6. The rejection of objective historiography does not disregard the truth of historiography. We are simply stating that bias and interpretation of the past can taint a historical record, in particular, we may not be questioning if something happened but when something actually happened. History can be accurate in its recording of what and when something actually happened or it may not. Historical bias and in-

terpretation can, but do not necessarily, negate the truth of the account in question having actually happened. This will become clearer as we move along.

7. http://www.ees.ac.uk/the-society/history.htm.

8. The first scientist interviewed, Dr. Richard Sternberg, was fired from the Smithsonian Institution for courageously publishing a peer-reviewed article that treated intelligent design seriously. George Mason University fired Dr. Carolyn Crocker because she mentioned intelligent design as a possible alternative to evolution to her second-year biology students. Guillermo Gonzalez, an astronomer with impressive credentials at Iowa State University, was denied tenure. He was ultimately fired because he openly supported intelligent design.

Chapter 8: When Timelines Don't Add Up

1. Leviticus 13:47-59 instructs the Israelites on the importance of getting rid of the greenish or reddish mildew from items made from such things as linen, leather, and wool. This mildew problem was considered so serious the items were to be burned with fire. When the greenish reddish mildew invaded a house, Leviticus 14:33-48 says that after seven days if the mold had spread, any contaminated stones were to be removed from the wall and replaced. If the mildew reappears, the entire house was to be destroyed and the building materials taken to an unclean place outside the village.

2. Encephalopathy is brain and nervous system damage that occurs as a complication of liver disorders. It causes different nervous system symptoms including changes in reflexes, changes in consciousness, and behavior changes that can range from mild to severe.

3. Rohl, *Pharaohs and Kings*, p. 119.

4. This discrepancy was originally pointed out by John Bimson in his article: "Shoshenq and Shishak: A Case of Mistaken Identity" in: *Catastrophism & Chronology Review* (*C&CReview*, formerly *SISReview*) VIII (1987), pp. 39-42. An updated version of this article appeared in *JACF* VI (1992/1993), pp. 19-32.

5. Rohl, Ibid, p. 135.

6. Cf. with comments made about the Egypt Exploration Fund in no. 7, "Who determined the first anchor points ..." in chapter seven. They are known today as the Egypt Exploration Society.

7. This would make King Merenptah, Ramesses' successor, the Pharaoh of the Exodus, which has its own set of problems. See Rohl, *Pharaohs and Kings*, pp. 164-165.

8. You may see this as Mitrsayama. The **a** in Mitrsayam**a** only adds the direction of descent into Egypt for the Hebrew reader.

9. Although Champollion is credited with being the first to decipher Egyptian hieroglyphics, there are those who claim he could not have done so without the help of

groundwork laid by his predecessors: Athanasius Kircher, Silvestre de Sacy, Johan David Akerblad, Thomas Young, and William John Bankes.

Athanasius Kircher (aka Kirchner) was a seventeenth century German Jesuit priest and scholar. He published around 40 works in the fields of oriental studies, geology, and medicine. He made an early attempt of Egyptian hieroglyphs, and has been considered the founder of Egyptology. In case you should need to know this someday, he also invented the first megaphone.

10. Third row, item no. 29.

11. The Biblical name Shishak and how it could have derived from Egyptian Sesi or Sisa, the nick name of Ramesses, is discussed at length by Peter van der Veen: *The Name Shishak*, *JACF* 8 (1999), pp. 22-25 and , *The Name Shishak – An Update*, *JACF* 10 (2005), pp. 8 and 42. An important critique of this name shift is found at Tektonics,org, *Is Shishak Equal to Shoshenq?* Their conclusion: The name issue can apparently go either way: the archaeological data seems stronger for Rohl. See http://www.tektonics.org/qt/shishkabob.html.

12. On this, again, see the articles by Peter van der Veen in *JACF* 8 and 10 referred to in note 11 above.

13. Moshe Garsiel, *Biblical Names – A Literary Study of Midrashic Derivations and Puns* (Ramat Gan: Bar Ilan University Press, 1987).

14. See van der Veen's article in *JACF* 8 for a detailed discussion of the name game and especially of the name Yezebel.

15. Again, this is fully discussed by van der Veen in *JACF* 8.

16. If you are familiar with the lunar dating of Ramesses, Papyrus Leiden I.350, which dates to the fifty-second year of Ramesses II, records lunar observations that place that year of Ramesses' reign in one of the following years: 1278; 1253; 1228; or, 1203 BC. Having questioned the value of the Ebers Papyrus, Rohl argues that since these lunar observations are only accurate every twenty-five years, they could also indicate dates 300 years later.

17. Besides the listing of these in Rohl's *Pharaohs and Kings*, also see Peter James, et al., *Centuries of Darkness*, ibid, pp. 220-259, where these arguments had already been discussed at great length.

18. The Apis cult lasted into the Hellenistic period when it transmuted (that is, blended) into the popular cult of Serapis. Serapis was a composite god of sorts. He was created by combining the Egyptian god Osorapis (who had been previously created by combining the Egyptian gods Osiris and Apis) with aspects of various Hellenistic gods such as Zeus, Hades and Dionysus during the reign of Ptolemy I Soter (305-285 BC). This was done to provide the Egyptians with an Egyptian god with ties to Greek theology.

19. Rohl, Pharaohs and Kings, p. 60. For further details study Rohl, pp. 43-60.

20. For further details study Rohl, Pharaohs and Kings, pp. 62-80.

21. Rohl, Pharaohs and Kings, p. 107. For further details study Rohl, ibid, pp. 91-107.

22. Not only is the historicity of the Bible restored, these fascinating synchronisms also appear. Several revised chronologists identify Sesostris III and his son Amenemhat III with the Pharaohs at the time of Joseph. The "new king who did not know Joseph" in Exodus 1:8 would then be identified with either Sobekhotep III or Neferhotep I. That would make Neferhotep I the adoptive grandfather of Moses; Khanefere Sebekhotep IV, brother and successor of Neferhotep, Khenephres, the Pharaoh from whom Moses fled to Midian according to the Jewish historian Artapan in the third century BC. Ibni, a late Middle Bronze Age ruler of Hazor may be identified with Jabin, king of Hazor in Joshua 11:10 as other scholars had suggested previously (personal communication of P. van der Veen with W. Horowitz of Hebrew University). Sheshi, a Hyksos ruler, could be the same Sheshai, a ruler of Hebron descended from Anak (Joshua 15:13-15).

Additionally, during the time of the first kings of Israel some conjectural identification is possible. There is some evidence that either the old Pharaoh Ramesses II or his son Merenptah, who both captured the city of Gezer, could have been Solomon's father-in-law. Egyptian finds in Jerusalem from exactly this time may support this view, although more straightforward evidence will be needed to confirm this. It appears plausible that the Biblical Shishak, who plundered the Jerusalem temple treasures at the time of Rehoboam, was a Ramesside Pharaoh (a hypocoristicon for Ramesses = Shysha).

23. Not all scholars proposing a revised chronology are non-believers, but a good many are.

24. P. van der Veen, C. Theis, M. Görg, Israel in Canaan: (Long) *Before Pharaoh Merenptah? in Journal of Ancient Egyptian Interconnections* 2:3 (2010): forthcoming.

25. See: M. Görg, *Israel in Hieroglyhen*, in *Biblische Notizen* (2001), pp. 21-27.

26. Although there is a difference by a whole century between the two existing models, both allow for very similar historical synchronisms in the overall time frame, e.g. a better match with the archaeology of Israel's Sojourn and Conquest by Joshua and the archaeology of the United Monarchy period during the flourishing Late Bronze Age II period (personal telephone communication with Peter van der Veen).

27. Rohl assigned a large statue of a high ranking western Semite official and the tomb in which the statue was found at Tell ed-Daba to the Biblical Joseph, *Pharaohs and Kings*, pages 327-368. The more general attribution of Joseph's Vizierate to the period of the later Twelfth Dynasty was first suggested by John Bimson, "*A Chronology for the Middle Kingdom and Israel's Egyptian Bondage*," *SISReview* III (1978/79), pp. 64-69.

28. The oppression is thus correctly dated to the Thirteenth Dynasty. A papyrus (Brooklyn Papyrus) from the reign of Pharaoh Sobekhotep III refers to many western Semite slaves and servants in an Upper-Egyptian household. Many of them bear Biblical names (e.g. Issakar, Shiphra). As with Velikovsky, the Exodus is dated to the period directly prior to the Hyksos invasion during the reign of a pharaoh called Tutimaios

(Manetho) who is identified with king Dudimose. See: John Bimson, *"A Chronology for the Middle Kingdom and Israel's Egyptian Bondage – II," SISReview* IV (1979), pp. 11-18. Also see Rohl, ibid, pp. 251-289.

29. See, for instance, John Bimson, *Exodus and Conquest – Myth or Reality? Can Archaeology Provide the Answer? JACF* 2 (1988), pp. 27-40; *IIB and not IIB? A Critique of David Rohl's Setting for the Exodus and Conquest, JACF* 10 (2005), pp. 69-77 and 92. Also see Rohl, ibid., pp. 263-273.

30. Bimson had already re-dated the Biblical conquest to the end of the Middle Bronze Age in his book, *Redating the Exodus and Conquest* (Sheffield: Almond Press, 1978). Bimson argued later that the end of the Middle Bronze Age (conventional c. 1550 BC) could only be revised to c. 1400 BC (on the Biblical chronology) by using a revised chronology. Rohl later adopted this view but dated the destruction of Jericho at the beginning of the last phase of the Middle Bronze Age (IIC) a view not shared by Bimson.

31. According to Rohl's new chronology model, Solomon reigned at the time of Pharaoh Haremhab – early Ramesses II. According to the CoD of Peter James et al. Solomon is a contemporary of Merenptah and his immediate successors. In both cases the archaeology in Israel witnessed a time of prosperity during the later part of the Late Bronze Age. In the latter model, impressive monumental building activity in Jerusalem (City of David) – which was started around 1200 BC (conventional date) – can be neatly realigned with the building activities of David and Solomon (c. 1000-930 BC).

32. Robert Morkot and Ad Thijs are members of the BICANE group, and have extensively published on the subject of Egypt's later history. See for instance: R. G. Morkot, *The Black Pharaoh – Egypt's Nubian Rulers* (London: The Rubicon Press, 2000), in which he uses conventional and revised dates side by side.

33. Ad Thijs (BICANE) has published extensively in the journals *Göttinger Miszellen* (*GM*) and *Zeitschrift für Ägyptische Sprache* (*ZÄS*) on the chronology of the late 20th and early 21st dynasties (e.g. *GM* 163, 167, 170, 173, 175, 177, 179, 181, 184, 199, 211; *ZÄS* 132, 134), etc.

34. For an overview of criticisms (especially on the shorter CoD chronology and answers to the critics), see: www.centuries.co.uk.

Chapter 9: 'The Facts on the Ground Are Speaking'

1. Eilat Mazar, *The Complete Guide to the Temple Mount Excavations* (Bar Ilan University Press, Ramat-Gan: Israel, 2002). (Mazar's worldview is theism.) The university's website is in Hebrew. The book is in English and can be purchased through multiple retailers. More specifically on the Davidic Palace and her finds from the Judean Monarchy Period see: E. Mazar, *The City of David Excavations 2005 at the Visitors Center Area* (Jerusalem: Shalem Press, 2005); *The Palace of King David – Excava-*

tions at the Summit of the City of David – Preliminary Report of Seasons 2005-2007 (Jerusalem: Shoham Academic Research and Publication, 2009).

2. Eilat Mazar's comment to Rachel Ginsberg of Aish. Ginsberg has written a superb account of Mazar's discovery titled *"Reclaiming Biblical Jerusalem"* which can be accessed at: http://www.aish.com/jw/j/48961251.html.

3. Kenneth A. Kitchen in the Foreword of John D. Currid, *Ancient Egypt and the Old Testament* (Grand Rapids MI: Baker Book House, 1997), p. 11.

4. Kitchen, *Reliable*, ibid, p. xiv.

5. See Kitchen, *Reliable*, ibid, p. 390, for example.

6. There is much division among Assyriologists about the apparent difficulties of AKL. This is an extremely complex topic but nonetheless bears mentioning.

7. For a summary discussion, see B. Newgrosh, *Chronology at the Crossroads – The Late Bronze Age in Western Asia* (Leicester: Matador: 2007), pp. 162-201. In a similar vein, Graham Hagens, who suggests a revision of some seventy years within the standard Mesopotamian chronology, suggests an overlap of dynasties during the late Middle Babylonian period, and discusses the questions that remain about this part of the chronology within mainstream scholarship. See: G. Hagens, *The Chronology of Tenth Century Assyria and Babylonia*, *JACF* 9 (2002), pp. 61-70.

8. In Arabic *waqf* means to stop or to prevent. In this case, it means the authority that prevents any property to be handled, sold, or bought without the permission of all Muslims worldwide. They are the ones who are responsible for the physical property that belongs to all Muslims. Waqf is all over the Islamic world and in many other countries as well. Israelis handed control of the Temple Mount to the Waqf in 1967. My thanks go to Alan, a devout Muslim in Jerusalem, and son of one of the top antiquities dealers on the Via Dolorosa, for clarifying this Arabic term for me.

9. Stephen J. Adler, *Israeli Court Finds Muslim Council Destroyed Ancient Remains on Temple Mount*, *BAR* 20:04 (July/Aug 1994).

10. Kristin M. Romey, *Jerusalem's Temple Mount Flap*, *Archaeology*, Volume 53 Number 2, (March/April 2000).

11. Steven Feldman, *Muslim Religious Body Snubs Israeli Law, Archaeological Concerns*, *BAR* 26:02 (March/April 2000).

12. Oral communication between G. Barkay and P. van der Veen kindly passed along to this author by P. van der Veen.

13. The most detailed reports on the work achieved by G. Barkay and his team have unfortunately so far only appeared in Hebrew: e.g. *New Light on the Temple Mount*, in: *Israel* 175 (Jerusalem, Ir David), pp. 6-46 (in Hebrew); G. Barkay & I. Zweig in: E. Baruch, Z. Greenhut, A. Faus (eds.), *New Studies on Jerusalem* Vol. 11 (Ramat Gan: The Ingeborg Rennert Center for Jerusalem Studies, 2006), pp. 213-237 (in Hebrew). For a brief summary of some finds see H. Shanks, Sifting the Temple Mount Dump, *BAR* 31:4 (2005), pp. 14-15.

14. Kenneth Kitchen, *Reliability*, ibid, p. 4. In keeping with 'no stone unturned' . . . before we leave this section, one must wonder if there isn't a hint of minimalism now coming also from Kenneth Kitchen. Discussing Solomon's Temple, Kitchen asks, "How far does such a structure and its embellishment correspond to known reality or arise from mere fantasy? This temple (if ever built) was replaced by a 'second temple 'in the late sixth century (537-520; Ezra 3:8ff.; 6:15), and was replaced under Herod from 19 B.C. onward (strictly a 'third temple'!). Of the first, or Solomonic Temple, no physical trace has been conclusively recovered or identified." Kenneth Kitchen, *Reliability*, ibid, p. 122. Note three important words: "This temple (if ever built) …" That's unfortunate. Kitchen systematically attacks the many failures of minimalist arguments against the Bible by marshaling pertinent evidence from antiquity's inscriptions and artifacts to make obvious the essential honesty of the Old Testament writers. But his comment questioning whether the Temple described in 1 Kings 6 was "ever built" seems to place a crack in the armor of his conservative position.

15. Ibid.

16. But many of the older priests and Levites and family heads, who had seen the former temple, wept aloud when they saw the foundation of this temple being laid, while many others shouted for joy.

17. I am indebted to John DeLancey for inviting me to co-lead several of his groups to Israel, Jordan, and Egypt and for his sharing his experiences and insights at this site in particular. DeLancey dug at this site in the 1980s.

18. Accessed January 22, 2010 at http://www.jpost.com/servlet/Satellite?cid=1238562926124&pagename=JPost/JPArticle/ShowFull.

19. Synagogues from the Second Temple period were rare because Jews during that time typically worshiped at the main temple in Jerusalem three times a year, as opposed to attending a local house of worship.

20. Accessed January 22, 2010 at http://www.cnn.com/2009/WORLD/meast/09/11/jerusalem.synagogue/index.html.

21. Eilat Mazar (The Hebrew University of Jerusalem), Takayoshi Oshima (University of Leipzig), Wayne Horowitz (The Hebrew University of Jerusalem), and Yuval Goren (Tel Aviv University), A Cuneiform Tablet from the Ophel in Jerusalem, Israel Exploration Journal, Volume 60, Number 1, Jerusalem, Israel, 2010, pp. 4-23.

22. Eilat Mazar, Takayoshi Oshima, Wayne Horowitz, Yuval Goren, A Cuneiform Tablet from the Ophel in Jerusalem, *Israel Exploration Journal*, Volume 60, Number 1, Jerusalem, Israel, 2010, p. 7.

Chapter 10: New Possibilities, New Questions

1. See Nikos Kokkinos, "Eratosthenes and the Dating of the Fall of Troy," Ancient West & East (2009) 37-56 (doi:10.2143/AWE.8.0.2045837). He has also authored The Herodian Dynasty: Origins, Role in Society and Eclipse (1998) and Antonia Augusta: Portrait of a Great Roman Lady (1989 and 1993). He edited The World of the Herods and the Nabataeans: 2001 International Conference (The British Museum), 17-19 April, 2001 and co-edited with David M. Jacobson of Herod and Augustus: Papers Presented at the IJS Conference, 21st-23rd June 2005.
2. Paraphrase based upon numerous conversations with Peter van de Veen.
3. In addition to his studies in Egyptology, David Rohl has also researched the Garden of Eden and proposes a location for the Garden of Eden in Iranian Azarbaijan, south-east of Tabriz in his published work, Legend: The Genesis of Civilisation (only available in the UK). In The Lost Testament, ibid, p. 53, Rohl assumes a local flood theory for the Genesis Flood based upon his rendering of the Biblical reference to the covering of "all the high mountains" as a description of the local flooding of cities in the plains of Mesopotamia. He bases his idea on the rendering of the Hebrew word 'har' (mountain) as 'hill' and/or 'city mound.'
4. Sturgis, ibid, p. 49.
5. David M. Rohl, The Lost Testament, ibid, p.474.
6. See Kitchen's remarks in the Preface to his 1996 edition of The Third Intermediate Period in Egypt, see §LL. (pp. xlii-xlvi).
7. To purchase Bernard Newgrosh's book go to http://www.troubador.co.uk/book_info.asp?bookid=509.

Chapter 11: Fact or Fiction?

1. Gary Greenberg, *The Moses Mystery: The African Origins of the Jewish People* (Birch Lane Press, 1997) was reprinted in paperback as *The Bible Myth: The African Origins of the Jewish People* (Citadel Press, 1998).
2. Ibid., *101 Myths of the Bible: How Ancient Scribes Invented Biblical History* (Naperville IL: Sourcebooks, 2000, paperback edition 2002), has been published in hardcover and paperback editions. It has also been published in Spanish, Korean, Greek, Serbian, and Croatian.
3. Greenberg, ibid. The first quotation is from p. 5 and the second is from p. 6 as noted.
4. Professor Jin Li of the Research Center of Contemporary Anthropology at Shanghai Fudan University (RCCASFU) says he can also prove that the modern Chinese people originated in Africa based on his DNA based research. Professor Jin published his research in 2001.

5. I have based our discussion here on an article written by Marvin Lubenow. For further study you can access *"The Apple (Computer) Bites the African Eve"* online at: http://www.icr.org/article/apple-computer-bites-african-eve/ You will find additional articles on this topic at: http://www.answersingenesis.org/docs/206.asp.

6. Henry Gee, *"Statistical Cloud over African Eden," Nature*, 355 (13 February 1992): 583.

7. S. Blair Hedges, Sudhir Kumar, Koichiro Tamura, and Mark Stoneking, *"Human Origins and Analysis of Mitochondrial DNA Sequences," Science*, 255 (7 February 1992): 737-739.

8. See Marvin L. Lubenow, *Bones of Contention* Grand Rapids MI: Baker Books, 2004.

9. Allan C. Wilson and Rebecca L. Cann, *"The Recent African Genesis of Humans," Scientific American*, April 1992: 68.

10. See H. Frankfort, *The Problem of Similarity in Ancient Near Eastern Religions*, (Oxford: Clarendon Press, 1951), pp.17ff. Also see Richard S. Hess, *Israelite Religions: An Archaeological and Biblical Survey*, (Grand Rapids MI: Baker Academic, 2007). Hess is a serious evangelical Old Testament scholar second to none from Denver Seminary. Check out his numerous publications. If you are serious about these issues, it will be well worth your time.

Chapter 12: Timing the Temples: Who Copied Whom?

1. See, for example, Leviticus 3:3,9; 7:16,17,29; 9:4,7; 14:19,30; 15:15,30; 16:9,24; 17:5,8,9; 19:5,6; 22:29; 23:12,19.

2. Hosea 13:2: "Now they sin more and more; they make idols for themselves from their silver, cleverly fashioned images, all of them the work of craftsmen. It is said of these people, 'They offer human sacrifice and kiss the calf-idols.'" Also see, for example, Isaiah 57:5: "You burn with lust among the oaks and under every spreading tree; you sacrifice your children in the ravines and under the overhanging crags."

3. The earliest example of human sacrifice may perhaps be found in the Predynastic burials in the south of Egypt where there is evidence of throats having been cut before decapitation. The position of E. A. Wallis Budge was that it was customary in the Predynastic period to slay slaves at the graves of the kings and nobles so that the souls of the sacrificed would protect them by warding off the evil spirits. The human heads discovered on the tombs of Osiris most likely reflect this custom when Osiris was buried; human sacrifices were offered at his tomb most likely for this same purpose. See E. A. Wallis Budge's two-volume set, *The Gods of the Egyptians* (Mineola NY: Dover Publications, 1969). Also see *Earthly Remains: The History and Science of Preserved Bodies* by Andrew Chamberlain and Mike Parker-Pearson (British Museum, 2001); *Dying for the Gods* by Miranda Green (Sutton, 2001); *The Archaeology of Death and Burial* by Mike Parker Pearson (Sutton,

1999); and, *The Highest Altar: The Story of Human Sacrifice* by Patrick Tierney (Viking, 1989).

4. See Utterances 273 - 274 of the Pyramid Texts.

5. Peter van der Veen e-mail correspondence with the author on 5 October 2009.

6. 2 Kings 25:26. For a detailed discussion on the archaeological evidence for the existence of Gedaliah see: P. G. van der Veen, *Gedaliah ben Ahiqam in the Light of Epigraphic Evidence (A Response to Bob Becking)*, in: M. Lubetski (ed.), *New Seals and Inscriptions, Hebrew, Idumean and Cuneiform* (Sheffield: Sheffield Phoenix Press, 2007), pp. 55-70.

7. Hophra was the fourth king of the Twenty-sixth Dynasty, the son of Psammetichus II. and grandson of Necho. When Nebuchadnezzar was moving in on Jerusalem, it was King Hophra who marched to assist Judah. He managed to delay the siege, but only for a short time (Jeremiah 37:5, 7, 11). Hophra also helped the Tyrians against Nebuchadnezzar. Ezekiel 29:18 most likely refers to this event. See Herodotus, ii. 161.

8. Amasis was the fifth king of the Twenty-sixth Dynasty. He has been referred to as the last great Egyptian pharaoh. The rule of his son, Psammetichus III, was very short-lived. Even in the last days of Amasis's life, the Persians were already advancing on Egypt. Amasis dethroned Apries aka Hophra.

9. See Herodotus, ii. 169. Herodotus was a Greek historian who lived in the fifth century BC (c. 484 BC–c. 425 BC) and is regarded as the "Father of History" in Western culture. Herodotus is the author of *The Histories*. The word "history" meant "inquiry" in ancient Greek. Herodotus often presents a number of different opinions on an issue, and then proceeds to state his own opinion and the reasons why he supported it.

10. The photo is from Ira Maurice Price, The Monuments and the Old Testament revised edition (Philadelphia: Judson, 1925) p.396. The original letter is located at Staatliche Museum in Berlin Germany Inventory no. 13495.

11. There was also a later Jewish presence that included a temple built by Onias IV in Leontoplis during the Late Period/Ptolemaic Period. Since this first temple was destroyed in the time of Emperor Vespasian we would not expect anything to exist today. Additionally, it is not certain that Tell el-Moqdam is the site of Leontopolis. There are two other possibilities: Tell es-Saba (Mound of the Lion) which has not been excavated; and Tell el-Yahudiya (Mound of the Jew). Both Arabic names suggest a connection to either Leonopolis or Onias. Hundreds of colored tiles with Egyptian motifs were found at Yahudiya with potter's marks on the back, which some have interpreted as Greek letters. This would date these tiles to the time of the Jewish temple of Onias IV. But this is all speculation, since there is no extent archaeological evidence for the Onais temple in the eastern delta. In early 1906 Egyptologist Sir William Flinders-Petrie spent six weeks at Yehudiyeh. As reported in the *Jewish Chronicle* of 18 May 1906, Petrie gave a lecture at King's College in London,

claiming to have found the Jewish temple at Yehudiyeh. Petrie made a model of the temple and presented it to University College. Unfortunately, the model has disappeared – as well as any traces of a temple at Yehudiya, although there is an identifiable ancient Jewish cemetery nearby. [I am indebted to David Rohl and Peter van der Veen for assisting with the details of this note.]

12. Text 34, AP 30/31; Berlin, St. Mus. P. 13495/ Cairo P. 3428 in Victor H. Matthews and Don C. Benjamin, *Old Testament Parallels: Laws and Stories from the Ancient Near East* (NY/NJ:Paulist Press, 2006), pp. 212-213.

13. Cambyses II successfully overthrew the indigenous Egyptian pharaoh, Psamtek III, making Psamtek III the last ruler of Egypt's Twenty-sixth Dynasty. Cambyses II thus becomes the first ruler of Egypt's 27th Persian Dynasty. His father had previously attempted an incursion against Psamtek III's predecessor, Amasis, but Cyrus the Great's death in 530 B.C. put a halt to that mission. For additional study see Pierre Briant, *From Cyrus to Alexander: A History of the Persian Empire* (Winona Lake IN: Eisenbrauns, 2002), pp. 55-61.

14. The temple built to honor Khnum can be seen in Esna farther north along the Nile.

15. Despite the scholarly criticisms, the issue of the reliability of Herodotus is not as easy as some scholars make it sound. Obviously something must have happened, but the whole thing seems to have been exaggerated at some point. *Anfänge politischen Denkens in der Antike* Von Kurt A. Raaflaub,Elisabeth Müller-Luckner, (Munich 1993) refers to a book by Professor Alan Llyod, an Egyptologist Professor, which can be found online in Google:
http://books.google.de/books?id=NySxd—wwYwC&printsec=frontcover#v=onepage&q=Lloyd&f=false
If you are interested in studying this matter further, this e-book will give you a more balanced view on this entire matter. Note that this is Lloyd's specialty and he has worked in detail on Herodotus.

Chapter 13: A Tour of Egyptian Temples

1. If your time is limited, you might want to bypass Esna because of the hassle of the walk through Esna's notorious bazaar to get to and from the temple. This is usually not a pleasant experience.
2. Amun (sometimes called Amen) was long the local god of Thebes.
3. David Rohl, *Pharaohs and Kings: A Biblical Quest* (New York: Crown Publishers, 1995), pp. 151ff.
4. E-mail correspondence between Rohl and the author on 11 March 11 2009.
5. Kenneth Kitchen, *Reliability*, ibid, pp. 124-125.
6. Ibid.
7. Alexander the Great died in 323 BC.

8. See http://www.touregypt.net/Map17.htm – accessed 12 March 2009. Also defines as the inner cell or sanctuary of a Greek temple, equivalent to the Roman cella, containing the statue of the deity.

9. http://www.msnbc.msn.com/id/30326676/ Accessed 20 January 2010.

10. Rafah is a Palestinian city in the southern Gaza Strip. It is about 19 miles (30 kilometers) south of Gaza. Interestingly, Rafah is the site of the Rafah Border Crossing, the only crossing between the Gaza Strip and Egypt, which nearly follows the ancient military highway or way of the Philistines.

11. "Then it came to pass, when Pharaoh had let the people go, that God did not lead them by way of the land of the Philistines, although that was near; for God said, 'Lest perhaps the people change their minds when they see war, and return to Egypt.' So God led the people around by way of the wilderness of the Red Sea. And the children of Israel went up in orderly ranks out of the land of Egypt (Exodus 13: 17-18 17 NKJ)."

12. http://www.huffingtonpost.com/2009/04/21/egyptian-temples-discover_n_189425.html.

13. Alexandria was founded by Alexander the Great in the fourth century. The city was the seat of the Greek-speaking Ptolemaic Dynasty, which ruled over Egypt for 300 years.

14. Solomon is dated 1052-974 BC.

15. Solomon's Temple also changed over the centuries, as many kings continued building and changing it. After the return from Exile, the old Temple (destroyed by the Babylonians) was rebuilt but never was revived to its old glories.

16. E-mail from Egyptologist Bill Manley on 30 September 2009. Manley, from the National Museum of Scotland, is one the world's top experts on New Kingdom inscriptions and knows the temples of Egypt very well. I highly recommend *How to Read Egyptian Hieroglyphs: A Step-by-Step Guide to Teach Yourself* (Revised Edition) that he did with Mark Collier. *The Seventy Great Mysteries of Ancient Egypt* (Hardcover) edited by Manley is also a fascinating volume.

17. Archaeologist Peter van der Veen in an e-mailed communication with the author, Monday, 23 March 2009.

18. See Kenneth Kitchen, *Reliability*, ibid, pp. 275-279.

19. See Lawrence T. Geraty, *The Jerusalem Temple of the Hebrew Bible in its Near Eastern Context*, in *The Sanctuary and the Atonement*, edited by Arnold V. Wallenkampf and W. Richard Lesher (Washington D.C.: Review and Herald, 1981).

Chapter 14: Temples to the North and Ritual Similarities

1. Lawrence T. Geraty, ibid, p. 55.

2. In 1999, the University of Chicago's Oriental Institute returned to the site to conduct a survey and to examine the original excavations. The University of Toronto sur-

veyed the site in 2003 and began new excavations in 2004. Excavations in the summer of 2005 unearthed more of the Iron Age temple. Excavations continue. The website for the current excavations as of this printing is http://www.utoronto.ca/tap/.

3. The late Fritz was professor of Old Testament studies and Biblical archaeology at the University of Mainz in Germany. He studied at Hebrew University in Jerusalem, and has excavated with Aharoni at Biblical Arad, Lachish and Beersheba. He co-directed a dig at Tel Masos in the Negev as well as directing a dig at ancient Kinneret, one of the Canaanite cities that fought Joshua and the Israelites.

4. Volkmar Fritz, "*Temple Architecture: What Can Archaeology Tell Us About Solomon's Temple?*" in *Biblical Archaeology Review*, July/August 1987, Volume 13 Number 4, p. 40.

5. From the third millennium BC, variations of this basic house have been found in Troy, Bey'çesultan, Karataş Seymayuk, Tarsus and Kültepe, all in modern Turkey.

6. Fritz, ibid, p. 49.

7. Fritz, ibid, p. 45.

8. Geraty, ibid, p. 59.

9. Angel Manuel Rodríguez, *Ancient Near Eastern Parallels to the Bible and the Question of Revelation and Inspiration, Journal of the Adventist Theological Society*, 12/1 (2001): 59.

10. Geraty, ibid, p. 59.

11. See Kenneth Kitchen, *Reliability*, ibid, pp. 121-127.

12. See discussion in David P. Wright, *The Disposal of Impurity: Elimination Rites in the Bible and in the Hittite and Mesopotamian Literature* (Atlanta: Scholars Press, 1987), p. 46.

13. See discussion in Wright, ibid, p. 64.

14. Cord Kühne, "Hittite Texts," in Walter *Beyerlin, Near Eastern Religious Texts* (Westminster John Knox Press, 1978), p. 180. Also see Kitchen, ibid, *Reliablity*. Kitchen has a brief presentation on similarities regarding rituals and offerings on pages 281-282 and he does an exceptional job on the similarities between God's covenants with Israel and the covenants of the ancient Near East. See pp. 283-307.

Chapter 15: Of Translators and Traitors

1. A. Leo Oppenheim, *Ancient Mesopotamia: Portrait of a Dead Civilization*, (University of Chicago Press, 1977), p. 3.

2. Victor H. Matthews and Don C. Benjamin, *Old Testament Parallels: Laws and Stories from the Ancient Near East* (Revised and Expanded Third Edition) New York and New Jersey: Paulist Press, 2006. See also W. W. Hallo, William Hallo, K. L.

Younger, eds. *The Context of Scripture: Canonical Compositions, Monumental Inscriptions and Archival Documents from the Biblical World,* Vol. 3 (Brill Academic, 2003).

3. That is, in the chronological book order of Christian Bibles as opposed to the chronological book order of the Jewish versions of the Hebrew Bible.

4. See their Foreword, p. xiii.

5. Alexander Heidel, *The Gilgamesh Epic and Old Testament Parallels* (Chicago: University of Chicago Press, 1946 and 1949). The typeset of this volume consists of copies of typewritten pages. Heidel calls this work a companion to his previous work *The Babylonian Genesis*. Heidel, ibid, p. v. *The Babylonian Genesis* (Chicago: University of Chicago Press, 1942, 1951, 1963), contains translations of the Babylonian accounts of creation with parallels from the Old Testament. It was not intended for the serious Assyriologists but for a wider audience of general readership.

6. Heidel, ibid, p. 224.

7. Heidel, ibid, p. 260.

8. David M. Rohl, *The Lost Testament: From Eden to Exile: The Five-Thousand-Year History of the People of the Bible* (London: Century Random House, 2002), pp. 45-55.

9. Heidel, ibid. p. 267.

10. Heidel, ibid. p. 268.

11. Ironically, John Gardner was killed in a motorcycle wreck just after he had finished the typescript of *Gilgamesh*, the ancient epic on death and the afterlife. The work had taken him ten years.

12. John Gardner and John Maier, *Gilgamesh*, p. vii.

13. Charles Martin, Flood Legends: Global Clues of a Common Event (Green Forest, AR: Master Books, 2009).

14. Also known as "Instruction of Amen-em-apt (Amenemope or Amenophis)," son of Kanakht.

15. Hieratic script was invented more or less at the same time as the hieroglyphic script. Scholars believe it was used in parallel with hieroglyphics for recording everyday records, accounts, and letters. It was much faster and easier to use than hieroglyphics. Hieratic script was used until around the Twenty-sixth Dynasty. Toward the end of its use, it was primarily used for religious texts. The new Demotic script was used for most other purposes from the around the Twenty-fifth Dynasty.

16. See, for example, L. G. Perdue, *Wisdom and Cult* (Missoula, MT: Scholars, 1977); G. E. Bryce, *A Legacy of Wisdom: The Egyptian Contribution to the Wisdom of Israel* (Lewisburg PA: Bucknell University Press, 1979); J. Blenkinsopp, *Wisdom and Law in the Old Testament* (Oxford: Oxford University Press, 1983); and E. Wurthwein, "Egyptian Wisdom and the Old Testament," in *Studies in Ancient Israelite Wisdom*, ed. J. L. Crenshaw (New York: Ktav, 1976).

17. *The New English Bible with the Apocrypha: Oxford Study Edition,* (NY: Oxford University Press) Corrected Impression, 1972. p. 675.

18. For our historical survey, we will build upon the outline set forth in John D. Currid, *Ancient Egypt and the Old Testament* (Grand Rapids, MI: Tyndale, 1997), pp. 207-211.

19. E. A. W. Budge, *Facsimiles of Egyptian Hieratic Papyri in the British Museum*, second series, London: British Museum, 1923), Plates 1 through 14. Sir Budge is better known for his publication of *The Egyptian Book of the Dead: The Papyrus of Ani in the British Museum* (1895) still available today.

20. Whether Budge meant there was a parallel between "Amen-em-Ope" 9.7-8 and Proverbs 15:16 or 15:17 can be debated depending upon how 9.7-8 is translated.

21. To emend is to correct, usually by textual alterations.

22. Hugo Gressmann, "Die neugefundene Lehre des Amen-em-Ope und die vorexilische Spruchdichtung Israels," in *Zeitschrift für die alttestamentliche Wissenschaft* 42 (1924) pp. 272-296.

23. D. C. Simpson, *The Hebrew Book of Proverbs and the Teaching of Amenophis*, in *Journal of Egyptian Archaeology* 12 (1926) pp. 232-265.

24. W. O. E. Oesterley, *The Wisdom of Egypt and the Old Testament in the Light of the Newly Discovered "Teaching of Amen-em-Ope"* (London:SPCK, 1927).

25. Their idea was revived in 1972 by Irene Grumach, who postulated the idea that the writer of Proverbs and "Amen-em-Ope" both drew from the same Eighteenth Dynasty source of Egyptian maxims. Irene Grumach, *Untersuchungen zur Lebenslehre des Amenemope* (Munich: Deutscher Kunstverlag, 1972).

26. D. Herzog, *Die Sprüche des Amen-em-Ope und Proverbien Kapp. 22, 17-24, 35*, in *Zeitschrift für Semitistik und verwandte Gebiete* 7 (1929) pp. 124-160.

27. Georges Posener, *Quatre tablettes scolaires de basse époque (Amenemope et Hardjedef)*, in *Revue d' Egyptologie* 18 (1966) pp. 45-65.

28. R.O. Kevin, *The Wisdom of Amen-Em-Apt and Its Possible Dependence upon the Hebrew Book of Proverbs*, in *Journal of the Society of Oriental Research* 14 (1930) pp. 115-157.

29. Currid, ibid., pp. 210-211.

30. Raymond B. Dillard and Tremper Longman III, *An Introduction to the Old Testament* (Grand Rapids MI: Zondervan, 1994), p. 241.

31. R. N. Whybray, *Proverbs*, in *New Century Bible Commentary* (Grand Rapids MI: Eerdmans, 1994), p.323.

32. John D. Currid earned his Ph.D. in archaeology from the Oriental Institute at the University of Chicago and chairs the division of Biblical Studies at Reformed Theological Seminary in Jackson, Mississippi.

33. See related discussion in A. Niccacci, *Proverbi 22:17-23:11*, in *Studii Biblici Franciscani* 29 (1979), pp. 42-72.

34. J. Currid, ibid., pp.215-216.

35. J. Ruffle, *The Teaching of Amenemope and Its Connection to the Book of Proverbs*, in *Tyndale Bulletin* 28 (1977), p. 65.

36. See *www.MyProfessorSays.com* for additional information.
37. 1 Kings 3:1; 7:8; 9:16; 9:24; 11:1-2; and, 2 Chronicles 8:11.
38. Rohl and NC: Horemheb; BICANE and CoD: Merenptah; van der Veen: Ramesses II (late) or Merenptah; and Thijs: Ramesses III; etc.
39. 1Kings 11:1:King Solomon, however, loved many foreign women besides Pharaoh's daughter – Moabites, Ammonites, Edomites, Sidonians and Hittites.
40. R. B. Dillard and T. Longman III, ibid, p.24.
41. If you need a refresher, the conventional and revised chronologies were discussed in chapters seven and eight.
42. David Rohl shared his position on this matter in a personal e-mail to the author on 1 June 2009.
43. In the E-mail from Rohl, ibid.
44. Excerpted from an e-mail between P. van der Veen and the author on 30 September 2009.
45. Diorite is a dark granular igneous rock. Today it is primarily used in surfacing roads.
46. Also check out the black granite statue of Sobekhotep IV, who is identified by several revised chronologists with Moses's stepfather. See Appendix A. This suggestion had already been made for them by the great German Egyptologist, Wolfgang Helck, in his book, *Untersuchungen zur Geschichte und Altertumskunde Aegyptens* (Berlin: Akademie Verlag, 1956), p. 36.
47. Hammurabi Code art 141 as translated in Matthews and Benjamin, ibid., p. 110.
48. Code of Hammurabi, art. 157.
49. Leviticus 18:7-8; 29. It is not sin for a son to have sexual relations with his mother under the Hittite code. See art 190.
50. Lines excerpted from the Lay of the Harpist.
51. Pyramid Text 1248-49; Story of Horus and Set; The Turin Papyrus contains various pictures of sexual activity.
52. Code of Hammurabi, art 199.
53. David Rohl, *The Lost Testament*, ibid, pp. 11-12.
54. Hittite Code art 98.
55. Hittite Code art 195.

Chapter 16: Zoroastrianism . . . Old or New?

1. See Mary Boyce, *Zoroastrians: Their Religious Beliefs and Practices*, (London: Routledge, 1979).
2. It is estimated that there are about 150,000 people who practice Parsism/Zoroastrianism in India, 60,000 in Iran, and possibly 50,000 in the rest of the world.
3. For the first four items below, see mainly Boyce, ibid, and John A. Simpson and Edmund S. Weiner, eds. *Zoroastrianism, Oxford English Dictionary* 20 Volume Set - 2nd ed. (London: Oxford University Press, 1989).

4. Although Zoroastrianism is considered a monotheistic religion with one single supreme god, Ahura Mazdah, six other deities were gradually added and named as emanations of Ahura Mazdah (called the Amesha Spentas). These theoretical representations of the single god were personified somewhat like archangels, and were said to be worthy of worship. The six Zoroastrian emanating gods had opposing evil spirits with whom they were constantly at war. As we mentioned above, the leader of these evil spirits was known as Ahriman.

Atenism is the other monotheistic system of which we're aware (cf Chapter 11, especially comments by Gary Greenberg).

5. See Boyce, ibid, and Richard P. Taylor, *Death and Afterlife: A Cultural Encyclopedia* (ABC-Clio, Inc. 2008 English edition), pp. 312ff. Taylor teaches courses on death, burial, and the afterlife at the University of California, Berkeley. He has also published on Hinduism and ancient religions. A strong word of caution is in order; several entries in this work are occultist in nature. See also Robert Kastenbaum, ed., *MacMillan Encyclopedia of Death and Dying*, – two-volume set, Gale Group, 2002) and James R. Lewis and Rudolf Steiner, *Encyclopedia of Afterlife Beliefs and Phenomena*, (Cengage Gale, 1994).

6. John. R. Hinnells, *Zoroastrian Saviour Imagery and Its Influence on the New Testament*, in *Numen*, Vol. 16, Fasc. 3 (Brill:Dec.,1969), pp. 161-185. Be sure to balance what is claimed in this article with what we are saying in the latter portion of this section.

7. Boyce, Zoroastrianism, ibid, p. 1.

8. http://www.hyperhistory.com/online_n2/people_n2/persons1_n2/zoroaster.html Accessed July 10, 2009.

9. http://wiki.answers.com/Q/When_did_zoroastrianism_begin Accessed July 20, 2009.

10. Visit www.gotquestions.org.

11. Ibid.

Chapter 17: Exchanging the Truth for a Lie

1. Samuel Sandmel, "Parallelomania," *Journal of Biblical Literature* 81 (1962): 1-13.

2. Sandmel, ibid, p.1.

3. See W. G. C. Gwaltney Jr., "Pan Babylonialism," in *Dictionary of Biblical Interpretation*, ed. John H. Haynes, (Nashville: Abingdon, 1999), 2:233-234.

4. Unfortunately Ishtar (goddess of fertility) is the name from whence we get Easter and Easter eggs. Linguistically adopting this name for resurrection Sunday on the church calendar was a tragic mistake. In the Babylonian pantheon, she is a goddess of fertility, love, war, and sex. In the Epic of Gilgamesh she asks the hero Gilgamesh to marry her. He refuses her, citing the ill fate that has befallen all her many lovers.

5. Hartmut Schmokel, *Mesopotamian Texts*, in Walter Beyerlin, *Near Eastern Religious Texts Relating to the Old Testament* (SCM Press, 1978), pp. 110-111.

6. See H. Ringgren, *Matay*, in *Theological Dictionary of the Old Testament*, ed. by G. Johannes Botterweek, Helmer Rinngren, and Heinz-Josef Fabry, (Grand Rapids MI: Eerdmans, 1998), 9:102.
7. Benjamin R. Forester, *Before the Muses: An Anthology of Akkadian Literature* (Bethesda MD: CDL Press, 1993), 2:494.
8. Hellmut Brunner, *Egyptian Texts*, in Walter Beyerlin, *Near Eastern Religious Texts Relating to the Old Testament* (SCM Press), 1978, p. 14.
9. KJV used to emphasize the shared translational use of the English "manifold" for many.
10. Marduk was a Babylonian god from around the time of the Hammurabi Code. His original character is obscure. He was connected with water, vegetation, judgment, and magic. Not to be confused with the current black metal band using this same name. Or is there an intended link in the underworld? Marduk's predominant lyrical topics are Satanism, anti-Christianity, Biblical tales, Third Reich history, and World War II.
11. The goddess Gula (aka Nintinugga)was associated with another goddess, known as Bau. However, scholars now believe that the two were originally independent. The name Bau is from the oldest period, and the name Gula is used later. Bau-Gula was the goddess of healing and she played a prominent role in incantation rituals used to bring healing to people suffering from disease.
12. Benjamin R. Forester, ibid, 2:527.
13. Isa 37:12a. Consider this; the Jews as a people are still intact. Even in spite of Hitler's plan to annihilate them all, they are still here.
14. See details in "Sources of the Standard Babylonian poem," School of Oriental and African Studies, University of London at http://www.soas.ac.uk/nme/research/gilgamesh/standard.
15. James R. Davila, *The Perils of Parallels* (Lecture) now available online at: http://www.st-andrews.ac.uk/divinity/rt/dss/abstracts/parallels. Be sure to check out his list on what parallels can and cannot prove. This is also well done.
16. The Q hypothesis is from the German Quelle for "source." It represents a postulated lost source for the Gospels of Matthew and Luke. Theoretically it is a collection of Jesus's sayings that the Gospel writers used in writing their gospels. Many scholars believe that "Q" was a real document, but no actual document or fragment has ever been found. For further study see Richard A. Edwards, *A Theology of Q* (Philadelphia: Fortress Press, 1976); Robert H. Gundry, *A Survey of the New Testament* (Grand Rapids MI: Zondervan, 2003), pp. 93-101; D. A. Carson and Douglas J. Moo, *An Introduction to the New Testament* (Grand Rapids MI: Zondervan, 2005), pp. 98-101.
17. Genesis 12:1-3 "The LORD had said to Abram, 'Leave your country, your people and your father's household and go to the land I will show you. I will make you into a great nation and I will bless you; I will make your name great, and you will

be a blessing. I will bless those who bless you, and whoever curses you I will curse; and all peoples on earth will be blessed through you.' "

18. Job 1:22: "In all this, Job did not sin by charging God with wrongdoing."
Job 2:10: "He replied, 'You are talking like a foolish woman. Shall we accept good from God, and not trouble?' In all this, Job did not sin in what he said."
Job 10:6: "(T)hat you must search out my faults and probe after my sin …"
Job 10:14: "If I sinned, you would be watching me and would not let my offense go unpunished."
Job 13:23: "How many wrongs and sins have I committed? Show me my offense and my sin."
Job 14:16: "Surely then you will count my steps but not keep track of my sin."
Job 31:30: "I have not allowed my mouth to sin by invoking a curse against his life …"
Job 34:37: "To his sin he adds rebellion; scornfully he claps his hands among us and multiplies his words against God."

19. The New American Standard version is more accurate to the context. While it is true the Hebrew *adam* can mean mankind in general (and some translations have translated this verse as such), the indictment here is by the Almighty against the individual, not mankind in general. See verse 35.

20. Henry Morris, "Job and Adam," Institute for Creation Research, December 29, 1999: http://www.icr.org/article/21922/ . For more detail see Henry M. Morris, *Remarkable Record of Job: The Ancient Wisdom, Scientific Accuracy, and Life-Changing Message of an Amazing Book* (New Leaf Publishing Group, 2001).

21. Rohl, *The Lost Testament*, ibid, pp. 27-29.

22. John Gardner and John Maier, *Gilgamesh*, ibid, p. vii.

Chapter 18: Does Biblical Faith Have to be Blind?

1. Robert Steven Bianchi, *Foreword*, in Rohl, *Pharaohs*, ibid, p. ii.

2. See Donald Hettinga's article, *A Wrinkle in Faith: The unique spiritual pilgrimage of Madeline L'Engle*, in *Christianity Today* (May, 1998).

3. See http://womenhistory.about.com/od/quoates/a/madeleinelengle.htm accessed 12 December 2008.

4. "How long, O LORD? Will you forget me forever? How long will you hide your face from me? How long must I wrestle with my thoughts and every day have sorrow in my heart (Psalm 13:1-2a)?"

5. Ken Ham and Stacia Byers, *The Slippery Slide to Unbelief: A Famous Evangelist Goes from Hope to Hopelessness, Creation Ex Nihilo* 22(3) (June 2000): 8-13.

6. Charles Templeton, *Farewell to God* (Toronto, Ontario: McClelland & Stewart, 1996), p. 232.

7. That is, Gary E. Parker, Southern Baptist pastor and author; not to be confused with Gary E. Parker, Christian biologist and author.
8. Gary E. Parker, *The Gift of Doubt: From Crisis to Authentic Faith*, (San Francisco: Harper & Row, 1990), p. 69.
9. See James 1:2-4.
10. Bertrand Russell, *Russell: Bertrand Russell's Best*, (New York: Routledge, 2009), pp. 19-20.
11. Edward Michael Bankes Green, known as Michael Green, is a British theologian, Anglican priest, Christian apologist and author of more than fifty Christian books.
12. See Michael Green and Gordan Carkner, *Ten Myths About Christianity (Pocketbooks series)*, (Colorado Springs: Chariot Victor Pub, 1988).
13. Ravi Zacharius, ibid, pp. xi,xii.
14. John R. W. Stott, *Your Mind Matters*. (Inter-Varsity, 1978), p. 14.
15. Stott, ibid, p. 11.
16. Joe Boot, *Broader Cultural and Philosophical Challenges*, in Zacharias, ibid. p.174.
17. Since its publication in 1850, theologians, conservative and liberal, have debated whether *In Memoriam* was the proverbial work of Victorian faith or the proverbial work of Victorian doubt. It is both, without contradiction. While much of the work is about doubt, it is just as much about faith. Ultimately, it is a brave story about overcoming doubt and the resultant stronger faith for having gone through the process.
18. Lillian Kwon, *"Survey: High School Seniors 'Graduating from God,'"* ChristianPost.com, August 10, 2006.

Chapter 19: Who Do You Say I Am?

1. Augustine was born in a Roman province. He was educated at Carthage. As a young man he was fascinated with philosophy but had no time of day for Christianity. In his thirties, he met Jesus Christ and became a man of great faith. In 396 A.D. he had become bishop of Hippo. His sermons were well-liked and his writings became quite famous to this day. He is best known for his *Confessions* and his discourse titled *The City of God*. His teachings on God's grace, the free will of man, and the concept of original sin had a great influence on Christian theology.

Chapter 20: Moving from Faith to Faith

1. Known as Rabbi Shaul in Jewish Messianic circles.
2. Dan Cohn-Sherbok, A Concise Encyclopedia of Judaism (Oxford, England: One World, 1998), p.73.
3. See Psalm 77, especially verses 7 through 12.
4. Max Lucado, *Facing Your Giants* (Nashville TN: Thomas Nelson, 2005), p. 166.

5. Some of these altars are still here today (that is, when dated correctly).
6. Max Lucado, *Facing Your Giants* (Nashville TN: Thomas Nelson, 2005), p. 168.

Appendix A: On Ancient Mesopotamia

1. James, Peter, in collaboration with I. J. Thorpe, Nikos Kokkinos, Robert Morkot & John Frankish, *Centuries of Darkness: A Challenge to the Conventional Chronology of Old World Archaeology* (New Brunswick, NJ: Rutgers University Press, 1993). Out of print.
2. And, in the interim, research was undertaken on scientific dating methods, debating these with Mike Baillie of the Palaeoecology Centre, Belfast in successive issues of *JACF* (2-5), leading up to a critical review of Baillie's *A Slice Through Time*, in *JACF* 8 (1999).

Appendix B: The Sovereignty Debate

1. William J. Murnane, *The Road to Kadesh: A Historical Interpretation of the Battle Reliefs of King Sety I at Karnak*, (Chicago: Oriental Institute of the University of Chicago, 1990), pp. 53-54.
2. Donald B. Redford, *Egypt, Canaan, and Israel in Ancient Times* (Princeton: Princeton University Press, 1992), p.180, citing Kenneth Kitchen, *Ramesside Inscriptions*, Vol. I, p.12.
3. See 1 Kings 4:7-21 and in particular verse 12.
4. Remember this is the 350-year reduction year model.
5. Peter is referring to the Bronze to Iron Age Chronology of the Ancient Near East international study group.

Appendix C: History of the Revised Chronology

1. For a more detailed history of the early days of revised chronology studies see: D. M. Rohl, *Pharaohs and Kings*, pp 400-405; Peter van der Veen & Uwe Zerbst (eds.), *Biblische Archäologie am Scheideweg? Fur und Wider einer Neudatierung archaologischer Epochen im alttestamentlichen Palastina* (Holzgerlingen: Hanssler-Verlag, 2002), pp. 19-20; Uwe Zerbst & Peter van der Veen (eds.), *Keine Posaunen vor Jericho? Beitrage zur Archaologie der Landnahme* (Holzgerlingen: Hanssler-Verlag, 2005, second edition 2009), pp. 11-14.
2. I am indebted to Peter van der Veen for helping me put this summary together for you.
3. The final version appeared under the title *Recherches sur l'histoire de l'ancienne Egypte* in 1914.

4. Both the book and the debate can be found in the reprinted edition: C. Torr, *Memphis and Mycenea – with complementary material on the great chronology debate*, edited by D. Rohl & M. Durkin, *ISIS Occasional Publications* No. 1, *ISIS*, 1988.

5. For example in his later works, Velikovsky equated Ramesses II of the Nineteenth Dynasty with Pharaoh Necho of the Twenty-sixth Dynasty c. 600 BC, and Ramesses III of the Twentieth Dynasty with Nectanebo I of the Thirtieth Dynasty c. 400 BC – and completely ignored straightforward evidence that the Twentieth Dynasty succeeded the Nineteenth, which can be clearly shown on the basis of many genealogies. Genealogies also clearly show that Ramesses II and III preceded the Twenty-sixth Dynasty by several centuries (let alone the Thirtieth Dynasty).

6. See John J. Bimson, *Redating the Exodus and Conquest, JSOT Supplement Series 5*, (Sheffield: The Sheffield Almond Press, 1981). For Bimson's revised dates concerning his conquest theory see: Bimson, "A Chart to Illustrate the Conquest of Canaan", *SISReview* II: 3 (1977/1976), pp. 57-58.

7. The papers presented at Glasgow were published in 1982 in the following publication: *Ages and Chaos? Proceedings of the Residential Weekend Conference, Glasgow, 7-9 April 1978*, in: *SISReview* Vol. VI: 1-3.

8. Rohl & P. James, *An Alternative to the Velikovskian Chronology for Ancient Egypt – A Preview of Some Recent Work in the Field of Ancient History*, in: *SIS Workshop* 5:2 (1982/1983), pp. 12-22.

9. The following list of scholars, who have played an important part in its inception (which eventually led to the two main models available, i.e. the 300-year reduction adhered to by David Rohl and the 200 plus year reduction suggested by Peter James and his colleagues), is not complete. But special mention should be made of the following persons: John Bimson, Geoffrey Gammon, Peter James, Nikos Kokkinos, Robert Morkot, Bernard Newgrosh, Robert Porter, David Rohl, and Peter van der Veen. You will find early discussions by some of these scholars on the initial debates in the pages of *SISWorkshop* from the 1980's, e.g.: *Workshop* 5:3 (1982/83), pp. 6-12 (by J. Clarke, G. Gammon, P. van der Veen, B. Newgrosh, D. Rohl and P. James; *Workshop* 5:4 (1982/83) J. Bimson, *It Ain't Necessarily So*, pp. 9-10; *Workshop* 6:1 (1985) discussions by P. van der Veen, B. Newgrosh, D. Rohl etc., *Workshop* 6: 2 (1985), pp. 21-26 (by D. Rohl and L. Mitcham). Also in *C&CWorkshop* (1986,1) pp. 16-23 (with a detailed discussion on the high priests of Amun by D. Rohl), etc.

10. Ten issues appeared (*JACF* 1-10) between 1987-2005. The articles published in *JACF* can still be accessed online at: http://www.newchronology.org/cgi-bin/open.cgi?page=index2.

11. Peter James and his colleagues published their findings in the first volume of *JACF*: *Bronze to Iron Age Chronology in the Old World: Time for a Reassessment?* in: *JACF* 1 (1987), pp. 6-82. Their work was later published as a book: Peter James, I. J. Thorpe, Nikos Kokkinos, Robert Morkot, *Centuries of Darkness: A Challenge to the Conventional Chronology of Old World Archaeology* (New Brunswick NJ: Rutgers

University Press, 1993). REPRINT of the 1991 edition by Jonathan Cape Publishing. For more recent developments of the *Centuries of Darkness* chronology (CoD) see their website: www.centuries.co.uk.

12. The last issue of *JACF* (No. 10, 2005) contains several critical articles which query the correctness of the new chronology model, especially so by John Bimson and Peter van der Veen, who both had come to the conclusion that a 300-plus-year reduction would probably be too radical, and that a 200-plus-year revision would be more in keeping with the evidence. See especially Bimson, *Does Tablet KTU 1.78 provide 'independent scientific confirmation of the New Chronology?'* pp. 57-62 and his *IIB or not IIB? A Critique of David Rohl's Setting for the Exodus and Conquest*, pp. 69-77; 92. Also Peter van der Veen, *The Name of Shishak, an Update*, pp. 8 and 42 (especially n. 1); *A Revised Chronology and Iron Age Archaeology*, pp. 49-51;56. Some of the ideas presented in the last paper are elaborated in van der Veen's PhD Thesis, *The Final Phase of Iron Age IIC and the Babylonian Conquest"* (unpublished Ph.D. thesis for the University of Bristol, 2005) forthcoming in the *AOAT* Series at Ugarit Verlag.

13. The following list is not complete: R. Chapman, *Putting Shoshenq I in His Place*, *Palestine Exploration Quarterly* 141:1 (2009), pp. 4-17; N. Franklin, *Jezreel – Before and After Jezebel*, in: L. L. Grabbe (ed.), *Israel in Transition – From the Late Bronze II to Iron IIA (c. 1250-850 B.C.E.)* Vol. 1, The Archaeology, (London: T. & T. Clarke, 2008), pp. 45-53; P. Furlong, *Aspects of Ancient Near Eastern Chronology (c. 1600-700 BC)*, (unpubl. PhD thesis for the University of Melbourne, forthcoming at Georgias Press); P. J. James, *The Alleged 'Anchor-Point' of 732 BC for the Destruction of Hazor V*, *Antiguo Oriente* 6 (2008), pp. 133-180 and *Mezad Hashavyahu Reconcidered: Ancient Strategy and Archaic Chronology*, in: *Conference Proceedings of the Centre of Egyptology and Mediterranean Archaeology (2006)*, Swansea (in print); J. M. Tebes, *The Influence of Egyptian Chronology in the Archaeology f the Iron Age Negev: A Reassessment*, in: *Göttinger Miszellen* 198 (2004), pp. 91-104. Ad Thijs, *The Lunar Eclipse of Takeloth II and the Chronology of the Libyan Period* in *Zeitschrift für Ägyptische Sprache* (forthcoming 2010). For a summary of the current views held by several members of the BICANE group: see P. James & P. van der Veen, *Geschichtsbild in Scherben?" Spektrum der Wissenschaft* (German branch of *Scientific American)* (December 2008), pp. 88-93.

Appendix D: The Jericho Dilemma

1. See critique by Bryant Wood: http://www.biblearchaeology.org/post/2007/05/david-rohls-revised-egyptian-chronology-a-view-from-palestine.aspx.
2. Jericho is now under the jurisdiction of the PLO.

3. See also the German article by P. van der Veen on "Jericho" in the Internet Lexicon of the German Bible Society under www.WiBiLex.dewith a full bibliography of the work accomplished by the new excavations.

Index

Don't just *read* Dr. Tom's book – *experience* it at
www.MyProfessorSays.com

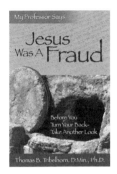

Coming Next!

My Professor Says
Jesus Was a Fraud

The most critical question in a Christian's life is the one that Jesus himself asked the apostle Peter: "Who do *you* say that I am?"

The Church once found the answer to this question very simple . . . but that was before the firestorms of controversy have raged over the last couple of hundred years. Before you jump to conclusions . . . and risk answering Jesus's question inaccurately . . . get the facts.

Dr. Tom's next book, *My Professor Says Jesus Was a Fraud,* will tackle the toughest current questions about the most debated figure in religious history . . . the one man who is at the very foundation of Christianity. It is a critical topic . . . for, if Jesus is not who He said He was, the entire Christian faith crumbles.

Get ready once again for solid, scholarly answers to the most common challenges to believing in Jesus as the promised Messiah . . .

**Come face-to-face with one of the most
controversial figures in history . . .
And see Him as you've never seen Him before!**